THE CONDITION OF TEACHING

A CARNEGIE FOUNDATION TECHNICAL REPORT

The Condition of Teaching

A STATE BY STATE ANALYSIS, 1985

C. EMILY FEISTRITZER

WITH A FOREWORD BY

ERNEST L. BOYER

THE CARNEGIE FOUNDATION FOR THE

ADVANCEMENT OF TEACHING

5 IVY LANE, PRINCETON, NEW JERSEY 08540

Feistritzer, C. Emily
  The condition of teaching.

  Includes bibliographical references.
  1. Elementary school teachers--United States--States
--Statistics. 2. High school teachers--United
States--States--Statistics. I. Title.
LB2832.2.F44 1985   373.11'0092'2   85-26898
ISBN 0-931050-29-4

Second printing, 1986

Copies are available from the
PRINCETON UNIVERSITY PRESS
3175 Princeton Pike
Lawrenceville, New Jersey 08648

CONTENTS

LIST OF TABLES

SOURCES OF DATA

While the basic data used for this report were obtained from many sources, the compilation and analyses are original. General population numbers were obtained from several documents published by the U. S. Department of Commerce, Bureau of the Census, and Bureau of Economic Analysis. Public school enrollments, numbers of teachers, salaries of teachers, and expenditures and revenues were obtained from the National Education Association because NEA has the most current data available. Personal income and per-capita income figures came from the U. S. Department of Commerce, Bureau of Economic Analysis. The U. S. Department of Labor, Bureau of Labor Statistics provided salary data for professions other than teaching. Basic data concerning who is going into teaching and qualifications of new teacher graduates were obtained from the U.S. Department of Education, National Center for Education Statistics and the National Education Association. The College Entrance Examination Board provided Scholastic Aptitude Test (SAT) data for each state. Teacher certification data were obtained from a survey The National Center for Education Information conducted among the states in summers 1984 and 1985, The National Association of State Directors of Teacher Education and Certification and the National Education Association.

FOREWORD

By Ernest L. Boyer

C. Emily Feistritzer, has done a remarkable job in bringing together information about the nation's teachers and providing an analysis of the changes that have occurred since the first Carnegie report on the condition of teaching was released in 1983. As in the case of her earlier work, this analysis will be a valuable tool for policy makers and others interested in the status of education in the nation.

In issuing the 1985 update, our goal once again is to put the spotlight on the teacher. It remains our view that excellence in education means excellence in teaching. The big push for school reform will accomplish little if we do not give greater status and recognition to those who meet with young people in the classroom every day.

In this latest report there is grounds for cautious hope. Teachers' salaries have gone up and there are indications that we may be improving the quality of prospective teachers and raising the standards of teacher certification. Still, the challenge confronting teaching in this country is far greater than its achievements. And if the teaching profession is to be strengthened, the following steps are urgently required.

First, outstanding people must be attracted into teaching

During the next five years, as many as half of today's teachers will be leaving the profession or retiring. The National Center for Education Statistics (NCES) projects a need for more than one million new elementary teachers and more than a half-million secondary teachers by 1993.

And yet, in the fall of 1982, only 4.7 percent of college freshmen said they planned to be a teacher. Compare that to 1972 when almost twenty percent (19.3) were attracted to the classroom. To compound the problem, the quality of those who choose teaching is not outstanding. Students now majoring in education have a combined average SAT score of 852. That is 73 points below the average of students overall.

Clearly, a national program of teacher recruitment is required. It must begin within the school itself, but national leadership is needed as well. Last year, Congress passed the Talented Teacher Act, which is on the books but still remains unfunded. This Act would provide $5,000 a year scholarships for outstanding high school graduates who agree to teach two years for each year they receive such national support.

Schools also have a role to play. For example, high school teachers should identify gifted students who might enter the profession, arrange for them to work as tutors and, occasionally, to have seminars with outstanding school and college teachers.

Teacher recruitment must involve higher education, too. Unfortunately, when colleges call for "excellence in the schools," there is, quite frankly, a lot of hypocrisy at work. On many campuses, there is open hostility toward teaching in the public schools. At one prestigious institution we visited several years ago, a college sophomore said he'd like to be a teacher but he couldn't tell his roommate or faculty advisor. "I'd just be ridiculed," he said.

Recruiting future teachers is at least as important as recruiting fullbacks. And all colleges and universities should give scholarships to outstanding students who plan to teach. Such a program is already in place at Trinity University in Texas and at several other higher learning institutions.

Second, the professional standards of teaching must be tightened

If the profession of teaching is to be improved, teacher candidates must be more carefully selected, teacher education must be dramatically overhauled, and apprentice teachers must spend more time learning from outstanding teachers already in the classroom.

Certification must also be split off from teacher education. Today, colleges not only enroll and educate students, they also recommend them for credentials. If teaching is to become a recognized profession this monopoly must be broken.

xiv

We proposed, in <u>High School</u>, that credentialing be separated from college preparation. To qualify for credentials, each candidate would submit written recommendations from a member of the faculty in his or her academic major; a member of the faculty in his or her education sequence; and a teacher who has supervised his or her school internship.

Before being credentialed, the candidate would also pass a written examination in English proficiency and subject matter competence administered by a Board of Teacher Licensure to be established in every state. We would urge that the majority membership on such boards be comprised of senior classroom teachers.

Once credentialed, a candidate would become an associate teacher. For two years this teacher would work under the mentoring of senior teachers. He or she would have a full teaching load. During this time, however, there would be continuous assessment and counseling by senior teachers to screen out individuals whose performance is inadequate.

After two years, a candidate's performance would be more formally reviewed. The evaluation of the teacher would be based upon testimony of the mentor, the written record, and testimony of other school personnel, including students. Direct observations would be crucial. Equally important are character, motivation, and, most especially, success in the classroom. If the review is favorable, the associate teacher would be given full teacher status.

The testing of prospective teachers also is essential. Paper and pencil examinations cannot identify those who will be successful in the classroom. However, they may help to weed out candidates who cannot read with understanding, who cannot use with accuracy the number system, or who have not acquired basic information about our world. Serious, not superficial, teacher testing is essential if students are to be well served and if public confidence is to be sustained and strengthened.

<u>Third, teachers must be given more recognition and rewards</u>
In his 1975 study <u>Schoolteacher</u>, Professor Dan Lortie talks about three kinds of rewards for teachers: psychic, extrinsic, and ancillary. Extrinsic rewards are those

that take the form of "earnings" of different kinds: financial compensation, to be sure, but also status, prestige, and "power over others." Ancillary rewards include security, spare time, convenient schedules, freedom from rivalry, and a subjective sense that what one is doing is "appropriate" for himself or herself—what we have just described as the working conditions of the teacher.

Psychic rewards come from the satisfaction of reaching students and helping them learn, the chance to work with young people, the opportunity to associate with other teachers, to study, and to read.

Today, psychic rewards appear to be harder to come by. Teachers say, for example, that many of today's students "don't like to study anymore," "aren't interested in learning."

Another complaint we frequently heard was that students are no longer motivated to learn. Even more devastating is the subtle disrespect many adults have for teachers.

The time has come to reaffirm the centrality of teaching, to support good teachers, and give them the recognition they deserve. Students and parents have the most frequent opportunities for extending such recognition. A student's "thank you" for making a difficult lesson clear, or a complimentary note from home are simple examples, rendered special by the infrequency with which they occur. Prompt parent responses to teachers' requests for conferences, and public participation in school events also signal community support.

Fourth, the salaries of teachers must improve
The cornerstone of recognition is, of course, renumeration. Here, progress has been made. In the Carnegie study, High School, we proposed a 25 percent salary increase over three years for beginning teachers. Our goal is now within reach. During the past two years, as Dr. Feistritzer reports, teachers' salaries have increased about 14 percent. And, in one state, the overall salary average has increased 23 percent.

But rejoicing should be muted. We still have states where beginning salaries are disgraceful, and the average annual average for all salaries is less than $18,000. If this nation continues to shortchange its teachers, we will surely shortchange our students, too.

xvi

Our society pays for what it values. Unless teacher salaries become more commensurate with those of other professions, teacher status cannot be raised; able students cannot be recruited.

Fifth, continuing education must be a centerpiece of every teacher contract

The continuing education of the teacher has been consistently neglected. It is fascinating that, while the corporate world is recognizing the importance of the worker, in education we increasingly try to fix "the system" from the top. And while doctors and business executives have lifelong learning programs, we keep teachers in the classrooms--except for an occasional in-service workshop where they listen to experts on leave from Mt. Olympus.

If we're serious about the quality of teaching, every school district should provide an authentic program of continuing education so that all teachers can be intellectually enriched. And the teachers should participate in shaping the program.

In High School we proposed that a two-week Teacher Professional Development Term be added to the school year, with appropriate compensation. This would be a time for study, a period to improve instruction, and an opportunity to expand knowledge. The planning of such a term would be largely controlled by teachers at the local school or district level. Local colleges would be actively involved.

We also recommend that every five years teachers be eligible to receive a special contract with pay to match to support a Summer Study Term. To qualify and to compete for this extended contract, each teacher would prepare a study plan. Such a plan would be subject to review and approval both by peer panels and by the school and district administrators.

Finally, there should be a Teacher Travel Fund. An informal survey of select math and science teachers reveals that their most urgent need was not higher salaries but contact with colleagues in the profession. The fund would make it possible for teachers, based on competitive applications, to travel occasionally to keep current in their field--a practice that is commonplace and respected in other professions.

We will need more, not less, outstanding new teachers in the years to come. We have the facts and the figures. Now it is time to move beyond the data. It is time to take the actions needed to advance teaching, not only to serve the profession but also the students who are taught.

INTRODUCTION

The Typical American Teacher

Any analysis of the current condition of teaching in the United States depends for success upon an understanding of who teachers are. We don't know very much about what kinds of people go into teaching, but we do have data about such things as their ages, years of experience, and job satisfaction, and all of these help explain who they are.

A "typical" American teacher today would be a woman in her early forties who had taught for fifteen years, mostly in her present district. Over those years, she would have returned to her local college or university often enough to acquire enough credits for a master's degree. She would be married and the mother of two children. She would be white and not politically active. Her formal political affiliation, if she had one, would be with the Democratic Party. She would teach in a suburban elementary school staffed largely by women, although, in all likelihood, the school principal would be male. She would have about twenty-three pupils in her class.[1] Counting her after-hours responsibilities, she would put in a work week slightly longer than that of the average worker. The median household income of the average teacher is comparable to that of college graduates in general. Both groups had a median household income of about $30,000 in 1982.[2]

Age: The typical American teacher is almost forty-one years of age, about five years older than the typical American worker.[3] Most of today's teachers in elementary and secondary schools are just entering middle age. Compared with teachers in 1970, they are both older and younger. Until now, the number of new or recently hired teachers has been reduced because of declining enrollments. Staff cuts fell heavily on young teachers: In 1970, almost 17 percent of all teachers were under twenty-five. Today that figure is around 1 percent. There are also fewer older teachers in the teaching force. In 1970, almost 14 percent of all teachers were over fifty-five. Today, teachers over fifty-five constitute only about 12 percent of the total teaching force.

Experience: The typical classroom teacher, having taught for fifteen years, with most of them in the current district, could be considered a top performer at the peak of her or his career. But another, less flattering interpretation is that opportunities for further development and substantive salary increases could be over. Many teachers, in fact, view themselves as having reached the plateau where they are stranded. They see no real opportunities for growth or reward. A number of teachers report this as a major problem.

Nearly half (48 percent) of all teachers have taught at least fifteen years, and 27 percent have taught for twenty years or more. Eighty-one percent of teachers hold tenured positions.[4]

Academic preparation: Teachers are a relatively experienced and nontransient lot. They also are going to school longer and getting more degrees. Today, more than half (52.0 percent) of the teachers in elementary and secondary schools have earned at least a master's degree compared with 25 percent in 1963.[5] This increase in proportion of teachers with a master's degree is directly related to the fact that the teaching force is older. The only requirement for getting one's certificate to teach renewed in most states is to take more college courses. Since 48 percent of current teachers have been teaching fifteen or more years, it is not surprising they have taken enough courses to get a master's degree.

Sex: The great majority of the 1,184,337 public elementary school teachers in the classrooms today are women. In 1984-85, there were 988,508 women teaching in elementary schools and approximately 195,829 men; as a result, the ratio of women to men in elementary schools remains high—as it has historically—at about five to one. In secondary schools, there is a relative balance between men and women. The 1984-85 estimates showed 479,956 (49.9 percent) men and 481,249 (50.1 percent) women.[6]

Marital Status: The typical American teacher is more likely to be married than is the average American worker. Seventy-four percent of teachers are married compared with 64 percent of the working public. In addition, 74 percent of all teachers have children. Only 51 percent of the working public have children.[7] Half of the current teachers have school-age children.

Ethnic background: If males are underrepresented in the teaching force, especially in elementary schools, so are minority groups. Almost nine of every ten teachers are white. It is estimated that blacks constitute 8.6 percent of the teaching force. The proportion of teachers from other minority groups is very small. Hispanics represent 1.8 percent of teachers in kindergarten through high school, and Asian American and American Indians represent less than 1 percent. There is great variation in the racial/ethnic distribution according to geographic location. Southern states have a much higher percentage of minority teachers than the national average, which is consistent with their share of the minority population. Examples of states with large percentages of minority teachers in 1980 include: Mississippi, 38.6 percent; Louisiana, 35.3 percent; Georgia, 27.6 percent; Alabama, 27.2 percent; and South Carolina, 26.1 percent. On the other hand, some non-Southern states fall short in proportions of minority teachers by comparison with their percentages of minority population and school enrollment. Examples of these states include New York, 7.8 percent minority teachers; Colorado, 6.8 percent; Iowa, 1.1 percent; Minnesota, 0.8 percent; and South Dakota, 0.8 percent.[8]

Where they teach: The basic administrative unit for the American school system is the local school district. There has been a continuing decrease in the number of districts as consolidations occurred to avoid duplication and conserve costs. In 1931, there were more than 127,000 school districts. Today there are 15,248. These districts contain 50,926 elementary schools, 9,785 junior high schools and 13,837 senior high schools. A fourth (27.4 percent) of the elementary schools enroll more than 500 students. A third (32.8 percent) of senior high schools enroll more than 1,000 students.[9]

Only 11 percent of our teachers work in what is considered the inner core of a city, while another 12 percent work elsewhere in urban areas. Almost one-third teach in a suburb (31 percent) or a small town (31 percent). Another 14 percent teach in schools characterized as rural.

Of the 2,145,542 teachers employed in K-12 schools in 1984-85, 1,184,337 were in elementary schools and 961,205 in secondary schools. In 1983, almost half of all teachers were categorized as strictly elementary (47.0 percent), nearly one quarter (21.0 percent) as middle or junior high school teachers, 30 percent as senior high school teachers, and 2 percent as teachers at more than one level.

Classroom demand: Although classroom size diminished over the past decade at both the elementary and secondary levels, it appears that teacher–pupil ratios are beginning to edge upward again. Difficult economic conditions offer one explanation for the turn-around.

Teachers estimate the average number of hours in the required school day to be 7.3. Since they also estimate that they spend about 50-55 hours per week on teaching-related duties, it would appear that teachers spend an additional two hours each day beyond normal school hours on their teaching responsibilities. The average school year across the country is 180 teaching days.[10]

Job Satisfaction: The data on job satisfaction for teachers are mixed. Ninety-six percent of all teachers report they love to teach. The vast majority of teachers say they are satisfied with their jobs, although teachers are less satisfied than are working people in general. Eighty-one percent of teachers are at least somewhat satisfied with their jobs, and 40 percent are very satisfied. Comparable figures for the working public are 87 percent and 52 percent. Eighteen percent of teachers and 13 percent of the working public report dissatisfaction with their jobs.[11]

Even though 8 out of 10 teachers report relative job satisfaction, nearly half of them say if they had to do it over again they would not go into teaching. In 1983, 13 percent of teachers said they certainly would not become a teacher again if they could go back to their college days. An additional 30 percent reported they probably would not become a teacher again.[12]

These are relatively high statistics compared with less than twenty years ago (1966) when only 9.1 percent of teachers said they would not choose teaching if they had it to do over again.[13]

The amount of time spent on record keeping and clerical duties is reported by teachers as the number one variable contributing to job dissatisfaction. Salary and treatment of education by the media are tied for second, followed by lack of clerical help available from teacher aides or other support staff.[14]

Regardless of whether they are satisfied or not, teachers tend to stick with it. More than half of all teachers surveyed in 1983 said they planned to remain in teaching either until required to retire (12 percent) or until eligible for retirement (39 percent). Another quarter (24 percent) said they would continue teaching unless something better came along. Only 9 percent said they definitely planned to leave teaching as soon as they could, and 16 percent said they were undecided.[15]

These proportions haven't changed much since 1976, when 59 percent of teachers said they wouldn't leave until retirement, 10 percent reported they would stay unless something better came along, 5 percent said they'd leave teaching as soon as they could and 26 percent were undecided.[16]

The remaining chapters in this report on the current condition of teaching in America will analyze variables for each state and the District of Columbia that affect teaching and will for decades to come--population changes, enrollment patterns, numbers of teachers, projected teacher shortages, salaries, school spending and the economy in general, who's going into teaching and the education and certification of teachers.

This project could not have been done without the help and support of many people. My deepest gratitude goes especially to my assistant Betty Moran and to Sarah Ince who tracked information for weeks and to Fred Quelle who told the computer to do what I wanted done.

CHAPTER I

Population Changes in the United States

The baby boomlet of the late 1970s is hitting our schools right now. Reversing fifteen years of steady decline, enrollment in elementary schools went up in the fall of 1984. Enrollments in elementary schools are expected to rise for the next decade while secondary enrollments will continue to decline until the current bumper crop of under six-year-olds gets to high school. About the time that happens—the mid-1990s—elementary school enrollments will start descending again.

Population shifts in the United States are such that school enrollment patterns are by no means uniform. While most states show either an increase in elementary enrollments or at least a slowing down of a downward trend since 1972, eight states are experiencing a continuation of declining enrollments across-the-board at both the elementary and secondary levels—the District of Columbia, Illinois, Maryland, Missouri, New Jersey, New Mexico, Pennsylvania and West Virginia.

The southern and western regions continue to grow in population at much faster rates than the Northeast and North Central regions. The net migration alone from the industrial Northeast and North Central states to the "sun belt" of the South and West totaled 3.2 million from 1970 to 1980, contributing to an overall increase of 21 million people (22 percent) for the South and West during the decade. This compares with a 3.3 million (3 percent) increase in total population in the Northeast and North Central states (Chart 1).

The Census Bureau expects a 22.2 percent increase in the West's population from 1980 to 1990, and an 18.1 percent rise from 1990 to the end of the century. Projections for the other regions from 1980 to 1990 are: South 15.9 percent

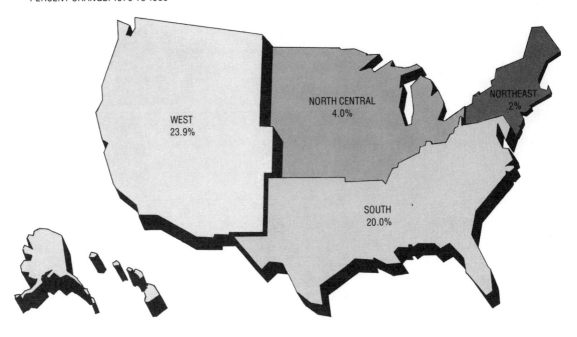

RESIDENT POPULATION—
PERCENT CHANGE: 1970 TO 1980

NORTH CENTRAL
4.0%

NORTHEAST
.2%

WEST
23.9%

SOUTH
20.0%

Chart 1

increase, North Central 2.1 percent increase, and Northeast 1.7 percent decrease; projections from 1990 to 2000: South 12.8 percent increase, North Central 0.9 percent decrease, and Northeast 4.2 percent decrease (Table 1 and Chart 2).

The ten fastest-growing states, in terms of numerical and percentage increases--all in the South and West--draw much of their gain from high growth rates for children under five years of age.

California had the largest growth in actual numbers from July 1, 1982 to July 1, 1984, a total of 925,000 that included 146,000 children under-five. Other leaders were Texas, which grew by 660,000 for the period (111,000 children under-five), and Florida, with another 510,000 (including 69,000 children under-five).

Percentage increases in total population for the ten fastest growing states for the period were: Alaska, 12.6 percent; Arizona, 5.6 percent; Utah, 5.2 percent; Florida, 4.9 percent; Texas, 4.3 percent; Hawaii and New Mexico, 4.2 percent; Nevada, 4.0 percent; California, 3.7 percent and Colorado, 3.5 percent. Their gains

2

TABLE 1. Percent change in population by region and by state: 1960-1980 and projected
1980-2000

	1960-1970	1970-1980	1980-1990	1990-2000
United States	13.4	11.4	9.7	7.3
REGIONS				
Northeast	9.8	.2	-1.7	-4.2
North Central	9.6	4.0	2.1	-.9
South	14.3	20.0	15.9	12.8
West	24.2	23.9	22.2	18.1
STATES				
Alabama	5.4	13.1	8.0	4.8
Alaska	34.1	32.8	29.7	20.8
Arizona	36.3	53.1	46.5	39.8
Arkansas	7.7	18.9	12.6	9.9
California	27.1	18.5	16.0	11.2
Colorado	26.0	30.8	29.5	24.0
Connecticut	19.6	2.5	.7	-2.3
Delaware	22.9	8.4	5.5	1.3
District of Columbia	-.9	-15.6	-21.4	-24.9
Florida	37.1	43.5	36.6	31.0
Georgia	16.4	19.1	12.6	8.6
Hawaii	21.6	25.3	17.5	12.3
Idaho	6.9	32.4	28.0	24.6
Illinois	10.2	2.8	.5	-2.7
Indiana	11.4	5.7	3.1	--
Iowa	2.4	3.1	2.1	-.4
Kansas	3.2	5.1	4.0	1.3
Kentucky	6.0	13.7	10.9	8.1
Louisiana	11.9	15.4	12.5	8.7
Maine	2.6	13.2	9.1	6.4
Maryland	26.5	7.5	6.2	2.0
Massachusetts	10.5	.8	-.8	-3.7
Michigan	13.5	4.3	1.2	-2.0
Minnesota	11.5	7.1	6.5	3.1
Mississippi	1.8	13.7	9.2	6.4
Missouri	8.3	5.1	3.0	.1
Montana	2.8	13.3	12.6	8.4
Nebraska	5.2	5.7	4.2	1.4
Nevada	71.6	63.8	59.1	50.4
New Hampshire	21.6	24.8	23.4	19.7
New Jersey	18.2	2.7	1.8	-1.1
New Mexico	6.9	28.1	17.7	12.5
New York	8.7	-3.7	-6.5	-8.9
North Carolina	11.6	15.7	9.9	6.1
North Dakota	-2.2	5.7	3.6	.5
Ohio	9.8	1.3	-.6	-3.8
Oklahoma	9.9	18.2	15.5	12.6
Oregon	18.3	25.9	25.7	21.3
Pennsylvania	4.3	.5	-1.4	-4.4
Rhode Island	10.6	-.3	.2	-2.6
South Carolina	8.7	20.5	13.6	9.8
South Dakota	-2.2	3.7	.9	-1.6
Tennessee	10.1	16.9	10.2	6.8
Texas	16.9	27.1	22.5	18.5
Utah	18.9	37.9	38.7	36.1
Vermont	14.1	15.0	12.0	8.8
Virginia	17.2	14.9	11.2	7.2
Washington	19.6	21.1	21.0	16.4
West Virginia	-6.2	11.8	4.2	1.5
Wisconsin	11.8	6.5	6.7	3.6
Wyoming	.6	41.3	48.3	42.9

SOURCE: Selected data from U.S. Bureau of the Census, Statistical Abstract of the United
States, 1984, (Washington: U.S. Government Printing Office, 1983), pp. 13
and 15.

PERCENT CHANGE IN POPULATION 1960-1980
AND PROJECTED 1980-2000

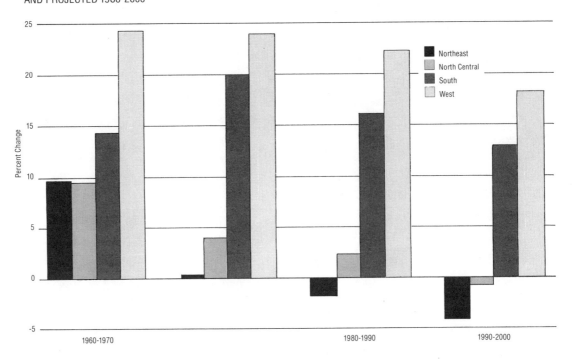

Chart 2

for children under five-years-old: Alaska, 21.7 percent; Florida, 10.6 percent; Arizona, 9.2 percent; Oklahoma, 8.9 percent; Colorado, 8.6 percent; Texas, 8.4 percent; Delaware, 7.7 percent; California, 7.6 percent; Hawaii, 7.1 percent; and Nevada, 6.1 percent (Tables 2 and 3).

The West and West South Central regions also are experiencing rapid growth among 25-to-44-year-olds—the child-bearing age group that began as the baby boomers after World War II and the Korean War. The West's 6.5 percent increases overall between 1980 and 1983 reflected gains of 15.8 percent for under-fives and 13.7 percent for the 25 to 44's (Table 4).

The West South Central's total increases of 8.6 percent included increases of 17.7 percent for children under-five and 17.0 percent for 22-44 year-olds, and the Northeast's 0.8 percent gain overall covered a 5 percent growth for children under-five and an 8.5 percent increase for the 25-44 year-old category.

Both of these age groups constituted a greater proportion of the entire

4

TABLE 2. Population (in thousands)

State	Percent change '72-'82	1982	1983	1984	Percent change '82-'83	Percent change '83-'84	Rank of percent change '82-'83	Rank of percent change '83-'84	1984 Rank
United States	10.6	231,786	233,975	236,158	0.9	0.9			
Alabama	11.4	3,941	3,959	3,990	0.4	0.7	37	26	22
Alaska	34.4	444	479	500	7.8	4.3	1	1	51
Arizona	42.4	2,892	2,963	3,053	2.4	3.0	5	2	28
Arkansas	13.5	2,307	2,328	2,349	0.9	0.9	22	20	33
California	20.1	24,697	25,174	25,622	1.9	1.7	10	8	1
Colorado	26.6	3,071	3,139	3,178	2.2	1.2	7	14	26
Connecticut	2.7	3,126	3,138	3,154	0.3	0.5	38	31	27
Delaware	4.9	600	606	613	1.0	1.1	20	16	48
District of Columbia	-15.2	626	623	623	-0.4	0.0	50	45	47
Florida	38.5	10,466	10,680	10,976	2.0	2.7	9	3	6
Georgia	17.3	5,648	5,732	5,837	1.4	1.8	12	6	11
Hawaii	20.0	997	1,023	1,039	2.6	1.5	3	11	39
Idaho	26.5	977	989	1,001	1.2	1.2	14	14	40
Illinois	1.7	11,466	11,486	11,511	0.1	0.2	43	42	5
Indiana	3.3	5,482	5,479	5,498	0.0	0.3	45	40	14
Iowa	1.5	2,906	2,905	2,910	0.0	0.1	45	44	29
Kansas	6.7	2,408	2,425	2,438	0.7	0.5	27	31	32
Kentucky	9.9	3,692	3,714	3,723	0.5	0.2	31	42	23
Louisiana	1.59	4,383	4,438	4,462	1.2	0.5	14	31	18
Maine	9.5	1,136	1,146	1,156	0.8	0.8	25	22	38
Maryland	4.5	4,270	4,304	4,349	0.7	1.0	27	19	19
Massachusetts	0.3	5,750	5,767	5,798	0.2	0.5	39	31	12
Michigan	0.9	9,116	9,069	9,075	-0.5	0.0	51	45	8
Minnesota	4.2	4,133	4,144	4,162	0.2	0.4	39	36	21
Mississippi	10.6	2,569	2,587	2,598	0.7	0.4	27	36	31
Missouri	4.2	4,942	4,970	5,008	0.5	0.7	31	26	15
Montana	11.4	805	817	824	1.4	0.8	12	22	44
Nebraska	4.5	1,589	1,597	1,606	0.5	0.5	31	31	36
Nevada	61.1	876	891	911	1.7	2.2	11	4	43
New Hampshire	21.6	948	959	977	1.1	1.8	16	6	41
New Jersey	1.4	7,427	7,468	7,515	0.5	0.6	31	29	9
New Mexico	26.1	1,367	1,399	1,424	2.3	1.7	6	8	37
New York	-3.8	17,567	17,667	17,735	0.5	0.3	31	40	2
North Carolina	13.7	6,019	6,082	6,165	1.0	1.3	20	13	10
North Dakota	6.2	672	680	686	1.1	0.8	16	22	46
Ohio	0.4	10,772	10,746	10,752	-0.2	0.0	48	45	7
Oklahoma	19.6	3,226	3,298	3,298	2.2	0.0	7	45	25
Oregon	20.7	2,668	2,662	2,674	-0.2	0.4	48	36	30
Pennsylvania	-0.3	11,879	11,895	11,901	0.1	0.0	43	45	4
Rhode Island	-1.8	953	955	962	0.2	0.7	39	26	42
South Carolina	17.8	3,227	3,264	3,300	1.1	1.1	16	16	24
South Dakota	2.1	694	700	706	0.8	0.8	25	22	45
Tennessee	13.8	4,656	4,685	4,717	0.6	0.6	30	29	17
Texas	29.9	15,329	15,724	15,989	2.5	1.6	4	10	3
Utah	36.9	1,571	1,619	1,652	3.0	2.0	2	5	35
Vermont	11.4	520	525	530	0.9	0.9	22	20	49
Virginia	13.7	5,485	5,550	5,636	1.1	1.5	16	11	13
Washington	36.9	4,276	4,300	4,349	00.5	1.1	31	16	19
West Virginia	8.4	1,961	1,965	1,952	0.2	-0.6	39	51	34
Wisconsin	5.9	4,745	4,747	4,766	0.0	0.4	45	36	16
Wyoming	44.7	509	514	511	0.9	-0.5	22	50	50

SOURCE: Compiled by the National Center for Education Information. Basic data from the U.S. Department of Commerce, Bureau of Economic Analysis, State Per Capita Personal Income, selected years (Washington: U.S. Department of Commerce, selected years).

TABLE 3. Population under age 5

State	Percent change '72-'82	1982	1983	1984	Percent change '82-'83	Percent change '83-'84	Rank of percent change '82-'83	Rank of percent change '83-'84	1984 Rank
United States	2.3	17,372,000	17,826,000	17,816,000	2.6	0.0			
Alabama	-0.7	302,000	302,000	296,000	0.0	-1.9	43	41	22
Alaska	31.4	46,000	52,000	56,000	13.0	7.6	1	1	47
Arizona	34.3	239,000	254,000	261,000	6.2	2.7	5	3	26
Arkansas	7.9	177,000	179,000	177,000	1.1	-1.1	37	30	34
California	18.3	1,917,000	2,008,000	2,063,000	4.7	2.7	12	3	1
Colorado	21.5	243,000	259,000	264,000	6.5	1.9	3	6	25
Connecticut	-17.2	193,000	193,000	195,000	0.0	1.0	43	10	33
Delaware	-10.4	43,000	43,000	43,000	0.0	0.0	43	16	49
District of Columbia	-33.9	39,000	41,000	42,000	5.1	2.4	10	5	50
Florida	20.1	651,000	691,000	720,000	6.1	4.1	6	2	7
Georgia	1.2	438,000	446,000	443,000	1.8	-0.6	28	27	10
Hawaii	13.5	84,000	89,000	90,000	5.9	1.1	8	9	39
Idaho	41.2	96,000	99,000	96,000	3.1	-3.0	17	49	38
Illinois	-3.7	881,000	896,000	885,000	1.7	-1.2	29	32	4
Indiana	6.5	420,000	420,000	409,000	0.0	-2.6	43	46	12
Iowa	1.8	227,000	226,000	220,000	-0.4	-2.6	50	46	29
Kansas	13.4	195,000	199,000	199,000	2.0	0.0	27	16	32
Kentucky	2.5	284,000	286,000	277,000	0.7	-3.1	40	50	24
Louisiana	13.6	392,000	407,000	405,000	3.8	-0.4	14	26	13
Maine	-3.6	81,000	82,000	82,000	1.2	0.0	35	16	40
Maryland	-11.9	289,000	298,000	301,000	3.1	1.0	17	10	21
Massachusetts	-19.7	351,000	359,000	362,000	2.2	0.8	25	12	16
Michigan	-12.2	686,000	682,000	664,000	-0.5	-2.6	51	46	8
Minnesota	4.4	329,000	336,000	330,000	2.1	-1.7	26	39	19
Mississippi	2.8	223,000	226,000	221,000	1.3	-2.2	33	43	28
Missouri	1.1	372,000	377,000	374,000	1.3	-0.7	33	28	15
Montana	19.0	69,000	71,000	70,000	2.8	-1.4	21	34	41
Nebraska	8.3	130,000	133,000	131,000	2.3	-1.5	23	36	37
Nevada	43.5	66,000	69,000	70,000	4.5	1.4	13	8	41
New Hampshire	3.1	66,000	68,000	68,000	3.0	0.0	19	16	43
New Jersey	-14.6	478,000	486,000	485,000	1.6	-0.2	30	25	9
New Mexico	24.8	126,000	133,000	133,000	5.5	0.0	9	16	36
New York	-16.8	1,171,000	1,182,000	1,183,000	0.9	0.0	38	16	3
North Carolina	-7.6	416,000	421,000	416,000	1.2	-1.1	35	30	11
North Dakota	1.8	59,000	61,000	61,000	3.3	0.0	16	16	45
Ohio	9.6	810,000	808,000	788,000	-0.2	-2.4	49	45	5
Oklahoma	24.0	258,000	280,000	281,000	8.5	0.3	2	15	23
Oregon	24.6	208,000	209,000	205,000	0.4	-1.9	41	41	31
Pennsylvania	-12.1	775,000	788,000	778,000	1.6	-1.2	30	32	6
Rhode Island	-17.8	60,000	60,000	60,000	0.0	0.0	43	16	46
South Carolina	3.7	250,000	254,000	252,000	1.6	-0.7	30	28	27
South Dakota	13.0	61,000	64,000	63,000	4.9	-1.5	11	36	44
Tennessee	0.0	331,000	334,000	329,000	0.9	-1.4	38	34	20
Texas	27.1	1,329,000	1,415,000	1,440,000	6.4	1.7	4	7	2
Utah	65.9	204,000	211,000	206,000	3.4	-2.3	15	44	30
Vermont	-2.6	38,000	39,000	39,000	2.6	0.0	22	16	51
Virginia	-3.3	380,000	389,000	391,000	2.3	0.5	23	13	14
Washington	21.5	333,000	343,000	345,000	3.0	0.5	19	13	18
West Virginia	1.4	143,000	143,000	136,000	0.0	-4.8	43	51	35
Wisconsin	0.8	363,000	364,000	358,000	0.2	-1.6	42	38	17
Wyoming	66.7	50,000	53,000	52,000	6.0	-1.8	7	40	48

SOURCE: Compiled by the National Center for Education Information. Basic data from the U.S. Bureau of the Census. Statistical Abstract of the United States, 1984 and 1985; (Washington: U.S. Bureau of the Census, 1983, 1984), and State Population Estimates by Age and Components of Change: 1980 to 1984, CPR Series P-25, No. 970, (Washington: U.S. Bureau of the Census, 1984.)

TABLE 4. Percent change in the resident population of regions by age: April 1, 1980
         to July 1, 1983

Regions	Total Resident	Under 5 Years	5-17 Years	18-24 Years	25-44 Years	45-64 Years	65 years and over
U.S.	3.3	9.0	-5.6	-0.4	10.9	0.1	7.2
Northeast	0.8	5.0	-9.4	--	8.5	-2.8	5.4
New England	1.1	6.0	-10.5	0.1	9.9	-2.9	6.4
Middle Atlantic	0.7	4.6	-9.1	--	8.0	-2.7	5.1
North Central	0.1	4.2	-8.3	-3.9	7.9	-3.5	5.9
East North Central	-0.4	3.0	-9.0	-3.9	7.3	-4.1	6.5
West North Central	1.4	7.3	-6.6	-3.8	9.6	-2.0	4.5
South	5.5	11.1	-3.3	2.0	13.1	3.4	8.1
South Atlantic	5.0	9.8	-5.4	2.8	12.0	2.9	9.8
East South Central	1.9	2.5	-5.7	-1.9	9.4	0.2	6.1
West South Central	8.6	17.7	1.1	3.1	17.0	6.3	6.3
West	6.5	15.8	-1.6	-0.4	13.7	3.2	9.9
Mountain	8.4	15.5	1.9	-0.4	15.6	5.8	12.9
Pacific	5.8	15.9	-2.9	-0.4	13.0	2.3	9.0

SOURCE: Selected data from U.S. Bureau of the Census, Estimates of the Population of
States, by Age: July 1, 1981 to 1983, CPR Series P-25, No. 951, (Washington: May
1984), p. 12.

population for 1983 than they did three years earlier--29.7 percent for the 25-44's
(up from 27.7 percent three years earlier). The population over 65 years of age rose
slightly during the period, from 11.3 percent to 11.7 percent, but every other age
group recorded a decline as a proportion of the total.[17]

Trends in Racial and Ethnic Composition of the U.S.

The new baby boom is disproportionately non-white. The number of under-
fives in the white population actually decreased 2.7 percent (14,464,000 in 1970 to
14,075,000 in 1982). Black children in this age group showed an 11.6 percent gain,
from 2,434,000 to 2,717,000 (Table 5 and Chart 3).

The number of white children between five and thirteen years of age dropped
19.8 percent as figures for the same age group for black children showed a 9.9
percent drop. Numbers of all children between fourteen and seventeen years old
decreased 5.6 percent, representing a 9.1 percent decline among white and 7.1
percent increase for black children fourteen to seventeen.

The percentage of black Americans increased from 11.1 percent in 1970 to
11.7 percent in 1980; of American Indians from 0.4 percent to 0.6 percent, of Asian

7

and Pacific Islanders from 0.8 percent to 1.5 percent, and of persons of Spanish origin from 4.5 percent to 6.4 percent.

From 1970 to 1980, the black population increased by 17.3 percent. There were also increases in the population of American Indians, by 71 percent; Chinese, 85.3 percent; Filipinos, 125.8 percent; Japanese, 18.5 percent, and Korean, 412.8 percent.

The white population in the United States increased by only 6 percent from 1970 to 1980. Still the overwhelming majority, it nevertheless dropped, as a percentage of total population, from 87.4 percent in 1970 to 83.2 percent in 1980.

Blacks, the second largest racial group in this country, represented about 12 percent of the total population in 1980. Fifty-three percent of all blacks, about the same proportion as a decade ago, live in the South. In 1980, the District of Columbia had the greatest proportion of blacks, 70.3 percent; followed by

PERCENT CHANGE IN POPULATION BY SELECTED AGE AND RACE: 1970-1982

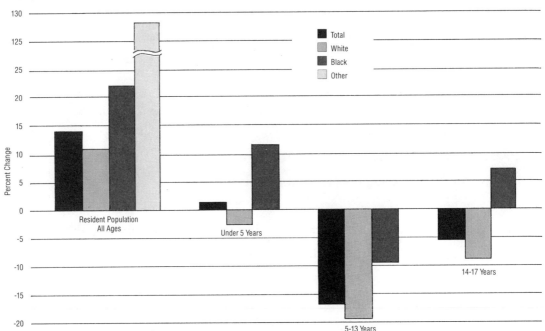

Chart 3

8

TABLE 5.   Population changes by selected age and race: 1970 and 1982, with percent changes

| | Population (in thousands) | | | | | | Percent Change | | |
| | 1970 | | | 1982 | | | | | |
Race	Under 5 years	5-13 yrs.	14-17 yrs.	Under 5 years	5-13 yrs.	14-17 yrs.	Under 5 years	5-13 yrs.	14-17 yrs.
All races	17,163	36,675	15,851	17,372	30,431	14,962	+1.2	-17.0	-5.6
White	14,464	31,171	13,579	14,075	24,989	12,342	-2.7	-19.8	-9.1
Black	2,434	5,009	2,073	2,717	4,515	2,220	+11.6	-9.9	+7.1

SOURCE: Compiled by the National Center for Education Information.   Basic data from U.S. Bureau of the Census, Statistical Abstract of the U.S., 1984, selected data, p. 33.

Mississippi, 35.2 percent; South Carolina, 30.4 percent; Louisiana, 29.4 percent; Georgia, 26.8 percent, and Alabama, 25.6 percent.

Although the West recorded the smallest proportion of blacks of any region in both 1970 and 1980, it was the only region that experienced an increase in the percentage of black residents—from 7.5 percent in 1970 to 8.5 percent in 1980. The Northeast had a slight decline in its black population, from 19.0 percent in 1970 to 18.0 percent in 1980. The proportion of blacks in the North Central region remained about the same, 20.6 percent.

The fastest growing minority group of significant size in the United States includes persons of Spanish origin. Their numbers increased by 61.0 percent— 9,294,500 in 1970 to 14,609,000 in 1980. In both 1970 and 1980, more than 60 percent of the nation's Hispanics lived in California, Texas, and New York. California ranks first in the number of Hispanics—4.5 million (19.2 percent of the state's total population); followed by Texas, with 3.0 million (21.0 percent), and New York, 1.7 million (9.5 percent). Other states with large Hispanic populations include New Mexico, 37.0 percent; Arizona, 16.0 percent, and Colorado, 12.0 percent.

Population Summary and Projections

For all age groups, the black population increased 49.5 percent from 1960 to 1983; the white, 25.8 percent; and the other-races group 294.7 percent.

According to the United States Bureau of the Census, our total population

TABLE 6. Resident population by race: 1960-1983 and projected 1985-2000, with percent changes

Resident population (in thousands)

Race	1960	1970	1980	1981	1982	1983	Percent change 1960-83
All Races	179,323	203,235	226,546	229,348	231,534	234,496	30.8
White	158,832	178,098	194,811	196,664	198,108	199,887	25.8
Blacks	18,872	22,581	26,631	27,153	27,589	28,215	49.5
Other Races	1,620	2,557	5,104	5,530	5,837	6,394	294.7

	Projected			
Race	1985	1990	2000	Percent change 1985-2000
Total	238,648	249,731	267,990	12.3
White	203,237	210,964	222,801	9.6
Black	29,107	31,452	35,795	23.0
By age, All races				
Under 5	18,462	19,200	17,624	-4.5
5-17 years	44,352	45,123	49,762	12.2
18-24 years	28,715	25,777	24,590	-14.4
25-44 years	73,779	81,351	80,105	8.6
45-64 years	44,668	46,481	60,873	36.3
65 years and over	28,673	31,799	35,036	22.2
16 years and over	183,054	191,901	208,222	13.7
18 years and over	175,834	185,409	200,604	14.1

SOURCE: Compiled by the National Center for Education Information. Basic data from U.S. Bureau of the Census, Statistical Abstract of the U.S. 1984, (Washington: 1983), p. 32.

will grow 12.3 percent from 1985 to 2000, with the white population increasing 9.6 percent and the black 23 percent. For the school-age category (ages five through seventeen), a 12.2 percent increase is projected for the next fifteen years, reversing declines of the past fifteen.

For the under-fives, who jumped 9 percent in the past three years (three times the rate of growth of all the population), a drop of 4.5 percent is expected toward the end of the century. The college-age category (eighteen to twenty-four) is forecast at a 14.4 percent decline by the end of the century.

The implications of these population changes for schooling in America are obvious. Enrollments in elementary schools will rise while secondary and college enrollments will fall in the next few years. Then enrollments at the secondary and college levels will pick up as the students pass through elementary schools. By the year 2000, enrollments in elementary grades will fall again.

CHAPTER II

Public Elementary and Secondary School Enrollment

Rapidly changing demographics are having a dramatic impact on schooling in America. Not only are elementary school enrollments on the rise, but the composition of enrollments is changing, making new demands on teachers.

o The population of children under five grew 9 percent—three times faster than the overall population in the U.S.—between 1980 and 1983.

o There are many more poor children coming to public schools today than there were fifteen years ago. Today, 13 million of the 62 million children under eighteen live below the poverty level, compared with 10 million of the 69 million children in 1970.

o Minority children made up 14.8 percent of all children under eighteen in 1970. They now comprise 18.3 percent of all children.

Classrooms today are filled with students from many different ethnic backgrounds. Minority enrollment in public elementary and secondary schools nationwide rose from 21.7 percent in 1972 to 26.7 percent in 1981 and is expected to reach one-third by the mid-1990s.

The rate of increase in minority school enrollments is in line with the general rate of growth of minority populations—up 25 percent for blacks, 150 percent for all other races, compared with 12 percent growth for whites since 1970.

Again, the rates of growth among minority populations and reflected in school enrollments differ radically from state to state. Further, in every state where minority populations are high, the greatest concentrations can be found in urban areas. Consequently, urban schools have the highest proportions of minorities enrolled.

Public School Enrollment Trends in the States

Enrollments in elementary and secondary schools started upward last fall for the first time since 1972-73, the highest year ever. After dropping 14.0 percent for a decade and continuing downward 1.1 percent from 1982-83 to 1983-84, public school enrollments rose 0.3 percent from 1983-84 to 1984-85 reaching a total of 39,373,476 (Table 7).

All but four states (New Jersey, New Mexico, Tennessee and West Virginia) had either more students enrolled in their public schools last fall than the year before or showed a slowing down of enrollment declines.

The positive turn-around in total enrollment is due to increases at the elementary level. Elementary school enrollment went up 1.3 percent last year over the year before while secondary enrollment continued to drop. There were 1.1 percent fewer students enrolled in secondary schools last year than in 1983-84 continuing the downward trend of 17.9 percent for the decade between 1972-73 and 1982-83.

There were 23,770,897 students enrolled in public elementary schools last year and 15,602,579 students in secondary schools.

Enrollments actually went up in twenty-six states in the last year—nine of them continuing the upward trend of the year before and seventeen states reversing the trend of decreasing enrollments of previous years.

Only seven states, all in the South and West, increased their enrollments in the decade between 1972-73 and 1982-83. These seven states still lead the pack in rates of growth in enrollments. Alaska had the sharpest enrollment increase last year over the year before—5 percent after a 2.4 percent increase for the decade between 1972-73 and 1982-83. Arizona followed at 3.8 percent after a decade growth of 4.4 percent. The remaining five states with continuing growth in enrollments since 1972-73 are: Utah, 3.1 percent increase in enrollment over the last year after a 20.7 percent jump for the earlier decade; Wyoming, 2.2 percent

12

TABLE 7. Public elementary and secondary enrollment

State	Percent change 1972-1982	1982-83	1983-84	1984-85	Percent change '82-'83	Percent change '83-'84	Rank of percent change '82-'83	Rank of percent change '83-'84	1984-85 Rank
United States	-14.0	39,698,833	39,223,841	39,373,476	-1.1	0.3			
Alabama	-7.6	724,037	721,901	727,567	-4.2	0.7	11	15	20
Alaska	2.4	89,324	89,517	94,990	0.2	5.0	7	1	48
Arizona	4.4	552,425	545,760	567,000	-1.2	3.8	30	2	26
Arkansas	-4.5	432,565	426,363	432,668	-1.4	1.4	35	12	32
California	-12.0	4,065,486	4,087,986	4,150,430	0.5	1.5	4	11	1
Colorado	-5.1	545,209	542,175	545,427	-0.5	0.6	16	16	27
Connecticut	-25.0	505,150	487,400	478,012	-3.5	-1.9	49	47	29
Delaware	-31.0	92,646	91,406	91,767	-1.3	0.3	34	20	49
District of Columbia	-37.4	91,105	88,843	87,397	-2.4	-1.6	45	46	51
Florida	-10.4	1,484,917	1,495,705	1,523,924	0.7	1.8	3	10	8
Georgia	-3.6	1,053,700	1,050,900	1,049,700	-0.2	-0.1	11	30	11
Hawaii	-9.0	161,874	161,932	163,364	0.0	0.8	9	13	40
Idaho	11.0	205,824	206,342	210,700	0.2	2.1	7	8	38
Illinois	-20.3	1,875,770	1,843,708	1,837,058	-1.7	-0.3	40	36	4
Indiana	-17.6	999,542	984,090	973,858	-1.5	-1.0	37	42	12
Iowa	-23.2	505,582	494,966	490,402	-2.1	-0.9	41	40	28
Kansas	-17.4	407,074	404,500	405,822	-0.6	0.3	20	20	33
Kentucky	-8.8	650,368	647,414	644,421	-0.4	-0.4	14	37	23
Louisiana	-8.5	775,700	768,450	795,800	-0.9	3.5	24	3	16
Maine	-14.3	211,986	207,000	207,839	-2.3	0.4	44	17	39
Maryland	-24.1	699,201	682,155	673,763	-2.4	-1.2	45	43	22
Massachusetts	-23.0	925,160	879,101	878,000	-4.9	-0.1	50	30	14
Michigan	-19.7	1,761,521	1,735,881	1,743,000	-1.4	0.4	35	17	6
Minnesota	-21.0	715,221	677,891	695,392	-5.2	2.5	51	6	21
Mississippi	-12.4	462,461	460,000	459,140	-0.5	-0.1	16	30	30
Missouri	-21.7	802,841	795,453	793,793	-0.9	-0.2	24	34	17
Montana	-11.7	152,400	153,700	154,240	0.8	0.3	2	20	42
Nebraska	-19.6	269,009	266,998	265,619	-0.7	-0.5	22	38	36
Nevada	14.7	151,100	151,200	151,600	0.0	0.2	9	25	43
New Hampshire	-4.0	160,199	158,597	158,615	-1.0	0.0	28	27	41
New Jersey	-22.8	1,172,520	1,147,841	1,117,782	-2.1	-2.6	41	50	9
New Mexico	-4.1	269,111	269,949	260,874	0.3	-3.3	5	51	37
New York	-22.9	2,705,413	2,633,600	2,625,900	-2.6	-0.2	47	34	3
North Carolina	-4.7	1,103,480	1,089,606	1,094,545	-1.2	0.4	30	17	10
North Dakota	-17.6	116,569	114,765	118,233	-1.5	3.0	37	5	46
Ohio	-23.4	1,856,500	1,828,100	1,806,100	-1.5	-1.2	37	43	5
Oklahoma	-4.3	593,825	588,038	590,000	-0.9	0.3	24	20	25
Oregon	-6.3	448,184	446,700	446,685	-0.3	0.0	13	27	31
Pennsylvania	-24.6	1,783,969	1,736,500	1,702,060	-2.6	-1.9	47	47	7
Rhode Island	-27.5	139,362	136,179	134,034	-2.2	-1.5	43	45	44
South Carolina	-3.1	605,519	600,800	602,720	-1.2	0.3	30	20	24
South Dakota	-23.8	123,625	122,656	122,818	-0.7	0.1	22	26	45
Tennessee	-6.3	830,224	826,470	820,753	-0.4	-0.6	14	39	15
Texas	5.3	2,985,659	2,995,000	3,059,845	0.3	2.1	5	8	2
Utah	20.7	369,338	378,208	390,141	2.4	3.1	1	4	34
Vermont	-14.0	91,510	91,038	90,900	-0.5	-0.1	16	30	50
Virginia	-8.8	975,727	966,110	965,222	-0.9	0.0	24	27	13
Washington	-6.6	738,618	734,364	740,886	-0.5	0.8	16	13	19
West Virginia	-8.5	375,115	371,251	362,941	-1.0	-2.2	28	49	35
Wisconsin	-21.1	784,830	774,646	767,542	-1.2	-0.9	30	40	18
Wyoming	18.9	101,665	100,965	103,187	-0.6	2.2	20	7	47

SOURCE: Compiled by the National Center for Education Information. Basic data from National Education Association, Estimates of School Statistics, selected years.

13

over the last year and 18.9 percent for the earlier decade; Idaho, 2.1 percent in the last year and 11.0 percent for the earlier decade; Texas, 2.1 percent and 5.3 percent; and Nevada, 0.2 percent last year following a 14.7 percent jump in enrollment from 1972-73 to 1982-83.

Three states showed a marked increase in enrollments after years of decline: Louisiana, up 3.5 percent last year over the year before and an 8.5 percent drop from 1972-73 to 1982-83; North Dakota, up 3.0 percent in the last year after a 17.6 percent decrease for the earlier decade; and Minnesota, up 2.5 percent following a decade decrease of 21.0 percent.

The remaining sixteen states that showed increased enrollments last year over the year before with their rates of change for the latest year and for the decade from 1972-73 to 1982-83 are shown in Table 9.

Public Elementary School Enrollment Trends

Thirty states increased their public elementary school enrollments last year, twenty of them reversing downward trends since 1972-73. With the exceptions of Delaware, Michigan, New York, Rhode Island, Vermont and Wisconsin, they are all located in the South and West (Table 10).

States registering the largest increases (3.5 percent or more) in elementary school enrollments over the past year with their enrollment changes for each of the last two years, and for the decade from 1972-73 to 1982-83 can be found in Table 11.

Twenty states and the District of Columbia showed a decrease in elementary school enrollments from 1983-84 to 1984-85, three of them actually reversing an increase in the year before--Nevada, New Mexico and Oklahoma. Nevada's public elementary school enrollment dropped 2.8 percent last year after increasing 12.2 percent between 1972-73 and 1982-83 and increasing 0.1 percent from 1982-83 to 1983-84. New Mexico's dropped 5.3 percent last year after increasing 0.9 percent the year before and 3.8 percent in the preceding decade. Oklahoma registered a 3.0 percent decline in elementary school enrollment last year over the previous year

TABLE 8. States showing continuous enrollment increases since 1972-73

Percent change in total enrollment

	1972-73 to 1982-83	1982-83 to 1983-84	1983-84 to 1984-85
Alaska	2.4	0.2	5.0
Arizona	4.4	-1.2	3.8
Utah	20.7	2.4	3.1
Wyoming	18.9	-0.6	2.2
Idaho	11.0	0.2	2.1
Texas	5.3	0.3	2.1
Nevada	14.7	0.0	0.2

SOURCE: Compiled by the National Center for Education Information. Basic data from the National Education Association, Estimates of School Statistics, selected years.

after showing an increase of 0.3 percent from 1982-83 to 1983-84 and a 0.1 percent decrease for the decade earlier.

With the exceptions of New Mexico, North Carolina, Oklahoma, Tennessee, Virginia, and West Virginia, states having decreased enrollments in public elementary schools are in the Northeast and North Central regions.

What we are seeing is a slight breakdown in regional barriers regarding public elementary school enrollment trends. As indicated above, six states in the Northeast and North Central regions showed increases in enrollments at the elementary school level and six states in the South and West registered decreases in elementary enrollments. The baby boomlet of the late 70s was not regional.

TABLE 9. Additional states showing enrollment gains in 1984-85

State	Percentage change 1983-84 to 1984-85	Percentage change 1982-83 to 1983-84	Percentage change 1972-73 to 1982-83
Alabama	0.7	-0.2	-7.6
Arkansas	1.4	-1.4	-4.5
California	1.5	0.5	-12.0
Colorado	0.6	-0.5	-5.1
Delaware	0.3	-1.3	-31.0
Florida	1.8	0.7	-10.4
Hawaii	0.8	0.0	-9.0
Kansas	0.3	-0.6	-17.4
Maine	0.4	-2.3	-14.3
Michigan	0.4	-1.4	-19.7
Montana	0.3	0.8	-11.7
North Carolina	0.4	-1.2	-4.7
Oklahoma	0.3	-0.9	-4.3
South Carolina	0.3	-1.2	-3.1
South Dakota	0.1	-0.7	-23.8
Washington	0.8	-0.5	-6.6

SOURCE: Compiled by the National Center for Education Information. Basic data from the National Education Association, Estimates of School Statistics, selected years.

TABLE 10. Public elementary school enrollment

State	Percent change 1972-1982	1982-83	1983-84	1984-85	Percent change '82-'83	Percent change '83-'84	Rank of percent change '82-'83	Rank of percent change '83-'84	1984-85 Rank
United States	-11.1	23,671,666	23,443,766	23,770,897	-0.9	1.3			
Alabama	-5.1	386,828	385,291	392,304	-0.3	1.8	16	12	22
Alaska	5.3	49,256	50,200	52,000	1.9	4.6	1	4	48
Arizona	2.2	388,873	387,175	401,000	-0.4	3.5	19	5	21
Arkansas	-1.7	233,645	232,536	232,337	-0.4	0.0	19	26	34
California	-1.2	2,801,818	2,835,050	2,855,780	1.1	0.7	4	21	1
Colorado	-0.5	320,798	319,064	322,416	-0.5	1.0	21	18	27
Connecticut	-29.5	337,299	325,936	315,794	-3.3	-3.1	49	50	28
Delaware	-33.6	45,963	45,545	46,901	-0.9	3.0	27	6	51
District of Columbia	-41.8	50,921	50,251	49,787	-1.3	-0.9	35	39	49
Florida	-10.2	783,685	778,909	795,797	-0.6	2.1	23	10	8
Georgia	-5.3	652,900	648,500	648,970	-0.6	0.0	23	26	11
Hawaii	-10.1	86,925	86,920	88,813	0.0	2.2	13	9	42
Idaho	28.7	115,237	115,550	118,647	0.2	2.6	8	8	39
Illinois	-12.5	1,286,858	1,271,447	1,266,937	-1.1	-0.3	32	34	4
Indiana	-19.3	523,733	515,914	505,758	-1.4	-1.9	36	44	17
Iowa	-26.4	268,213	262,581	262,733	-2.1	0.0	45	26	30
Kansas	-11.5	248,496	249,000	253,789	0.2	1.9	8	11	32
Kentucky	-3.9	434,426	431,243	427,966	-0.7	-0.7	25	38	19
Louisiana	7.6	556,000	555,390	579,900	-0.1	4.4	14	1	14
Maine	-17.2	146,848	144,500	144,136	-1.6	-0.2	40	32	37
Maryland	-32.6	344,147	335,757	328,320	-2.4	-2.2	47	46	26
Massachusetts	-9.0	613,974	586,482	578,000	-4.4	-1.4	50	42	15
Michigan	-21.5	1,156,597	1,132,701	1,140,000	-2.0	0.6	44	22	5
Minnesota	-23.8	353,137	348,193	347,678	-1.4	-0.1	36	31	24
Mississippi	-16.1	256,325	255,000	257,101	-0.5	0.8	21	20	31
Missouri	-24.8	547,057	546,155	545,062	-0.1	-0.2	14	32	16
Montana	-8.5	106,900	108,300	108,905	1.3	0.5	3	23	40
Nebraska	-16.8	151,105	149,519	149,497	-1.0	0.0	28	26	36
Nevada	12.2	81,640	81,730	79,400	0.1	-2.8	12	47	45
New Hampshire	-3.4	93,887	92,948	92,632	-1.0	-0.3	28	34	41
New Jersey	-25.0	738,245	725,703	712,027	-1.6	-1.8	40	43	10
New Mexico	3.8	149,900	151,332	143,196	0.9	-5.3	5	51	38
New York	-30.3	1,314,575	1,285,800	1,306,300	-2.1	1.5	45	15	3
North Carolina	-3.6	770,952	761,053	758,402	-1.2	-0.3	33	34	9
North Dakota	-14.5	80,647	80,903	83,157	0.3	2.8	6	7	44
Ohio	-24.0	1,148,400	1,130,800	1,108,400	-1.5	-1.9	38	44	6
Oklahoma	-0.1	343,317	344,611	334,000	0.3	-3.0	6	48	25
Oregon	-1.3	276,238	275,330	278,672	-0.3	1.2	16	16	29
Pennsylvania	-28.2	872,629	844,640	832,850	-3.2	-1.3	48	41	7
Rhode Island	-40.8	73,591	68,642	68,615	-6.7	0.0	51	26	46
South Carolina	8.9	424,363	420,000	422,420	-1.0	0.5	28	23	20
South Dakota	-22.3	85,718	85,920	86,228	0.2	0.3	8	25	43
Tennessee	8.6	592,002	590,148	583,578	-0.3	-1.1	16	40	13
Texas	23.3	1,663,304	1,668,000	1,687,880	0.2	1.1	8	17	2
Utah	35.3	221,521	225,244	234,437	1.6	4.0	2	3	33
Vermont	-26.3	48,166	47,415	48,300	-1.5	1.8	38	12	50
Virginia	-9.8	600,396	588,476	585,028	-1.9	-0.5	42	37	12
Washington	-7.6	381,411	377,303	383,657	-1.0	1.6	28	14	23
West Virginia	-2.0	225,253	220,825	214,029	-1.9	-3.0	42	48	35
Wisconsin	-22.6	449,982	446,807	451,474	-0.7	1.0	25	18	18
Wyoming	30.6	58,254	57,505	59,887	-1.2	4.1	33	2	47

SOURCE: Compiled by the National Center for Education Information. Basic data from National Education Association, _Estimates of School Statistics_, selected years.

16

TABLE 11. States showing greatest elementary school enrollment gains in 1984-85

State	Percentage change 1983-84 to 1984-85	Percentage change 1982-83 to 1983-84	Percentage change 1972-73 to 1982-83
Alaska	3.6	1.9	-5.3
Arizona	3.5	-0.4	2.2
Delaware	3.0	-0.9	-33.6
Louisiana	4.4	-0.1	7.6
Utah	4.0	1.6	35.3
Wyoming	4.1	-1.2	30.6

SOURCE: Compiled by the National Center for Education Information. Basic data from the National Education Association Estimates of School Statistics, selected years.

Public Secondary School Enrollment Trends

As predicted, school enrollments at the secondary levels continue to fall. Last year, secondary enrollments dropped 1.1 percent following a 1.5 percent decline the year before and a 17.9 percent decrease from 1972-73 to 1982-83 (Table 12).

Only six states had an increase in secondary school enrollments in the decade from 1972-73 to 1982-83. Four of them continue to enroll more students in their public secondary schools. Two of them are now enrolling fewer secondary school students than they did two years ago. These six states, with their percentage change over the last year and change in the earlier decade are: Alaska, 6.8 percent and 14.1 percent; Arizona, 4.6 percent and 10.1 percent; Nevada, 3.9 percent and 17.9 percent; Utah, 1.8 percent and 4.0 percent; Vermont, -2.3 percent and 5.7 percent; and Wyoming, -0.3 percent and 5.6 percent.

Nearly half (24) of the states and the District of Columbia showed a decrease in secondary school enrollments in 1984-85 over 1983-84, compared with 36 that had declines in secondary enrollments from 1982-83 to 1983-84.

Ten of the states that had a decrease in secondary enrollments in both of the last two years showed a greater rate of decrease in the latter year—Alabama, Delaware, Kansas, Mississippi, Nebraska, New Jersey, New Mexico, Oregon, Pennsylvania, and Wisconsin.

An additional five states had a decrease in enrollment last year showing an increase the year before--Georgia, Rhode Island, Vermont, West Virginia, and Wyoming.

TABLE 12. Public secondary school enrollment

State	Percent change 1972-1982	1982-83	1983-84	1984-85	Percent change '82-'83	Percent change '83-'84	Rank of percent change '82-'83	Rank of percent change '83-'84	1984-85 Rank
United States	-17.9	16,027,167	15,780,075	15,602,579	-1.5	-1.1			
Alabama	-10.2	337,209	336,610	335,263	-0.1	-0.4	16	33	17
Alaska	14.1	40,068	39,317	41,990	-1.8	6.8	31	1	48
Arizona	10.1	163,552	158,585	166,000	-3.0	4.6	43	4	31
Arkansas	-7.6	198,920	193,827	200,331	-2.5	3.3	38	7	28
California	-29.0	1,263,668	1,252,936	1,294,650	-0.8	3.3	25	7	3
Colorado	-10.6	224,411	223,111	223,011	-0.5	0.0	22	22	24
Connecticut	-13.8	167,851	161,464	162,218	-3.8	0.4	47	19	32
Delaware	-28.0	46,683	45,861	44,866	-1.7	-2.2	30	44	45
District of Columbia	-30.8	40,184	38,592	37,610	-3.9	-2.5	48	47	49
Florida	-10.8	701,232	716,796	728,127	2.2	1.5	4	14	5
Georgia	-0.4	400,800	402,400	400,730	0.4	-0.4	7	33	11
Hawaii	-7.8	74,949	75,012	74,551	0.0	-0.6	13	36	39
Idaho	-6.5	90,587	90,792	92,053	0.2	1.4	10	15	38
Illinois	-33.5	588,912	572,261	570,121	-2.8	-0.3	41	31	8
Indiana	-15.7	475,809	468,176	468,100	-1.6	0.0	29	22	9
Iowa	-19.3	237,389	232,385	227,669	-2.1	-2.0	35	42	23
Kansas	-25.0	158,578	155,500	152,033	-1.9	-2.2	33	44	34
Kentucky	-17.0	215,942	216,171	216,455	0.1	0.1	11	21	25
Louisiana	-33.1	219,700	213,060	215,900	-3.0	1.3	43	16	26
Maine	-7.0	56,138	62,300	63,703	11.0	2.2	1	12	43
Maryland	-13.6	355,054	346,398	345,443	-2.4	-0.2	37	28	15
Massachusetts	-40.9	311,186	292,619	300,000	-5.9	2.5	50	10	19
Michigan	-17.6	604,924	603,180	603,000	-0.2	0.0	17	22	7
Minnesota	-18.1	362,084	329,698	347,714	-8.9	5.4	51	2	14
Mississippi	-7.5	206,136	205,000	202,039	-0.5	-1.4	22	40	27
Missouri	-13.9	255,784	249,298	248,731	-2.5	-0.2	38	28	21
Montana	-18.3	45,500	45,400	45,335	-0.2	-0.1	17	27	44
Nebraska	-23.1	117,904	117,479	116,122	-0.3	-1.1	19	39	37
Nevada	17.9	69,460	69,470	72,200	0.0	3.9	13	5	40
New Hampshire	-4.9	66,312	65,649	65,983	-1.0	0.5	26	18	41
New Jersey	-18.5	434,275	422,138	405,755	-2.7	-3.8	40	51	10
New Mexico	-12.4	119,211	118,617	117,678	-0.4	-0.7	21	37	36
New York	-14.4	1,390,838	1,347,800	1,319,600	-3.0	-2.0	43	42	2
North Carolina	-7.1	332,528	328,553	336,143	-1.1	2.3	27	11	16
North Dakota	-23.9	35,922	33,862	35,076	-5.8	3.6	49	6	51
Ohio	-22.5	708,100	697,300	697,700	-1.5	0.0	28	22	6
Oklahoma	-9.5	250,508	243,427	256,000	-2.8	5.1	41	3	20
Oregon	-13.4	171,946	171,370	168,013	-0.3	-1.9	19	41	30
Pennsylvania	-20.7	911,340	891,860	869,210	-2.1	-2.5	35	47	4
Rhode Island	-6.1	65,771	67,537	65,419	2.7	-3.1	3	49	42
South Carolina	-22.6	184,156	180,800	180,300	-1.8	-0.2	31	28	29
South Dakota	-27.1	37,907	36,736	36,590	-3.1	-0.4	46	33	50
Tennessee	-30.1	238,222	236,322	237,175	-0.7	0.3	24	20	22
Texas	-16.4	1,322,355	1,327,000	1,371,965	0.3	3.3	8	7	1
Utah	4.0	147,817	152,964	155,704	3.5	1.8	2	13	33
Vermont	5.7	43,344	43,623	42,600	0.6	-2.3	5	46	47
Virginia	-7.1	375,331	377,634	380,194	0.6	0.6	5	17	12
Washington	-5.4	357,207	357,061	357,229	0.0	0.0	13	22	13
West Virginia	-16.7	149,862	150,426	148,912	0.3	-1.0	8	38	35
Wisconsin	-19.2	334,848	327,839	316,068	-2.0	-3.5	34	50	18
Wyoming	5.6	43,411	43,460	43,300	0.1	-0.3	11	31	46

SOURCE: Compiled by the National Center for Education Information. Basic data from National Education Association, _Estimates of School Statistics_, selected years.

18

Racial and Ethnic Composition of Public Elementary and Secondary Schools

The rate of growth among minorities is the biggest contributing factor to increased enrollments in schools. The new baby boomlet hitting the schools this fall is disproportionately non-white. There were 400,000 fewer white children under five years old in 1982 than in 1970—which had the highest number in a decade—but there were 280,000 more black children.

Since 1970, the population of white children under five decreased 2.7 percent while the population of black children in this age group increased 12 percent. Numbers of white children five to thirteen years old decreased 20 percent and numbers of black children of elementary school age decreased only 10 percent in the last fifteen years. White high school age children (ages fourteen to seventeen) decreased 9 percent, compared with a 7 percent increase for black children in this age group.[18]

The fastest growing minority populations in the United States are Hispanics. While Hispanics make up 6.4 percent of the total population, they make up 8.0 percent of public school enrollment.

Minorities represented almost 14 percent of the total population in 1980 and 26.7 percent of public elementary and secondary school enrollment. By the year 2000, minorities are expected to make up 17 percent of the total United States population and well over a third of school enrollments.

Between 1972 and 1981 (the latest year for which state-by-state data is available), public elementary and secondary school enrollments declined, but the minority proportion of a diminishing pool of students increased—from 21.7 percent in 1972 to 26.7 percent in 1981 (Table 13).

Some states are experiencing dramatic increases in minority enrollments, whereas others have very small numbers of minorities in their schools. The range is from 96.4 percent minority enrollment in the District of Columbia, 57.0 percent in New Mexico and 51.6 percent in Mississippi to a low of 0.9 percent in Maine.

In seven states and the District of Columbia, more than 40 percent of students enrolled in school were minority students in 1981: Hawaii, 75.2 percent minority; California, 42.9 percent; the District of Columbia, 96.4 percent;

TABLE 13. Minority enrollment as a percentage of total enrollment

	Percent Change '72 to '81	1972	1976	1981
United States	5.0	21.7	24.0	26.7
Alabama	-0.9	34.5	34.2	33.6
Alaska	12.1	16.3	25.8	28.4
Arizona	6.5	27.2	31.4	33.7
Arkansas	-5.9	29.4	23.2	23.5
California	15.3	27.6	34.9	42.9
Colorado	3.7	18.4	20.3	22.1
Connecticut	4.0	13.0	15.4	17.0
Delaware	7.5	21.3	24.3	28.8
District of Columbia	0.9	95.5	96.5	96.4
Florida	4.2	28.0	29.1	32.2
Georgia	0.6	33.7	35.2	34.3
Hawaii	0.0	0.0	79.5	75.2
Idaho	3.7	4.5	5.7	8.2
Illinois	3.7	24.9	25.4	28.6
Indiana	0.7	11.3	11.4	12.0
Iowa	1.3	2.8	3.2	4.1
Kansas	2.4	10.3	10.7	12.7
Kentucky	-0.4	9.5	10.1	9.1
Louisiana	2.4	41.0	41.9	43.4
Maine	0.2	0.7	0.9	0.9
Maryland	8.7	24.8	30.2	33.5
Massachusetts	4.2	6.5	7.7	10.7
Michigan	5.1	16.2	18.3	21.3
Minnesota	3.1	2.8	4.1	5.9
Mississippi	0.5	51.1	49.0	51.6
Missouri	-2.1	16.9	12.8	14.8
Montana	5.2	6.9	9.0	12.1
Nebraska	2.4	8.1	7.5	10.5
Nevada	4.7	14.2	17.0	18.9
New Hampshire	0.4	0.9	1.1	1.3
New Jersey	6.8	21.6	24.5	28.4
New Mexico	9.7	47.3	53.5	57.0
New York	5.3	26.7	29.7	32.0
North Carolina	1.1	30.8	31.4	31.9
North Dakota	1.1	2.4	6.2	3.5
Ohio	0.7	14.0	14.0	14.7
Oklahoma	4.4	16.4	22.0	20.8
Oregon	3.9	4.6	6.5	8.5
Pennsylvania	1.5	13.3	14.4	14.8
Rhode Island	3.1	5.1	6.5	8.2
South Carolina	2.3	41.2	41.8	43.5
South Dakota	5.4	7.8	7.9	2.5
Tennessee	3.0	21.6	21.9	24.6
Texas	7.9	38.0	40.8	45.9
Utah	1.2	6.1	6.7	7.3
Vermont	0.5	0.8	1.0	0.5
Virginia	2.7	24.8	25.8	27.5
Washington	7.1	7.0	10.1	14.1
West Virginia	-0.6	4.9	4.5	4.3
Wisconsin	2.6	6.7	8.0	9.3
Wyoming	-1.8	9.3	8.7	7.5

SOURCE: U.S. Department of Education, Office of Planning, Budget, and Evaluation; National Center for Education Statistics, State Education Statistics (chart), 1984.

Louisiana, 43.4 percent; Mississippi, 51.6 percent; New Mexico, 57.0 percent; South Carolina, 43.5 percent; and Texas, 45.9 percent.

In seven states, less than 5 percent of all enrolled students were members of minorites in 1981: Iowa, 4.1 percent minority enrollment; Maine, 0.9 percent; New Hampshire, 1.3 percent; North Dakota, 3.5 percent; South Dakota, 7.9 percent; Vermont, 1.0 percent; and West Virginia, 4.3 percent.

California led the states in increases in minority enrollment between 1972 and 1981 (15.3 percent increase), followed by Alaska (12.1 percent), then New Mexico (9.7 percent), Maryland (8.7 percent), Texas (7.9 percent) and New Jersey (6.8 percent).

CHAPTER III

Numbers of Public School Teachers

After dropping at both the elementary and secondary levels from 1982-83 to 1983-84, the total number of teachers in the United States increased last year—by 1.1 percent in elementary schools and by 1.6 percent in secondary schools for a total increase of 1.3 percent (Table 14).

There were 2,145,542 teachers employed in the nation's public schools in 1984-85—1,184,337 in elementary schools and 961,205 in secondary schools. These numbers represent a net increase of 13,284 elementary school teachers and 15,201 secondary school teachers representing a total of 28,485 more teachers last year than the year before.

One-third of the 2.14 million public school teachers in the United States teach in just five states—California, Illinois, New York, Pennsylvania, and Texas. New York, California and Illinois rank in the top ten in average teacher salary. Pennsylvania ranks eighteenth and Texas fourteenth in average salary for teachers.

Sixty percent of all teachers are employed by only thirteen states, each of which employed 50,000 teachers more last fall than it did in fall 1983. These states are: Florida, Georgia, Massachusetts, Michigan, New Jersey, North Carolina, Ohio, and Virginia in addition to the above-mentioned five states.

Massachusetts increased its teaching force by 16.8 percent last year over the previous year, 8,066 teachers—6,899 at the secondary level (a 24.4 percent increase) and 1,167 at the elementary level (a 5.8 percent increase).

Michigan had 6,945 additional teachers—4,734 at the elementary level (a 12.7 percent increase) and 2,211 at the secondary level (a 6.3 percent increase). California increased its total teaching force by 2.7 percent (4,700 teachers) which

TABLE 14. Numbers of public elementary and secondary teachers

State	Percent change 1972-1982	1982-83	1983-84	1984-85	Percent change '82-'83	Percent change '83-'84	Rank of percent change '82-'83	Rank of percent change '83-'84	1984-85 Rank
United States	1.4	2,135,511	2,117,057	2,145,542	-0.8	1.3			
Alabama	15.0	39,084	39,200	36,099	0.2	-7.9	17	50	21
Alaska	35.9	6,027	6,387	6,090	5.9	-4.6	2	48	49
Arizona	34.8	25,753	25,662	25,920	-0.3	1.0	23	26	30
Arkansas	14.0	23,712	23,897	24,085	0.7	0.7	14	29	33
California	-9.1	173,270	170,435	175,135	-1.6	2.7	39	10	1
Colorado	16.6	29,375	29,447	28,822	0.2	-2.1	17	47	28
Connecticut	-7.2	33,210	32,715	32,467	-1.5	-0.7	37	41	25
Delaware	-14.1	5,409	5,436	5,516	0.4	1.4	16	21	51
District of Columbia	-24.8	5,344	5,648	5,792	5.6	2.5	3	13	50
Florida	22.8	82,008	83,074	86,223	1.3	3.7	10	8	7
Georgia	16.1	56,520	56,270	56,321	-0.4	0.0	24	36	12
Hawaii	16.6	8,226	8,073	8,141	-1.8	0.8	42	28	42
Idaho	24.8	9,810	9,900	10,160	0.9	2.6	12	12	39
Illinois	-5.1	103,586	101,056	100,497	-2.4	-0.5	45	38	5
Indiana	-3.1	50,442	49,456	49,646	-1.9	0.3	43	34	14
Iowa	0.2	30,814	30,686	30,336	-0.4	-1.1	24	44	27
Kansas	2.1	26,052	25,802	26,260	-0.9	1.7	33	19	29
Kentucky	2.5	32,237	32,000	32,400	-0.7	1.2	30	23	26
Louisiana	6.2	42,460	41,620	41,720	-2.0	0.2	44	35	17
Maine	9.2	12,277	12,273	12,510	0.0	1.9	20	17	38
Maryland	-10.8	37,493	37,437	37,694	-0.1	0.6	21	30	20
Massachusetts	-9.6	52,000	48,267	56,333	-7.1	16.8	51	1	11
Michigan	-14.4	76,837	72,955	79,900	-5.1	9.6	50	2	8
Minnesota	-10.6	39,736	38,544	39,400	-3.0	2.2	47	15	19
Mississippi	6.0	24,982	24,864	24,772	-0.4	-0.3	24	37	31
Missouri	2.6	45,957	46,714	47,240	1.6	1.1	9	25	15
Montana	4.8	9,520	9,350	9,756	-1.7	4.3	41	4	41
Nebraska	-7.6	17,378	16,785	17,513	-3.4	4.3	48	4	35
Nevada	37.5	7,222	7,293	7,496	0.9	2.7	12	10	45
New Hampshire	21.6	9,758	9,718	10,104	-0.4	3.9	24	6	40
New Jersey	-5.5	74,303	73,262	72,858	-1.4	-0.5	35	38	9
New Mexico	16.9	14,650	15,530	14,200	6.0	-8.5	1	51	37
New York	-12.8	165,200	164,000	164,900	-0.7	0.5	30	32	3
North Carolina	12.8	55,261	54,709	56,084	-1.0	2.5	34	13	13
North Dakota	4.7	7,499	7,385	7,300	-1.5	-1.1	37	44	46
Ohio	-9.2	94,130	92,765	94,429	-1.4	1.8	35	18	6
Oklahoma	20.2	35,073	35,693	35,000	1.7	-1.9	8	46	23
Oregon	10.7	25,272	23,990	24,413	-5.0	1.7	49	19	32
Pennsylvania	-8.0	103,855	102,150	101,150	-1.6	-0.9	39	42	4
Rhode Island	-7.7	7,399	7,441	7,548	0.5	1.4	15	21	44
South Carolina	19.2	32,030	32,070	33,340	0.1	3.9	19	6	24
South Dakota	-2.3	7,812	7,989	8,022	2.2	0.4	6	33	43
Tennessee	5.6	39,409	39,136	40,008	-0.7	2.2	30	15	18
Texas	27.8	167,298	171,096	172,639	2.2	0.9	6	27	2
Utah	20.8	15,077	15,433	16,188	2.3	4.8	5	3	36
Vermont	9.3	6,251	6,235	6,200	-0.2	-0.5	22	38	48
Virginia	6.1	56,428	56,154	56,863	-0.4	1.2	24	23	10
Washington	5.4	34,121	33,979	35,155	-0.4	3.5	24	9	22
West Virginia	23.5	22,159	22,417	22,557	1.1	0.6	11	30	34
Wisconsin	2.1	49,038	47,600	45,350	-2.9	-4.7	46	49	16
Wyoming	62.4	6,747	7,059	6,990	4.6	-0.9	4	42	47

SOURCE: Compiled by the National Center for Education Information. Basic data from National Education Association, Estimates of School Statistics, selected years.

23

TABLE 15. States that added teachers in 1983-84 and in 1984-85

State	Percentage change 1983-84 to 1984-85	Percentage change 1982-83 to 1983-84	Percentage change 1972-73 to 1982-83
Arkansas	0.7	0.7	14.0
Delaware	1.4	0.4	-14.1
District of Columbia	2.5	5.6	-24.8
Florida	3.7	1.3	22.8
Idaho	2.6	0.9	24.8
Missouri	1.1	1.6	2.6
Nevada	2.7	0.9	37.5
Rhode Island	1.4	0.5	-7.7
South Carolina	3.9	0.1	19.2
South Dakota	0.4	2.2	-2.3
Texas	0.9	2.2	27.8
Utah	4.8	2.3	20.8
West Virginia	0.6	1.1	23.5

SOURCE: Compiled by the National Center for Education Information. Basic data from the National Education Association, Estimates of School Statistics, selected years.

represented an actual decrease in the number of elementary school teachers (1,456 or 1.3 percent fewer) and a 10.0 percent increase (6,156 teachers) in secondary schools.

Florida, another big growth state, employed a total of 3,149 more teachers in 1984-85 than it had in 1983-84—1,751 at the elementary level (a 3.8 percent increase) and 1,398 in secondary schools (a 3.8 percent increase).

Noteworthy also in this story of increasing numbers of teachers is the fact that many teachers who had been teaching two years ago were not teaching last year. The National Center for Education Statistics estimates that the annual rate of turnover (teachers leaving) is 6 percent.

Thirty-five states and the District of Columbia increased the number of teachers in their public elementary and secondary schools last year over the previous year, compared with eighteen states and the District of Columbia that increased their numbers of teachers from 1982-83 to 1983-84.

Twelve states and the District of Columbia added teachers in both of the last two years, four of them reversing a trend of fewer teachers in 1982-83 than in 1972-73 (Table 15).

It is important to note that states that added a lot of teachers two years ago may not have added very many additional teachers last year and vice-versa—states that increased their rolls of teachers in 1984-85 may have decreased their numbers of teachers from 1982-83 to 1983-84. For example, Massachusetts had the largest drop in number of teachers from 1982-83 to 1983-84 (7.1 percent) but had the biggest rate of increase in number of teachers the following year (16.8 percent).

Fifteen states had fewer teachers last year than they had the year before and thirty-two had fewer teachers in 1983-84 than they had in 1982-83.

Nine states dropped teachers in both the 1983-84 and 1984-85 school years. These states with their percentage changes in numbers of teachers from 1983-84 to 1984-85, from 1982-83 to 1983-84 and from 1972-73 to 1982-83 are listed in Table 16.

It is noteworthy that all of these states experienced declines in their public elementary and secondary school enrollments over the past two years, except North Dakota which had an increase in elementary enrollments both years and an increase in secondary enrollment last year.

In addition to North Dakota, five states decreased their numbers of teachers last year even though their enrollments went up. It makes more sense to analyze these data separately for elementary schools and for secondary schools since the overall trend reflects an increase at the elementary level and a decrease at the secondary level.

TABLE 16. States that decreased numbers of teachers in 1983-84 and 1984-85

State	Percentage change 1983-84 to 1984-85	Percentage change 1982-83 to 1983-84	Percentage change 1972-73 to 1982-83
Connecticut	-0.7	-1.5	-7.2
Illinois	-0.5	-2.4	-5.1
Iowa	-1.1	-0.4	0.2
Mississippi	-0.3	-0.4	6.0
New Jersey	-0.5	-1.4	-5.5
North Dakota	-1.1	-1.5	4.7
Pennsylvania	-0.9	-1.6	-8.0
Vermont	-5.5	-0.2	9.3
Wisconsin	-4.7	-2.9	2.1

SOURCE: Compiled by the National Center for Education Information. Basic data from the National Education Association, Estimates of School Statistics, selected years.

Numbers of Public Elementary School Teachers

With elementary school enrollments on the rise it is no surprise that the number of elementary school teachers is on the ascendant. Thirty-one states and the District of Columbia added more teachers for their elementary schools last year. The year earlier, 1983-84, when enrollments were still on the wane, only sixteen states and the District of Columbia added teachers at the elementary school level (Table 17).

Six states decreased their numbers of elementary school teachers last year even though they had an increase in elementary enrollments. These states' percentage changes in numbers of teachers and in school enrollments, respectively, at the elementary level are: Alabama, a 6.5 percent drop in teachers and 1.8 percent increase in enrollment; California, 1.3 percent drop in teachers and 0.7 percent increase in enrollment; Mississippi, 0.5 percent drop in teachers and 0.8 percent increase in enrollment; North Dakota, 2.1 percent drop in teachers and 2.8 percent increase in enrollment; Vermont, 4.1 percent drop in teachers and 1.8 percent increase in enrollment; and Wisconsin, 3.8 percent drop in teachers and 1.0 percent increase in enrollment.

Eighteen states had increases in both elementary school enrollments and numbers of teachers in 1984-85 over the previous year. An additional nine states and the District of Columbia added teachers even though their elementary school enrollments went down last year. Four states maintained the same number of teachers in 1984-85 as they had in 1983-84.

Numbers of Public Secondary School Teachers

Secondary schools employed more teachers last year even though their enrollments continued to drop. The most obvious explanation is the demand for more secondary school teachers in mathematics, science and English following the increased number of courses required in the subjects for high school graduation in many states (Table 18).

Nine states whose secondary school enrollments dropped last year over the year before actually added more teachers last year: Hawaii, Illinois, Maryland,

TABLE 17. Numbers of public elementary school teachers

State	Percent change 1972-1982	1982-83	1983-84	1984-85	Percent change '82-'83	Percent change '83-'84	Rank of percent change '82-'83	Rank of percent change '83-'84	1984-85 Rank
United States	3.0	1,179,282	1,171,053	1,184,337	-0.6	1.1			
Alabama	17.7	19,862	19,950	18,634	0.4	-6.5	13	51	25
Alaska	32.7	2,793	3,214	3,800	15.0	18.2	1	1	47
Arizona	32.0	18,488	18,343	18,700	-0.7	1.9	30	24	24
Arkansas	15.3	11,589	11,657	11,773	0.5	0.9	11	30	34
California	-7.6	108,756	108,496	107,040	-0.2	-1.3	21	42	1
Colorado	21.2	15,434	15,287	15,283	-0.9	0.0	34	33	28
Connecticut	-1.3	19,214	18,902	18,907	-1.6	0.0	39	33	22
Delaware	-9.1	2,439	2,451	2,600	0.4	6.0	13	5	51
District of Columbia	-23.9	3,154	3,355	3,526	6.3	5.0	2	11	49
Florida	38.8	46,030	46,435	48,186	0.8	3.8	10	16	6
Georgia	17.6	33,916	33,660	34,420	-0.7	2.3	30	23	10
Hawaii	23.4	4,499	4,400	4,459	-2.2	1.3	46	26	45
Idaho	41.0	5,090	5,120	5,315	0.5	3.8	11	16	42
Illinois	7.8	67,627	66,374	65,620	-1.8	-1.1	42	41	4
Indiana	-3.1	25,251	24,813	24,811	-1.7	0.0	41	33	16
Iowa	-4.2	14,452	14,264	14,002	-1.3	-1.8	37	45	31
Kansas	11.6	14,375	14,320	14,723	-0.3	2.8	24	22	29
Kentucky	7.9	20,931	20,778	21,000	-0.7	1.0	30	29	20
Louisiana	10.6	26,480	26,510	27,580	0.1	4.0	16	14	13
Maine	14.8	7,778	7,773	8,187	0.0	5.3	18	8	37
Maryland	16.2	17,344	17,318	17,370	-0.1	0.3	19	32	27
Massachusetts	-24.3	22,000	20,103	21,270	-8.6	5.8	51	7	18
Michigan	-17.3	39,615	37,766	42,500	-4.7	12.7	49	2	8
Minnesota	-9.6	19,025	18,454	19,000	-3.0	2.9	47	20	21
Mississippi	3.7	13,634	13,507	13,431	-0.9	-0.5	34	38	32
Missouri	-3.8	23,003	23,342	23,726	1.4	1.6	8	25	17
Montana	-3.2	6,430	6,300	6,726	-2.0	6.7	44	3	39
Nebraska	-14.7	9,159	8,787	9,327	-4.0	6.1	48	4	36
Nevada	34.8	3,838	3,876	4,076	0.9	5.1	9	10	46
New Hampshire	19.2	5,122	5,101	5,370	-0.4	5.2	26	9	41
New Jersey	0.2	42,479	41,884	41,893	-1.4	0.0	38	33	9
New Mexico	8.0	8,160	8,120	7,990	-0.4	-1.6	26	43	38
New York	-19.0	74,500	74,000	76,200	-0.6	2.9	29	20	3
North Carolina	3.7	33,303	32,970	32,915	-1.0	-0.1	36	37	12
North Dakota	3.5	4,719	4,708	4,608	-0.2	-2.1	21	47	44
Ohio	-4.8	52,940	52,800	50,820	-0.2	-3.8	21	48	5
Oklahoma	19.8	18,294	18,682	18,300	2.1	-2.0	5	46	26
Oregon	23.1	14,817	14,070	14,256	-5.0	1.3	50	26	30
Pennsylvania	-12.5	48,917	48,114	47,744	-1.6	-0.7	39	40	7
Rhode Island	-17.0	3,573	3,581	3,723	0.2	3.9	15	15	48
South Carolina	24.8	20,408	20,430	21,270	0.1	4.1	16	13	18
South Dakota	1.3	5,200	5,334	5,387	2.5	0.9	4	30	40
Tennessee	10.4	24,713	24,264	25,192	-1.8	3.8	42	16	14
Texas	34.2	92,793	94,607	95,758	1.9	1.2	6	28	2
Utah	44.8	9,251	9,416	9,984	1.7	6.0	7	5	35
Vermont	-6.9	2,941	2,930	2,809	-0.3	-4.1	24	50	50
Virginia	10.4	33,303	33,141	32,975	-0.4	-0.5	26	38	11
Washington	-1.3	18,165	18,028	18,904	-0.7	4.8	30	12	23
West Virginia	32.3	12,229	12,652	12,427	3.4	-1.7	3	44	33
Wisconsin	5.8	26,674	26,100	25,100	-2.1	-3.8	45	48	15
Wyoming	78.1	4,575	4,566	4,720	-0.1	3.3	19	19	43

SOURCE: Compiled by the National Center for Education Information. Basic data from National Education Association, Estimates of School Statistics, selected years.

27

TABLE 18: Numbers of public secondary school teachers

State	Percent change 1972-1982	1982-83	1983-84	1984-85	Percent change '82-'83	Percent change '83-'84	Rank of percent change '82-'83	Rank of percent change '83-'84	1984-85 Rank
United States	-0.4	956,229	946,004	961,205	-1.0	1.6			
Alabama	12.5	19,222	19,250	17,465	0.1	-9.2	19	49	19
Alaska	40.1	3,234	3,173	2,290	-1.8	-27.8	39	51	49
Arizona	41.5	7,265	7,319	7,220	0.7	-1.3	16	37	35
Arkansas	12.8	12,123	12,240	12,312	0.9	0.5	13	22	27
California	-11.5	64,514	61,939	68,095	-4.0	10.0	47	2	3
Colorado	11.9	13,941	14,160	13,539	1.5	-4.3	9	45	26
Connecticut	-15.0	13,996	13,813	13,560	-1.3	-1.8	33	40	25
Delaware	-18.0	2,970	2,985	2,916	0.5	-2.3	17	42	46
District of Columbia	-26.1	2,190	2,293	2,266	4.7	-1.1	3	35	51
Florida	6.8	35,978	36,639	38,037	1.8	3.8	6	6	6
Georgia	13.8	22,604	22,610	21,901	0.0	-3.1	21	43	15
Hawaii	7.2	3,727	3,673	3,682	-1.4	0.2	34	27	42
Idaho	10.6	4,720	4,780	4,845	1.2	1.3	11	18	38
Illinois	22.3	35,959	34,682	34,877	-3.6	0.5	44	22	9
Indiana	-3.1	25,191	24,643	24,835	-2.1	0.7	40	20	11
Iowa	4.6	16,362	16,422	16,334	0.3	-0.5	18	31	21
Kansas	-7.6	11,677	11,482	11,537	-1.6	0.4	36	26	29
Kentucky	-0.6	11,306	11,222	11,400	-0.7	1.5	29	16	30
Louisiana	1.2	15,980	15,110	14,140	-5.4	-6.4	49	47	24
Maine	0.6	4,499	4,500	4,323	0.0	-3.9	21	44	40
Maryland	-5.2	20,149	20,119	20,324	-0.1	1.0	25	19	17
Massachusetts	5.4	30,000	28,164	35,063	-6.1	24.4	51	1	8
Michigan	-11.1	37,222	35,189	37,063	-5.4	6.3	49	5	7
Minnesota	-11.4	20,711	20,090	20,400	-2.9	1.5	42	16	16
Mississippi	9.0	11,348	11,357	11,341	0.0	-0.1	21	29	31
Missouri	9.9	22,954	23,372	23,514	1.8	0.6	6	21	13
Montana	17.0	3,090	3,050	3,030	-1.2	-0.6	32	32	45
Nebraska	0.8	8,219	7,998	8,186	-2.6	2.3	41	13	34
Nevada	40.7	3,384	3,417	3,420	0.9	0.0	13	28	43
New Hampshire	24.2	4,636	4,617	4,734	-0.4	2.5	27	12	39
New Jersey	-11.7	31,824	31,378	30,965	-1.4	-1.3	34	37	10
New Mexico	26.8	6,490	7,410	6,210	14.1	-16.1	2	50	36
New York	-6.7	90,700	90,000	88,700	-0.7	-1.4	29	39	1
North Carolina	30.6	21,958	21,739	23,169	-0.9	6.5	31	4	14
North Dakota	6.9	2,780	2,677	2,692	-3.7	0.5	45	22	47
Ohio	-14.3	41,190	39,965	43,609	-2.9	9.3	42	3	5
Oklahoma	20.8	16,779	17,011	16,700	1.3	-1.8	10	40	20
Oregon	-4.4	10,455	9,920	10,157	-5.1	2.3	48	13	32
Pennsylvania	-3.9	54,938	54,036	53,406	-1.6	-1.1	36	35	4
Rhode Island	5.8	3,826	3,860	3,825	0.8	-0.9	15	34	41
South Carolina	10.8	11,622	11,640	12,070	0.1	3.6	19	9	28
South Dakota	-8.6	2,612	2,655	2,635	1.6	-0.7	8	33	48
Tennessee	-1.5	14,696	14,872	14,816	1.1	-0.3	12	30	23
Texas	20.6	74,505	76,489	76,881	2.6	0.5	5	22	2
Utah	-4.0	5,826	6,017	6,204	3.2	3.1	4	10	37
Vermont	27.8	3,310	3,305	3,391	-0.1	2.6	25	11	44
Virginia	0.4	23,125	23,013	23,888	-0.4	3.8	27	6	12
Washington	14.3	15,956	15,951	16,251	0.0	1.8	21	15	22
West Virginia	13.2	9,930	9,765	10,130	-1.6	3.7	36	8	33
Wisconsin	-2.2	22,364	21,500	20,250	-3.8	-5.8	46	46	18
Wyoming	47.1	2,172	2,493	2,270	14.7	-8.9	1	48	50

SOURCE: Compiled by the National Center for Education Information. Basic data from National Education Association, Estimates of School Statistics, selected years.

28

Missouri, Nebraska, Oregon, South Carolina, Vermont, and West Virginia.

The most noticeable increases in the number of additional secondary school teachers in 1984-85 over the previous year occurred in Massachusetts which increased its stable of teachers in secondary schools by 24.4 percent (6,899 in number), followed by California which increased its secondary teachers by 10.0 percent (6,156); then Ohio by 9.3 percent (3,644); North Carolina by 6.5 percent (1,430); Michigan by 6.3 percent (2,211); and Florida by 3.8 percent (1,398).

Noteworthy about these six states is the fact that, with the exception of Florida, they all had a decrease in the number of secondary school teachers from 1982-83 to 1983-84. Massachusetts showed a 6.1 percent drop and California a 4.0 percent drop in secondary school teachers during that period. Ohio's secondary school teachers dropped 2.9 percent, Michigan's secondary school teachers decreased 5.4 percent, and North Carolina's by 0.9 percent two years ago.

At the secondary level, seven states decreased the number of teachers while registering higher enrollments in secondary schools. Their teacher and enrollment percentage changes last year over 1983-84 are: Alaska, -27.8 percent and 6.8 percent (Alaska went from 3,173 secondary school teachers in 1983-84 to 2,290 in 1984-85); Arizona, -1.3 percent (from 7,319 to 7,220) and 4.6 percent; Connecticut, -1.8 percent (from 13,813 to 13,560) and 0.4 percent; Louisiana, -6.4 percent (from 15,110 to 14,140) and 1.3 percent; Maine, -3.9 percent (from 4,500 to 4,323) and 2.2 percent; Oklahoma, -1.8 percent (from 17,011 to 16,700) and 5.1 percent; and Tennessee, -0.3 percent (from 14,872 to 14,816) and 0.3 percent.

CHAPTER IV

Projected Shortage of Teachers

If the latest projections by the National Center for Education Statistics hold up, the teacher-shortage picture could be a lot grimmer than it has already been painted.

NCES is now projecting we will need to hire 1.65 million additional public and private elementary and secondary school teachers between fall 1985 and fall 1993 to meet demand. That's more than two-thirds of the 2.40 million teachers in classrooms today. Due to retirements, leaving for other jobs or simply quitting, many of the current teachers will no longer be teaching eight years from now. NCES estimates there will be a total of 2,737,000 public and private elementary and secondary teachers in 1993 (Table 19).

NCES bases its teacher supply and demand estimates on a constant annual 6 percent rate of attrition (teachers leaving due to retirements or whatever), enrollments rising and teacher-pupil ratios improving only slightly.

More than two-thirds (68 percent) of the 1,651,000 additional teachers needed by 1993 will be elementary school teachers. NCES projects we will need 1,118,000 elementary school teachers and 533,000 teachers for secondary schools between 1985 and 1993. These figures represent 139 percent of the elementary school teachers and 27 percent of the secondary school teachers we have in this nation now. That means nearly one and a half times as many elementary school teachers as we currently have will have to be hired within the next eight years to meet demand.

Broken down by public and private school teachers, the nation will need 1,395,000 additional public school teachers (65 percent of the current public school

30

TABLE 19. Trends in estimated demand for classroom teachers in elementary/secondary
schools and estimated supply of new teacher graduates: fall 1980 to fall 1993
(numbers in thousands)

Fall of year	Total estimated teacher demand	Estimated demand for additional teachers					Estimated supply of new teacher graduates	Supply as percent of demand
		Total	Public	Private	Elementary	Secondary		
1980	2,439	127	110	17	69	58	144	113.4
1981	2,403	110	85	25	66	44	141	128.2
1982	2,401	143	120	23	94	49	143	100.0
1983	2,404	148	125	23	82	66	146	98.6
1984	2,401	142	127	15	78	64	146	102.8
1985	2,413	158	134	24	96	62	146	92.4
1986	2,438	165	139	26	109	56	144	87.3
1987	2,452	171	144	27	125	46	142	83.0
1988	2,468	162	140	22	124	38	139	85.8
1989	2,493	177	146	31	130	47	139	78.5
1990	2,527	188	160	28	136	52	139	73.9
1991	2,569	204	176	28	138	66	138	67.6
1992	2,624	215	181	34	135	80	137	63.7
1993	2,737	211	175	36	125	86	133	63.0

SOURCE: Selected data from the U.S. Department of Education, National Center for
Education Statistics, The Condition of Education 1983, (Washington: U.S.
Government Printing Office, 1983) and upcoming The Condition of Education 1985.

teaching force) by 1993. By that time, it will also need an additional 256,000 teachers to accommodate the demands of a rapidly burgeoning private elementary and secondary school system. That's 98 percent of the estimated 267,000 teachers in private schools today.

In other words, in just eight years, private schools could be employing twice as many teachers as they do today. This is no small threat to an already threatened public school system. Even though exact numbers are not available, it is a well known fact that many public school teachers leave and go into private schools-- usually taking pay cuts--because, they argue, the schools are better managed, offer greater autonomy for teachers, and the parents are more involved in their children's education.

Supply of New Teachers

The National Center for Education Statistics further estimates that, by 1993, the supply of new teacher graduates will be less than two-thirds (63 percent) of demand. The Center projects that supply will be 92.4 percent of demand in fall 1985.

Data collected from a survey of colleges and universities that have teacher education programs in spring and summer of 1984 by the National Center for

Education Information (NCEI) substantiate NCES' findings that demand for teachers is exceeding supply. The NCEI data showed a 53 percent drop in the number of new teacher graduates between fall 1973 and fall 1983.[19]

Results of the NCEI survey indicated there were approximately 135,000 graduates of teacher education programs in 1983. The estimate of graduates of teacher education programs in 1973 was approximately 289,000. These findings are consistent with estimates from both the National Center for Education Statistics and the National Education Association. NCES estimates there were 284,000 newly qualified graduates in 1970 and 143,000 in 1982.

According to the NCEI survey, an estimated 688,000 students were enrolled in undergraduate teacher education programs in 1973. By 1983, there were 115 more institutions in the business of teacher education, but the total number of students enrolled dropped to 444,000—35 percent fewer than in 1973 (Table 20).

NCEI's estimated number of persons admitted into teacher education programs in fall 1983 was 110,000. NCEI also found in its survey that approximately 80 percent of all students admitted into teacher education programs graduate. NCES estimates that only about 80 percant of those who do graduate apply to teach and that only about 80 percent of those who apply become teachers.

These combined statistics paint a very dismal picture. If only 110,000 persons entered a teacher education program in 1983 and only 80 percent graduate, that takes the number down to 88,000. If only 80 percent of them apply to teach, the number drops further to 70,400. Lastly, if the estimated 80 percent of these wind up in the classroom with teaching jobs, it means that out of a class of 110,000 new entrants into teacher education programs in 1983, only 56,320 will become teachers around 1986. NCES projects a demand for 165,000 additional teachers in fall 1986—More than 100,000 more than the crop of people enrolled in college today studying to be teachers will produce.

Many educators are counting on a big "reserve pool" of teachers to meet the projected demands. This reserve pool is composed of all the people certified to teach who got laid off or never got hired in the first place in the years when enrollments plummeted and the supply of teachers exceeded demand. There were

TABLE 20: Teacher education graduates, undergraduate enrollment in teacher education programs, and newly admitted teacher education students by control of institution and enrollment size: 1973 and 1983

Type IHE	Number of Graduates			Total Enrollment			No. of Newly Admitted		
	1983	1973	Percent Change	1983	1973	Percent Change	1983	1973	Percent Change
Total	134,870	288,738	-53	443,900	687,504	-35	110,059	195,333	-44
Public	107,896	236,765	-54	350,681	550,003	-36	82,554	154,313	-48
Private	26,974	51,973	-58	93,219	137,501	-32	27,514	41,020	-42
<1 K*	8,383			30,912			9,099		
1-5 K	34,504			117,448			31,293		
5-10 K	28,953			104,580			21,638		
10 K+	63,030			190,960			48,029		

*K = thousand

SOURCE: The National Center for Education Information, The Making of a Teacher, 1984, pp. 3, 4 and 6.

about twice as many new teacher graduates than were in demand as recently as 1971, according to NCES. If every teacher graduate who was not needed between 1970 and 1982, because supply exceeded demand in that period, applied for a job today, there would be 861,000 additional teachers.

However, there is no evidence that people who got certified to teach and make up this reserve pool ever go into teaching. For one thing, certification rules change so frequently in most states that one's certification to teach can quickly become outdated.

Projections Versus Reality

Checking NCES' projections against what actually happened in numbers of teachers in the last year shows that more teachers were actually added than NCES projected would be needed. There were 2,117,057 teachers employed in the nation's public elementary and secondary schools in 1983-84 and 2,145,542 in 1984-85. If 6 percent of the teachers in 1983-84 left due to retirement, other jobs or whatever, 127,023 teachers would have had to be hired just to replace them. NCES projected 127,000 additional teachers would be needed in 1984-85 to meet demand. It turns out there were 28,485 more teachers in 1984-85 than there were in 1983-84 which implies that as many as 155,508 new teachers were hired last year—28,485 plus 127,023 (the number needed to replace the 6 percent who left).

Doing the same arithmetic for elementary and secondary schools shows that there were 2,547 more elementary school teachers and 18,961 more secondary school teachers hired last year than NCES projected would be needed.

Several things could be happening, not the least of which is that teachers aren't leaving at the predicted 6 percent attrition rate. Also, raising standards, requiring more science, math, and English courses for high school graduation could very well account for the 36 percent more high school teachers added last year than NCES estimated would be needed.

But the big unanswered question is: Where are they coming from? It's an indisputable fact that the number of new teacher graduates in 1983-84 wasn't over 146,000.

Research further shows that a rather large proportion of people who get education degrees and are qualified to teach never do. Approximately one-third of the recent bachelor's degree recipients newly qualified to teach in 1979-80 were not teaching full-time in May 1981. Of these 48,400 qualified-to-teach, but not teaching, 38 percent did not even apply for a teaching position. Ninety percent of those who did not apply said they simply did not want to teach. In addition, 27 percent of those newly qualified to teach in 1979-80 who taught in 1980 were no longer teaching in May 1981.[20]

It's a confusing set of facts. Maybe there is something to the concept of "reserve pool" of teachers, but I suspect there is a lot more to be told about emergency certificates being issued all over the place.

CHAPTER V

Salaries of Teachers

Salaries of teachers have been outstripping the inflation rate since 1981-82, reversing decades of lagging behind inflation. The average salary of public school teachers rose from $19,270 in 1981-82 to $20,715 in 1982-83, representing a 7.5 percent increase. Teachers' salaries climbed to $22,019 in 1983-84, for a 6.2 percent increase and on to $23,546 in 1984-85 for a 6.9 percent increase over the year before. The inflation rate was 6.1 percent in 1982, 3.2 percent in 1983 and 4.3 percent in 1984.

Teachers earned 22.2 percent more last year, on the average, than they did just three years ago.

The debate about whether or not teachers get paid enough is a tough one. Joe Q. Public certainly seems to think they don't, and of course, the teachers' unions argue teachers are underpaid.

A survey conducted by the Gallup Organization for the National Education Association in summer 1985 indicated that 59 percent of the public thought its local school system was having a hard time getting good teachers because teachers' salaries were low. In response to the question, "If there is a teacher shortage in the coming years, what things do you think should be done to recruit teachers?" 61 percent responded, "Increase pay." The next highest response was 12 percent who said "Increase professional responsibilities and status of teachers" followed by 10 percent who said, "Improve working conditions."[21]

When asked how much they thought a full-time high school teacher and a full-time elementary school teacher who have graduated from college and have about fifteen years' experience should be paid per year, the public suggested about

$29,000 for a high school teacher and about $27,000 for an elementary school teacher.[22]

The average salary of a high school teacher in 1984-85 was $24,276 and for an elementary school teacher was $23,092. The median experience for teachers is about fifteen years. But teachers get paid on a nine or ten-month basis. Using the ten-month figure and converting the average salaries for teachers to a full twelve-month year takes them up to $29,131 for high school teachers and $28,255 for elementary school teachers which is certainly in line with what the public says they should be paid.

Many say you can't do the arithmetic this way. They argue that teachers work nine or ten months, and that their annual salary is what they get for working ten-twelfths of a year. The average teacher works 180 days a year. The average number of working days in a year is 250.

The 1984 survey of American teachers conducted by Louis Harris and Associates for the Metropolitan Life Insurance Company revealed that the median household income of the average teacher is comparable to that of college graduates in general. Both groups had a median household income of about $30,000 in 1983 (Table 21).

It is also interesting that 67 percent of the teachers had household incomes between $20,000 and $50,000 compared with 53 percent of total college graduates. Only 4 percent of teachers, compared with 16 percent of total college graduates, had household incomes of $15,000 or less in 1983. But, at the other end of the scale, one-fifth (20 percent) of college graduates had household incomes of $50,000 or more, compared with 13 percent of teachers.

Of course, the fact that any teacher has a household income of $50,000 or more may come as a shock to many, much less that about 275,000 of them do. And they can't all be in Alaska! (Alaska paid its teachers, on the average, $36,564 in 1983-84—the year it employed a total of 6,387 teachers.)

These statistics support three things we already know about teachers. First, there are relatively few "new" teachers, and secondly, teachers' salaries have a lower "cap" than those of the general working public; and thirdly, 74 percent of teachers are married and, consequently, are likely to be in two-income households.

TABLE 21. Percentage distribution of teachers and college graduates by household
income: 1983

Income Range	Total Teachers	Type of School Elementary	Type of School Junior High	Type of School High School	Total College Graduates*
$15,000 - or less	4	4	3	3	16
$15,001 - $20,000	15	17	13	12	11
$20,001 - $30,000	30	29	27	36 }	
$30,001 - $40,000	23	23	26	21 }	53
$40,001 - $50,000	14	13	16	13 }	
$50,001 and over	13	13	15	12	20
Not sure	1	1	1	1	--
Median income (in thousands of dollars)	$30.0	$29.8	$32.6	$29.4	$30.6

* Household income of college graduates from U.S. Bureau of the Census, Statistical
Abstract of the United States, 1984 edition.

SOURCE: The Metropolitan Life Survey of the American Teacher, 1984, p. 17.

In the general population, 60 percent of all households are married-couple
households.

Only 8 percent of the teaching force has been teaching less than five years,
compared with 16 percent of the total working public who have been employed less
than five years. Even so, it is worth noting that while 16 percent of college
graduates had a household income of $15,000 or less, and 8 percent of teachers have
been teaching less than five years, only 4 percent of teachers are in households
making $15,000 or less (Table 22).

Starting, Average, and Peak Salary Comparisons

The average starting salary for a teacher with a bachelor's degree was around
$14,000 and for a teacher with a master's degree about $16,000 in 1982.

Starting salaries in 1982 for selected other occupations that usually require a
bachelor's degree were: accountants--$18,700; architects--$12,000; chemists--
$21,000; computer programmers--$16,700; psychologists (federal)--$14,550; public
relations specialists--$11,500; and reporters--$18,750 (Table 23).

Average salaries for these occupations in 1982 were: teachers--$20,715;
accountants--$24,850; architects--$21,000; chemists--$29,000; computer
programmers--$23,000; psychologists (federal)--NA; public relations
specialist--$21,000; and reporters--$24,650.

Another comparison between teachers' salaries and those of other professionals is in the area of peak salaries. The National Education Association says the peak salary range for teachers was $28,000 to $35,000 in 1982. The Bureau of Labor Statistics says the peak salary for a reporter in 1982 was $38,350, for a chemist with a Ph.D.--$42,000, for an architect--$40,000+, and for a computer programmer--$27,250.

Salaries of Teachers Compared with State and Local Government Employees

Teachers generally make more than state and local government employees. The average salary of teachers has risen faster than that of government employees in the last two years. Both have outstripped the inflation rate for the period.

State and local government employees earned an average of $20,136 in 1983, an increase of 5.7 percent from the previous year. Teachers got paid an average of $22,019 that year, up 6.2 percent from the year before. Inflation rose only 3.2 percent.

From 1981 to 1982, state and local government employees' average salary rose 8.4 percent and the average salary for teachers increased 7.5 percent, while inflation grew by 6.1 percent. From 1981 to 1983, teachers' salaries gained, on the

TABLE 22. Percentage distribution of teachers by years taught and by whether or not they have tenure compared with the working public: 1983

| | Total Teachers | The Total Type of School | | | Total Working Public |
		Elementary	Junior High	High School	
Years taught					
Less than 5	8	7	9	8	16
5 to 9	19	20	15	17	24
10 to 14	25	25	28	23	16
15 to 19	21	23	29	31	13
20 or more	27	25	29	31	31
Median years	14.7	14.6	14.6	15.5	12.5
Tenure					
Have tenure	81	82	82	76	X
Do not have tenure	19	17	17	23	X

X = Not applicable

SOURCE: The Metropolitan Life Survey of the American Teacher, 1984, p. 13.

average, 15 percent and state and local government employees' salaries grew by 14.6 percent.

The variation from state to state in comparisons of gains from 1981 to 1983 between teachers' salaries and those of state and local government employees is noteworthy. Michigan, for example, increased its average salary for teachers 29.2 percent between 1981 and 1983 and its government employees' average salary by 10.8 percent for the period. Louisiana, on the other hand, raised its government salary average 10.4 percent while raising its teachers' average salary only 3.2 percent—the smallest two-year gain for teachers in the nation between 1981 and 1983 (Table 24).

Average Salaries for Teachers State-by-State

Average teachers' salaries ranged from a high of $39,751 in Alaska and $29,000 in New York to a low of $15,971 in Mississippi in 1984-85 (Table 25). Analyzing changes in average salaries of teachers requires taking into account several variables in addition to the face dollar amount. The way teachers are paid in every state in this nation is determined by two major factors: 1) How many years they have been teaching and 2) How many college courses they accumulate. (In most states the only requirement for getting a teaching certificate renewed is to acquire additional college credits.)

The increases in average salaries of teachers may be largely due to the fact that the current teaching force is composed of persons who have been teaching a relatively long time, and consequently, have more college courses to their credit since that is the only way they could keep their certificates to teach.

Some states, however, have taken significant steps to raise the salaries of all their teachers. These are reflected in noticeable jumps in their average salary figures in the last two years.

Arkansas heads the list of such states. Arkansas, which ranked fiftieth in average teacher salary in 1982-83, increased its average salary for teachers by 12.6 percent the following year (the highest rate of change of all the states) and by an additional 11.8 percent last year. Arkansas added teachers in both of the last two

TABLE 23. Salaries by occupation: 1982

Occupation	Starting Salaries	Average Salaries	Peak Salaries
Accountant	$18,700	$24,850	NA
Architects	12,000	21,000	$40,000+
Bank Officers	17,400	24,500	46,800+
Bank Tellers	NA	10,300	16,800+
Biological Scientists	16,500	NA	NA
Chemical Engineer	27,072	36,726*	66,938*
Chemist	21,000	29,000	42,000
w/Ph.D.			
Commercial Artist	NA	17,900	40,000
Computer Programer	16,700	23,000	27,250
Computer System Analyst	22,300	25,750	42,500
Dental Hygienist	NA	15,750	NA
Dentists	NA	55,000	NA
Economist	18,500	30,200	46,800
Editor	28,000	33,000	60,000
Health Services Admin.	24,000 w/Masters	NA	NA
Lawyers (private ind.)	28,000	NA	85,000
Legal Assistant	NA	21,000*	30,000+*
Mail Carrier	20,130	21,591	22,792
Mathematician	21,300	28,600	33,400+*
Mechanical Engineer	25,176	36,726*	66,938*
Nuclear Engineer	24,468	36,726*	66,938*
Physician	NA	100,000	NA
Principal (elementary)	NA	27,419	NA
(secondary)	NA	37,602	NA
Protestant Ministers	NA	16,500	NA
Psychologist (federal)	14,550	NA	NA
PR Specialist	11,500	21,000	38,500
Rabbis	NA	35,000	NA
Receptionist	10,332	12,876	NA
Recreation Worker	13,000	17,200	NA
Registered Nurse	17,600	23,300	28,500
Reporter	18,750	24,650	38,350
Roman Catholic Priests	NA	3,350	NA
Secretary	NA	15,549	20,232
Social Worker	14,300	18,100	23,800
Sociologist (federal)	14,550	NA	NA
Teachers (elementary)	14,000 (BA)	20,042	28,000-35,000
(secondary)	16,000	21,000	28,000-35,000
Telephone Operators	13,500	20,760	32,840
Typist	11,428	15,085	18,000+
Veterinarian	NA	45,000	NA

* 1983 statistics

SOURCE: Selected data from U.S. Department of Labor, Bureau of Labor Statistics,
Occupational Outlook Handbook, 1984-85 Edition, (Washington: U.S Department of
Labor, Bureau of Labor Statistics).

40

years, which would tend to bring the average down since new teachers usually get paid less.

Mississippi, which ranked fifty-first in 1982-83 in average teachers' salary, raised its average by 10.9 percent the following year and an additional 0.4 percent last year. Mississippi still ranks fifty-first in average salary for teachers.

Eleven states showed a greater than 10 percent jump in average salaries for teachers last year over the year before. Five states registered a greater than 10 percent increase in their average teachers' salaries between 1982-83 and 1983-84. These states, with their changes in numbers of teachers for the two years are shown in Table 26.

Only seven of these fifteen states (Arkansas is on both lists) increased their number of teachers both years. The remaining eight dropped teachers in at least one of the last two years. Illinois, Mississippi, North Dakota, and Vermont had a decrease in number of teachers in both years.

Four states--California, Michigan, Nevada, and North Dakota--showed a decrease in their average salary for teachers in 1984-85 from the year before. With the exception of North Dakota, which did increase its average teachers' salary by 10.7 percent the year before, these states all added teachers. New teachers usually cost less, so adding teachers at lower salaries than the average is likely to bring down the average.

The states whose average salary for teachers decreased in 1984-85 over 1983-84 did add teachers in that period. California increased its teaching force by 2.7 percent (4,700 teachers), and its average salary for teachers went down 0.3 percent last year, having gone up 9.8 percent the year before when the number of teachers declined from 173,270 to 170,435.

Michigan's average salary for public school teachers declined 1.6 percent last year, having risen 8.7 percent the year before. Michigan had 6,945 more teachers in 1984-85 than it had in 1983-84 representing a 9.6 percent jump. Interestingly enough, from 1982-83 to 1983-84, the year the average salary for teachers went up 8.7 percent, Michigan went from 76,837 teachers down to 72,955.

Nevada follows the pattern of a decrease in average salary following an

TABLE 24. Salaries of state and local government employees compared with salaries of teachers: 1983 and 2-year gain

State	State/Local Salaries 1983	2-Year Gain	Teachers' Salaries 1983	2-Year Gain
United States	$20,136	14.6%	$22,019	15.0%
Alabama	15,912	11.9	18,000	15.4
Alaska	32,844	14.3	36,564	14.5
Arizona	21,840	14.3	21,605	19.9
Arkansas	14,616	13.0	16,929	16.7
California	25,272	12.7	26,403	16.0
Colorado	21,048	13.7	22,895	16.9
Connecticut	21,180	25.4	22,624	19.8
Delaware	18,696	14.6	20,925	8.5
District of Columbia	27,312	16.8	27,659	14.0
Florida	18,948	22.6	19,545	16.5
Georgia	15,840	14.1	18,505	13.1
Hawaii	19,992	8.8	24,357	8.1
Idaho	17,064	11.9	18,640	13.7
Illinois	22,104	15.3	23,345	11.1
Indiana	17,796	14.0	21,587	15.9
Iowa	18,900	13.0	20,140	12.0
Kansas	17,076	13.9	19,598	17.3
Kentucky	16,920	12.0	19,780	14.4
Louisiana	16,524	10.4	19,100	3.2
Maine	16,416	14.0	17,328	14.7
Maryland	21,288	15.0	24,095	14.1
Massachusetts	20,472	18.5	22,500	19.8
Michigan	23,808	10.8	28,877	29.2
Minnesota	22,212	23.6	24,480	23.0
Mississippi	14,076	13.3	15,895	12.5
Missouri	17,184	18.9	19,300	17.6
Montana	19,560	20.8	20,657	16.2
Nebraska	17,436	12.5	18,785	13.4
Nevada	22,008	17.7	23,000	14.4
New Hampshire	17,028	18.1	17,376	18.2
New Jersey	21,204	16.0	23,044	15.7
New Mexico	17,556	13.8	20,760	11.1
New York	23,604	17.5	26,750	14.1
North Carolina	16,656	12.7	18,014	6.3
North Dakota	19,740	7.5	20,363	15.1
Ohio	18,948	14.3	21,421	15.5
Oklahoma	16,548	15.8	18,490	14.1
Oregon	20,928	12.9	22,833	12.5
Pennsylvania	19,584	12.6	22,800	17.0
Rhode Island	21,408	14.4	24,641	13.8
South Carolina	15,696	9.7	17,500	15.4
South Dakota	15,888	12.5	16,480	12.0
Tennessee	16,224	10.6	17,900	9.9
Texas	18,372	14.9	20,100	14.3
Utah	19,356	17.5	20,256	11.6
Vermont	17,412	17.3	17,931	21.6
Virginia	18,276	15.1	19,867	16.8
Washington	22,764	10.0	24,780	8.0
West Virginia	15,744	8.8	17,482	2.1
Wisconsin	20,688	12.7	23,000	18.6
Wyoming	20,676	13.0	24,500	15.3

SOURCE: Compiled by the National Center for Education Information. Basic data from the Advisory Commission on Intergovernmental Relations unpublished data, and the National Education Association, Estimates of School Statistics 1982-83 (Washington: National Education Association, 1983)

42

TABLE 25. Total teachers' salaries

State	Percent change* 1972-1982	1982-83	1983-84	1984-85	Percent change '82-'83	Percent change '83-'84	Rank of percent change '82-'83	Rank of percent change '83-'84
United States	-12.2	20,715	22,019	23,546	6.2	6.9		
Alaska	0.6	33,983	36,564	39,751	7.8	8.8	12	15
New York	-12.0	25,000	26,750	29,000	7.0	8.4	19	16
District of Columbia	-12.0	25,610	27,659	28,621	8.0	3.4	11	41
Michigan	-12.8	26,556	28,877	28,401	8.7	-1.6	9	49
Rhode Island	-5.0	23,175	24,641	27,384	6.3	11.1	26	9
Wyoming	12.3	23,690	24,500	26,709	3.4	9.0	41	12
California	-15.2	24,035	26,403	26,300	9.8	-0.3	6	48
Minnesota	-7.0	22,296	24,480	25,920	9.7	5.8	7	34
Maryland	-11.2	22,786	24,095	25,861	5.7	7.3	31	23
Illinois	-12.2	22,315	23,345	25,829	4.6	10.6	37	11
Washington	-3.9	23,488	24,780	25,610	5.5	3.3	33	42
New Jersey	-19.8	21,536	23,044	25,125	7.0	9.0	19	12
Oregon	1.2	21,746	22,833	24,889	4.9	9.0	34	12
Wisconsin	-12.6	21,496	23,000	24,780	6.9	7.7	22	21
Hawaii	2.4	24,796	24,357	24,628	-1.7	1.1	51	46
Connecticut	-16.7	20,731	22,624	24,520	9.1	8.3	8	18
Colorado	-3.3	21,470	22,895	24,456	6.6	6.8	24	29
Pennsylvania	-12.2	21,178	22,800	24,435	7.6	7.1	14	25
Massachusetts	-21.5	21,440	22,500	24,110	4.9	7.1	34	25
Arizona	-18.4	19,962	21,605	23,380	8.2	8.2	10	19
Delaware	-15.2	20,625	20,925	23,300	1.4	11.3	46	8
Indiana	-13.2	20,123	21,587	23,089	7.2	6.9	17	27
Ohio	-8.0	20,004	21,421	22,737	7.0	6.1	19	31
Texas	-2.4	19,550	20,100	22,600	2.8	12.4	43	3
Nevada	-16.3	22,070	23,000	22,520	4.2	-2.0	39	50
New Mexico	2.9	20,470	20,760	22,064	1.4	6.2	46	30
Montana	-5.0	19,488	20,657	21,705	5.9	5.0	28	39
Virginia	-15.5	18,535	19,867	21,536	7.1	8.4	18	16
Utah	0.6	19,859	20,256	21,307	1.9	5.1	45	38
Kansas	-6.5	18,231	19,598	21,208	7.4	8.2	16	19
Florida	-13.0	18,275	19,545	21,057	6.9	7.7	22	21
Iowa	-15.2	19,257	20,140	20,934	4.5	3.9	38	40
North Carolina	-15.4	17,585	18,014	20,691	2.4	14.8	44	1
Georgia	-7.7	17,412	18,505	20,494	6.2	10.7	27	10
Missouri	-15.0	17,521	19,300	20,452	10.1	5.9	5	33
Alabama	-4.2	17,850	18,000	20,209	0.8	12.2	50	4
Nebraska	-13.3	17,412	18,785	20,153	7.8	7.2	12	24
Kentucky	2.6	18,385	19,780	20,100	7.5	1.6	15	45
Tennessee	-8.7	17,380	17,900	20,080	2.9	12.1	42	5
North Dakota	-1.0	18,390	20,363	19,900	10.7	-2.2	3	51
South Carolina	-11.6	16,523	17,500	19,800	5.9	13.1	28	2
Idaho	-0.4	17,585	18,640	19,700	5.9	5.6	28	36
Louisiana	-5.2	18,420	19,100	19,690	3.6	3.0	40	43
West Virginia	-7.0	17,322	17,482	19,563	0.9	11.9	49	6
Vermont	-25.0	16,271	17,931	19,014	10.2	6.0	4	32
Arkansas	-9.9	15,029	16,929	18,933	12.6	11.8	1	7
Oklahoma	0.9	18,270	18,490	18,930	1.2	2.3	48	44
New Hampshire	-27.1	16,549	17,376	18,577	4.9	6.9	34	27
Maine	-23.4	16,248	17,328	18,329	6.6	5.7	24	35
South Dakota	-14.2	15,595	16,480	17,356	5.6	5.3	32	37
Mississippi	-10.1	14,320	15,895	15,971	10.9	0.4	2	47

* After adjusting for inflation

SOURCE: Compiled by the National Center for Education Information. Basic data from National Education Association, Estimates of School Statistics, selected years.

TABLE 26. Change in numbers of teachers and in teachers' salaries: 1984 to 1985 and 1983 to 1984

State	1984 to 1985 salary percent change	1984 to 1985 no. teachers percent change	1983 to 1984 salary percent change	1983 to 1984 no. teachers percent change
North Carolina	14.8	2.5	2.4	-1.0
South Carolina	13.1	3.9	5.9	0.1
Texas	12.4	0.9	2.8	2.2
Alabama	12.2	-7.9	0.8	0.2
Tennessee	12.1	2.2	2.9	-0.7
West Virginia	11.9	0.6	0.9	1.1
Arkansas	11.8	0.7	12.6	0.7
Delaware	11.3	1.4	1.4	0.4
Rhode Island	11.1	1.4	6.3	0.5
Georgia	10.7	0.0	6.2	-0.4
Illinois	10.6	-0.5	4.6	-2.4
Mississippi	0.4	-0.3	10.9	-0.4
North Dakota	-2.2	-1.1	10.7	-1.5
Vermont	6.0	-0.5	10.2	-0.2
Missouri	5.9	1.1	10.1	1.6

SOURCE: Compiled by the National Center for Education Information. Basic data from the National Education Association, Estimates of School Statistics, selected years.

addition of more teachers. North Dakota, on the other hand, breaks the mold. North Dakota decreased its teaching force both years, which should have driven up the average salary of its teachers (and did from 1982-83 to 1983-84). However, the average salary of North Dakota's teachers went down by 2.2 percent last year, and its number of teachers dropped from 7,385 to 7,300 (1.1 percent).

Comparisons Between Elementary and Secondary School Teachers' Salaries
Secondary school teachers still make more, on the average, than their elementary school counterparts. However, the gap is closing. Salaries of elementary teachers are gaining faster than those of teachers in secondary schools (Tables 27 and 28).

The average salary of an elementary school teacher in 1984-85 was $23,092, compared with $24,276 for secondary teachers. The rates of increase in average salary for elementary teachers in each of the last two years were 6.1 percent for 1983-84 and 7.6 percent for 1984-85 and for the decade ending in 1982-83, 102.9 percent. For secondary teachers, the rates of increase were slightly lower--6.0 percent, 7.0 percent and 101.0 percent, respectively.

Florida and Georgia paid their elementary school teachers more, on the average, than they paid their teachers in secondary schools in 1984-85.

The states having the greatest increases in salaries for elementary teachers also had the largest jumps in average secondary teachers' salaries (Table 29).

44

TABLE 27. Elementary teachers' salaries

State	Percent change 1972-1982	1982-83	1983-84	1984-85	Percent change '82-'83	Percent change '83-'84	Rank of percent change '82-'83	Rank of percent change '83-'84	1984-85 Rank
United States	102.9	20,205	21,452	23,092	6.1	7.6			
Alabama	116.8	17,400	18,000	20,209	3.4	12.2	41	7	34
Alaska	129.0	33,784	36,292	39,520	7.6	8.9	14	13	1
Arizona	96.2	19,860	21,546	23,247	8.4	7.8	10	19	20
Arkansas	105.1	14,579	16,436	18,382	12.7	11.8	1	9	47
California	99.2	23,465	25,492	26,170	8.6	2.6	9	45	7
Colorado	112.0	21,066	22,452	24,150	6.5	7.5	26	20	18
Connecticut	101.0	20,405	22,384	24,250	9.6	8.3	6	16	16
Delaware	92.1	20,078	20,378	22,712	1.4	11.4	48	10	21
District of Columbia	N/A	25,610	27,659	28,582	8.0	3.3	11	43	2
Florida	105.7	18,633	19,928	21,442	6.9	7.5	23	20	26
Georgia	116.2	17,111	18,184	21,370	6.2	17.5	28	1	27
Hawaii	138.2	25,335	25,300	24,628	-0.1	-2.6	50	50	12
Idano	125.5	16,920	17,925	18,970	5.9	5.8	29	35	44
Illinois	102.4	21,400	22,324	25,759	4.3	15.3	40	3	8
Indiana	101.1	19,693	21,147	22,652	7.3	7.1	17	27	22
Iowa	96.7	18,542	19,366	20,135	4.4	3.9	39	40	35
Kansas	118.5	18,146	19,507	21,110	7.5	8.2	16	18	29
Kentucky	134.5	17,929	19,340	20,095	7.8	3.9	13	40	36
Louisiana	118.1	18,120	18,700	19,400	3.2	3.7	43	42	41
Maine	76.0	15,755	16,839	17,849	6.8	5.9	25	34	49
Maryland	99.6	21,780	23,052	24,742	5.8	7.3	32	23	11
Massachusetts	79.9	21,193	22,240	23,835	4.9	7.1	36	27	19
Michigan	104.6	26,340	28,650	28,191	8.7	-1.6	8	49	4
Minnesota	118.5	22,115	23,660	24,970	6.9	5.5	23	36	10
Mississippi	107.9	14,083	15,632	15,710	10.9	0.4	2	48	51
Missouri	93.8	17,031	18,800	19,824	10.3	5.4	3	37	38
Montana	122.0	18,987	20,126	21,110	5.9	4.8	29	38	29
Nebraska	103.0	16,650	17,976	19,292	7.9	7.3	12	23	42
Nevada	92.0	21,710	22,000	22,110	1.3	0.5	49	46	24
New Hampshire	69.6	16,438	17,357	18,638	5.5	7.3	33	23	45
New Jersey	83.9	21,142	22,622	24,596	7.0	8.7	19	15	13
New Mexico	133.7	19,730	20,360	21,340	3.1	4.8	44	38	28
New York	102.5	24,150	25,850	28,500	7.0	10.2	19	11	3
North Carolina	99.9	17,476	18,299	20,620	4.7	12.6	38	6	33
North Dakota	129.2	17,680	19,503	19,610	10.3	0.5	3	46	39
Ohio	111.7	19,550	20,922	22,183	7.0	6.0	19	33	23
Oklahoma	132.3	17,780	19,503	18,380	9.6	-5.7	6	51	48
Oregon	132.4	21,309	22,374	24,358	4.9	8.8	36	14	14
Pennsylvania	101.5	21,098	22,720	24,289	7.6	6.9	14	29	15
Rhode Island	134.0	24,070	25,593	27,497	6.3	7.4	27	22	5
South Carolina	101.4	16,027	16,980	19,206	5.9	13.1	29	5	43
South Dakota	101.4	15,386	16,200	17,300	5.2	6.7	35	30	50
Tennessee	116.6	17,330	17,850	20,020	3.0	12.1	45	8	37
Texas	121.2	19,007	19,379	21,965	1.9	13.3	46	4	25
Utah	128.0	19,066	19,447	20,700	1.9	6.4	46	32	32
Vermont	73.5	15,794	17,373	18,539	9.9	6.7	5	30	46
Virginia	95.7	17,875	19,170	20,767	7.2	8.3	18	16	31
Washington	124.6	23,120	24,392	25,221	5.5	3.3	33	43	9
West Virginia	119.8	16,923	16,726	19,530	-1.1	16.7	51	2	40
Wisconsin	102.2	21,062	22,540	24,190	7.0	7.3	19	23	17
Wyoming	148.4	23,210	24,000	26,172	3.4	9.0	41	12	6

SOURCE: Compiled by the National Center for Education Information. Basic data from National Education Association, Estimates of School Statistics, selected years.

45

TABLE 28. Secondary teachers' salaries

State	Percent change 1972-1982	1982-83	1983-84	1984-85	Percent change '82-'83	Percent change '83-'84	Rank of percent change '82-'83	Rank of percent change '83-'84	1984-85 Rank
United States	101.0	21,380	22,667	24,276	6.0	7.0			
Alabama	121.4	18,000	18,000	20,209	0.0	12.2	50	4	41
Alaska	134.7	34,154	36,841	39,900	7.9	8.4	9	16	1
Arizona	82.2	20,220	21,753	23,683	7.5	8.8	12	15	21
Arkansas	108.7	15,459	17,396	19,456	12.5	11.8	1	7	46
California	93.4	25,331	27,232	27,890	7.5	2.4	12	46	6
Colorado	119.5	22,291	23,789	24,800	6.7	4.2	23	39	16
Connecticut	89.1	21,250	23,031	24,940	8.3	8.2	7	17	15
Delaware	97.6	21,075	21,375	23,788	1.4	11.2	48	8	20
District of Columbia	0.0	25,610	27,659	28,679	8.0	3.6	8	41	4
Florida	92.8	18,058	19,156	20,569	6.0	7.3	27	20	37
Georgia	107.2	17,847	18,948	20,960	6.1	10.6	26	10	34
Hawaii	131.2	24,024	24,000	24,628	0.0	2.6	50	44	17
Idaho	133.9	18,300	19,400	20,500	6.0	5.6	27	33	38
Illinois	99.6	24,036	25,297	27,842	5.2	10.0	33	11	7
Indiana	98.4	20,554	22,031	23,544	7.1	6.8	17	25	22
Iowa	92.9	19,892	20,808	21,629	4.6	3.9	37	40	30
Kansas	111.9	18,317	19,690	21,290	7.4	8.1	14	18	31
Kentucky	136.5	19,270	20,680	20,110	7.3	-2.7	15	50	43
Louisiana	116.7	18,915	19,615	20,210	3.7	3.0	40	43	40
Maine	76.3	17,073	18,171	19,238	6.4	5.8	24	32	48
Maryland	102.7	23,142	24,471	26,265	5.7	7.3	31	20	10
Massachusetts	80.8	21,626	22,700	24,350	4.9	7.2	35	23	19
Michigan	98.5	26,800	29,140	28,700	8.7	-1.5	6	49	3
Minnesota	105.8	23,574	25,220	26,790	6.9	6.2	21	29	9
Mississippi	105.2	14,604	16,210	16,280	10.9	0.4	3	47	51
Missouri	96.9	18,012	19,799	21,084	9.9	6.4	5	27	32
Montana	105.5	20,532	21,764	22,830	6.0	4.8	27	35	26
Nebraska	95.4	18,173	19,598	21,008	7.8	7.1	10	24	33
Nevada	93.2	22,480	23,000	22,960	2.3	-0.1	45	48	25
New Hampshire	65.5	16,678	17,394	18,505	4.2	6.3	39	28	49
New Jersey	85.4	22,061	23,605	25,732	6.9	9.0	21	13	13
New Mexico	140.0	21,130	21,810	22,770	3.2	4.4	42	37	27
New York	102.4	25,700	27,500	30,000	7.0	9.0	19	13	2
North Carolina	89.4	17,697	18,530	20,788	4.7	12.1	36	5	35
North Dakota	121.1	19,110	21,231	20,340	11.0	-4.1	2	51	39
Ohio	111.9	20,590	22,072	23,383	7.1	5.9	17	31	24
Oklahoma	132.2	18,790	19,000	19,490	1.1	2.5	49	45	45
Oregon	138.0	22,536	23,663	25,822	5.0	9.1	34	12	12
Pennsylvania	101.1	21,241	22,875	24,561	7.6	7.3	11	20	18
Rhode Island	100.1	22,154	23,555	28,075	6.3	19.1	25	1	5
South Carolina	108.4	17,183	18,200	20,592	5.9	13.1	30	2	36
South Dakota	93.7	15,988	16,700	17,450	4.4	4.4	38	37	50
Tennessee	101.1	17,470	17,990	20,180	2.9	12.1	43	5	42
Texas	128.8	20,225	20,763	23,390	2.6	12.6	44	3	23
Utah	138.8	20,970	21,389	22,388	1.9	4.6	46	36	29
Vermont	71.5	16,747	18,489	19,407	10.4	4.9	4	34	47
Virginia	98.3	19,426	20,830	22,535	7.2	8.1	16	18	28
Washington	118.5	23,906	25,221	26,056	5.5	3.3	32	42	11
West Virginia	108.8	17,813	18,461	19,603	3.6	6.1	41	30	44
Wisconsin	100.0	22,024	23,570	25,190	7.0	6.8	19	25	14
Wyoming	157.6	24,710	25,100	27,817	1.5	10.8	47	9	8

SOURCE: Compiled by the National Center for Education Information. Basic data from National Education Association, Estimates of School Statistics, selected years.

TABLE 29. Percentage changes for elementary and secondary teachers' salaries: 1983-84 to
          1984-85 and 1982-83 to 1983-84

State	1983-84 to 1984-85		1982-83 to 1983-84	
	Elementary	Secondary	Elementary	Secondary
Georgia	17.5	10.6	6.2	6.1
Washington	16.7	3.3	5.5	5.5
Illinois	15.3	10.0	4.3	5.2
Texas	13.3	12.6	1.9	2.6
South Carolina	13.1	13.1	5.9	5.9
North Carolina	12.6	12.1	4.7	4.7
Alabama	12.2	7.0	3.4	6.0
Tennessee	12.1	12.1	3.0	2.9
Arkansas	11.8	11.8	12.7	12.5
Delaware	11.4	11.2	1.4	1.4
New York	10.2	9.0	7.0	7.0

SOURCE: Compiled by the National Center for Education Information. Basic data from the
         National Education Association, Estimates of School Statistics, selected years.

CHAPTER VI

Teachers and Schools in the Context of the Overall Economy

It doesn't make sense to talk about salaries of teachers outside the context of school expenditures in general, and it doesn't make sense to discuss either salaries or school expenditures without understanding how they fit into the overall economy of each state.

Mississippi's average salary for teachers is lowest in the nation. But so is Mississippi's per capita income, and its per pupil expenditure ranks second last. The cost of living in Mississippi is right at the bottom. The proportion of Mississippi's population that lived below the poverty level in 1979 (the latest year for which state-by-state data are available) was 23.9 percent—the highest in the nation that year when the national average was 12.4 percent.

The same relationship holds in the state with the highest average salary for teachers, Alaska. Alaska pays its teachers an average of $39,751—$10,751 more than the next highest state, New York. Alaska has the highest per capita income of any state in the United States and spends more per pupil enrolled in its schools than any other state.

But, once away from the extremes, some interesting comparisons show up. Michigan, for example, has the fourth highest average teacher salary in the nation but ranks twenty-third in per capita income and twentieth in per pupil expenditure. New Jersey, on the other hand, ranks third in per pupil expenditure, fourth in per capita income, and twelfth in average teacher salary. One more example: California has the sixth highest per capita income in the country, yet the state ranks twenty-sixth in per pupil expenditure but seventh in average salary for teachers (Tables 30 and 31).

48

TABLE 30. Average teachers' salaries, per pupil expenditures, rank of per pupil expenditures, per capita income, rank of per capita income: 1985

	Average teacher salary	Per pupil expenditure	Rank of per pupil expenditure	Per capita income	Rank of per capita income
United States	$23,546	$3,429		$12,707	
1. Alaska	39,751	6,867	1	17,155	1
2. New York	29,000	5,226	2	14,121	7
3. D.C.	28,621	4,753	5	16,845	2
4. Michigan	28,401	3,434	20	12,518	23
5. Rhode Island	27,384	4,097	9	12,730	18
6. Wyoming	26,709	4,809	4	12,586	21
7. California	26,300	3,291	26	14,344	6
8. Minnesota	25,920	3,408	23	13,219	13
9. Maryland	25,861	4,101	8	14,111	8
10. Illinois	25,829	3,517	18	13,728	10
11. Washington	25,610	3,437	19	12,728	19
12. New Jersey	25,125	5,220	3	15,282	4
13. Oregon	24,889	3,963	12	11,582	34
14. Wisconsin	24,780	3,880	14	12,309	27
15. Hawaii	24,628	3,596	17	12,761	17
16. Connecticut	24,520	4,447	6	16,369	3
17. Colorado	24,456	3,898	24	13,742	9
18. Pennsylvania	24,435	4,002	10	12,343	25
19. Massachusetts	24,110	3,889	13	14,574	5
20. Arizona	23,380	2,801	40	11,629	33
21. Delaware	23,300	4,155	7	13,545	11
22. Indiana	23,089	2,638	44	11,799	31
23. Ohio	22,737	3,315	25	12,314	26
24. Texas	22,600	3,287	27	12,636	20
25. Nevada	22,520	2,998	34	13,216	14
26. New Mexico	22,064	3,278	28	10,330	43
27. Montana	21,705	3,968	11	10,216	44
28. Virginia	21,536	3,043	32	13,067	16
29. Utah	21,307	2,182	51	9,719	50
30. Kansas	21,208	3,668	16	13,319	12
31. Florida	21,057	3,409	21	12,553	22
32. Iowa	20,934	3,409	22	12,090	30
33. North Carolina	20,691	2,588	45	10,758	38
34. Georgia	20,494	2,692	42	11,441	35
35. Missouri	20,452	2,993	35	12,129	29
36. Alabama	20,209	2,241	49	9,981	47
37. Nebraska	20,153	3,128	31	12,280	28
38. Kentucky	20,100	2,792	41	10,374	42
39. Tennessee	20,080	2,349	46	10,400	41
40. North Dakota	19,900	3,249	30	12,461	24
41. South Carolina	19,800	2,650	43	10,075	46
42. Idaho	19,700	2,290	48	10,174	45
43. Louisiana	19,690	2,821	38	10,850	37
44. West Virginia	19,563	2,866	37	9,846	48
45. Vermont	19,014	3,783	15	10,692	39
46. Arkansas	18,933	2,344	47	9,724	49
47. Oklahoma	18,930	3,264	29	11,745	32
48. New Hampshire	18,577	2,964	36	13,148	15
49. Maine	18,329	3,038	33	10,678	40
50. South Dakota	17,356	2,813	39	11,049	36
51. Mississippi	15,971	2,182	50	8,857	51

SOURCE: The National Center for Education Information. Basic data from U.S. Department of Commerce, Bureau of Economic Analysis, State Per Capita Personal Income, selected years; and the National Education Association, Estimates of School Statistics, selected years.

TABLE 31: Teachers' salaries as proportion of total school expenditures
(in percents)

State	1984-85	1983-84	1982-83	1972-73
United States	36.6	36.7	37.2	41.9
Alabama	42.7	50.0	44.7	55.8
Alaska	35.1	35.5	34.0	36.8
Arizona	40.7	38.7	38.6	45.2
Arkansas	44.6	40.8	39.3	49.3
California	31.1	34.4	34.2	37.1
Colorado	37.6	37.7	38.6	37.7
Connecticut	37.4	37.3	37.1	42.5
Delaware	34.2	34.4	34.3	34.2
District of Columbia	43.6	44.8	44.7	NA
Florida	34.2	33.4	33.9	42.9
Georgia	39.7	39.8	40.4	46.3
Hawaii	34.7	31.7	37.7	33.9
Idaho	40.1	38.8	38.3	41.5
Illinois	43.2	40.0	43.2	44.7
Indiana	33.4	39.5	39.7	45.9
Iowa	38.1	38.6	38.3	40.4
Kansas	36.4	36.2	36.6	44.3
Kentucky	37.1	39.1	39.3	46.9
Louisiana	37.1	37.3	37.6	43.7
Maine	35.9	35.9	35.6	44.5
Maryland	37.1	37.3	36.4	35.2
Massachusetts	40.1	35.8	37.2	42.8
Michigan	37.5	35.7	35.9	39.0
Minnesota	41.3	38.5	37.9	38.5
Mississippi	38.6	42.9	40.0	39.7
Missouri	42.6	43.3	41.3	45.1
Montana	33.9	34.2	34.9	46.3
Nebraska	42.4	41.1	41.3	48.5
Nevada	36.3	39.4	39.2	40.4
New Hampshire	41.2	39.4	38.7	47.8
New Jersey	33.2	31.8	32.9	43.3
New Mexico	30.1	31.7	34.2	40.9
New York	36.5	36.0	35.6	38.2
North Carolina	42.6	37.8	39.8	44.4
North Dakota	36.4	36.9	36.0	43.4
Ohio	36.6	35.7	37.1	42.6
Oklahoma	32.8	32.6	34.4	45.1
Oregon	35.5	33.1	34.2	43.7
Pennsylvania	35.2	35.5	35.7	39.0
Rhode Island	40.8	39.1	38.6	46.8
South Carolina	38.5	35.7	36.3	40.4
South Dakota	38.1	39.3	39.4	45.1
Tennessee	40.1	38.3	38.9	44.4
Texas	35.1	39.5	40.0	44.9
Utah	33.8	32.6	34.6	38.0
Vermont	35.4	37.3	36.6	37.3
Virginia	40.4	39.1	38.8	45.9
Washington	32.2	32.9	32.9	40.4
West Virginia	41.7	39.6	40.7	43.1
Wisconsin	38.3	40.3	41.0	47.0
Wyoming	30.6	30.9	32.0	45.3

SOURCE: The National Center for Education Information. Basic data from the National
Education Association, Estimates of School Statistics, selected years.

Teacher Salaries as Percentage of Total School Expenditures

Regardless of any state's economy, every state in the union is still spending less than fifty cents of every education dollar on salaries for its teachers.

Teachers' salaries, as a proportion of total expenditures for elementary and secondary schools, dropped to 36.6 percent in 1984-85—down from 36.7 percent in 1983-84, 37.2 percent in 1982-83 and 41.9 percent in 1972-73.

Twenty-four states have increased their proportion of total school expenditures that goes to teachers' salaries since 1982-83. Ten of them have steadily increased the share of total school expenses for teachers' salaries in both of the last two years—Arizona, Arkansas, Connecticut, Idaho, Maryland, Minnesota, Missouri, New Hampshire, New York, North Dakota, Rhode Island, Utah, and Virginia.

However, a mere ten states increased the share of the pie that goes to teachers in the form of salary between 1972-73 and 1982-83 and only two (Idaho and Maryland) have gotten that piece larger than it was in 1972-73.

Thirteen states have continued to cut the share of school spending going to teachers' salaries smaller and smaller since 1982-83—Colorado, Georgia, Indiana, Kentucky, Louisiana, Montana, New Mexico, Pennsylvania, South Dakota, Texas, Washington, Wisconsin and Wyoming. These states spend less than forty cents on the education dollar for teachers' salaries.

With the exceptions of South Dakota and Texas, all of these states decreased their teaching force in either one or both of the last two years. Except for Georgia and Texas in the last year, these states did not raise their average teachers' salaries dramatically in comparison with the national averages. However, all of them, except Indiana and Louisiana, spent noticeably more per student enrolled in their public schools in either one or both of the last two years than they had the year before (Table 32).

Total Expenditures for Public Elementary and Secondary Schools

Public education for the nation's 39,373,841 elementary and secondary students cost $138,117,496 last year—up 8.8 percent (nearly twice the inflation rate) from

TABLE 32. States continuing to cut share of school expenditures going for teachers salaries

State	Teachers' salaries as percent of total expenditure		Number of teachers		Average salary of teachers		Per pupil expenditure	
	'84-85	'83-84	'84-85	'83-84	'84-85	'83-84	'84-85	'83-84
United States	36.6	36.7	1.3	-0.8	6.9	6.2	8.0	7.7
Colorado	37.6	37.7	-2.1	0.2	6.8	6.6	4.2	10.1
Georgia	39.7	39.8	0.0	-0.4	10.7	6.2	16.5	7.5
Indiana	33.4	39.5	0.3	-1.9	6.9	7.2	-3.3	7.8
Kentucky	37.1	39.1	1.2	-0.7	1.6	7.5	9.4	7.6
Louisiana	37.1	37.3	0.2	-2.0	3.0	3.6	0.0	3.7
Montana	33.9	34.2	4.3	-1.7	5.0	5.9	9.2	5.4
New Mexico	30.1	31.7	-8.5	6.0	6.2	1.4	12.2	2.7
Pennsylvania	35.2	35.5	-0.9	-1.6	7.1	7.6	7.4	10.0
South Dakota	38.1	39.3	0.4	2.2	5.3	5.6	5.8	10.2
Texas	35.1	39.5	0.9	2.2	12.4	2.8	23.1	4.8
Washington	32.2	32.9	3.5	-0.4	3.3	5.5	10.6	7.9
Wisconsin	38.3	40.3	-4.7	-2.9	7.7	6.9	9.2	5.1
Wyoming	30.6	30.9	-0.9	4.6	9.0	3.4	7.1	11.5

SOURCE: Compiled by the National Center for Education Information. Basic data from the National Education Association, Estimates of School Statistics, selected years.

1983-84. School expenditures rose 6.5 percent from 1982-83 to 1983-84 when the rate of inflation averaged 3.2 percent (Table 33).

Three states spent less last year for their public elementary and secondary schools than they did in 1983-84—Hawaii (6.8 percent less), North Dakota (down 2.0 percent) and Oklahoma (down 0.4 percent). All three of these states also spent less per student enrolled in 1984-85 than they did the year before. Oklahoma's per capita income also dropped 2.3 percent.

Expenditures Per Pupil

Probably the best simple indicator of a state's effort to support education is how much it spends on each pupil. Per pupil expenditure in average daily attendance is computed by comparing total current expenditures with total number of pupils in average daily attendance (ADA) for the school year. The ADA formula is about 92 percent of fall enrollment.

Per pupil expenditures rose 22.5 percent, after adjusting for inflation, between 1972-73 and 1982-83. This was the decade in which per capita income increased 6.5 percent and the average salary for a teacher decreased 12.2 percent in real terms.

Spending per pupil continues to increase above the rate of inflation. Public

TABLE 33. Total current expenditures (in thousands)

State	Percent change 1972-1982	1982-83	1983-84	1984-85	Percent change '82-'83	Percent change '83-'84	Rank of percent change '82-'83	Rank of percent change '83-'84	1984-85 Rank
United States	126.3	119,093,398	126,883,778	138,117,496	6.5	8.8			
Alabama	133.8	1,561,110	1,569,844	1,708,000	0.5	8.8	51	19	28
Alaska	264.2	602,174	658,207	690,000	9.3	4.8	10	36	38
Arizona	204.7	1,333,600	1,434,753	1,490,000	7.5	3.8	18	39	31
Arkansas	217.9	906,628	992,574	1,022,194	9.4	2.9	9	43	35
California	64.5	12,180,000	13,070,000	14,787,179	7.3	13.1	19	3	1
Colorado	157.7	1,636,181	1,788,412	1,877,796	9.3	4.9	10	35	24
Connecticut	117.2	1,858,683	1,985,760	2,130,513	6.8	7.2	23	27	21
Delaware	77.7	325,146	331,500	376,000	1.9	13.4	49	2	49
District of Columbia	45.5	306,258	349,461	380,600	14.1	8.9	3	17	48
Florida	188.9	4,421,307	4,855,811	5,312,743	9.8	9.4	7	11	9
Georgia	192.7	2,437,020	2,613,777	2,911,622	7.2	11.3	20	5	13
Hawaii	135.7	541,100	621,200	578,400	14.8	-6.8	2	51	42
Idaho	197.9	450,000	475,140	499,130	5.5	5.0	32	34	44
Illinois	104.6	5,356,892	5,892,580	6,011,380	10.0	2.0	6	46	6
Indiana	131.7	2,554,628	2,702,700	2,702,700	5.7	0.0	30	48	16
Iowa	122.4	1,548,288	1,602,882	1,666,376	3.5	3.9	43	38	29
Kansas	162.1	1,297,833	1,396,455	1,532,211	7.6	9.7	17	9	30
Kentucky	175.4	1,508,400	1,618,300	1,756,220	7.2	8.5	20	21	25
Louisiana	142.3	2,078,800	2,130,900	2,213,500	2.5	3.8	48	39	20
Maine	147.1	560,262	592,554	639,740	5.7	7.9	30	24	39
Maryland	75.2	2,350,020	2,416,618	2,627,891	2.8	8.7	46	20	17
Massachusetts	111.4	2,993,931	3,035,535	3,383,865	1.3	11.4	50	4	10
Michigan	131.1	5,683,799	5,908,979	6,056,439	3.9	2.4	41	44	5
Minnesota	92.0	2,335,900	2,452,700	2,471,700	5.0	0.7	36	47	18
Mississippi	143.3	895,242	922,098	1,025,112	3.0	11.1	44	6	34
Missouri	113.6	1,948,607	2,081,002	2,266,361	6.7	8.9	24	17	19
Montana	178.2	532,000	565,700	625,900	6.3	10.6	26	8	40
Nebraska	116.8	732,600	767,927	833,000	4.8	8.4	39	22	37
Nevada	181.0	407,465	426,125	465,300	4.5	9.1	40	13	45
New Hampshire	138.7	417,996	429,585	456,478	2.7	6.2	47	31	46
New Jersey	125.8	4,864,300	5,308,300	5,506,600	-9.1	3.7	12	41	8
New Mexico	260.4	876,815	1,018,109	1,041,640	16.1	2.3	1	45	33
New York	84.4	11,600,000	12,200,000	13,100,000	5.1	7.3	35	26	2
North Carolina	192.9	2,439,684	2,609,253	2,727,800	6.9	4.5	22	37	15
North Dakota	187.7	383,480	408,165	399,860	6.4	-2.0	25	50	47
Ohio	117.1	5,080,000	5,570,000	5,865,000	9.6	5.2	8	33	7
Oklahoma	246.9	1,865,000	2,026,876	2,017,362	8.6	-0.4	13	49	22
Oregon	238.7	1,607,012	1,653,664	1,711,191	2.9	3.4	45	42	27
Pennsylvania	99.5	6,160,900	6,553,000	7,014,130	6.3	7.0	26	28	4
Rhode Island	126.9	444,947	469,419	506,670	5.5	7.9	32	24	43
South Carolina	154.5	1,459,657	1,572,445	1,715,435	7.7	9.0	16	16	26
South Dakota	117.0	309,340	335,000	365,500	8.3	9.1	14	13	50
Tennessee	160.7	1,763,898	1,830,126	2,004,746	3.7	9.5	42	10	23
Texas	207.1	8,184,426	8,700,000	11,125,151	6.2	27.8	28	1	3
Utah	228.0	865,510	958,585	1,020,541	10.7	6.4	5	30	36
Vermont	85.8	278,687	300,651	333,494	7.9	10.9	15	7	51
Virginia	139.9	2,697,940	2,855,848	3,031,039	5.8	6.1	29	32	11
Washington	180.0	2,435,243	2,559,104	2,798,353	5.0	9.3	36	12	14
West Virginia	177.0	943,036	989,465	1,057,037	4.9	6.8	38	29	32
Wisconsin	134.5	2,571,853	2,714,810	2,933,731	5.5	8.0	32	23	12
Wyoming	369.5	499,800	559,275	610,666	11.9	9.1	4	13	41

SOURCE: Compiled by the National Center for Education Information. Basic data from National Education Association, Estimates of School Statistics, selected years.

53

TABLE 34. Per pupil expenditures in Average Daily Attendance (ADA)

State	Percent change 1972-1982	1982-83	1983-84	1984-85	Percent change '82-'83	Percent change '83-'84	Rank of percent change '82-'83	Rank of percent change '83-'84
United States	181.8	2,944	3,173	3,429	7.7	8.0		
Alaska	320.0	6,383	7,026	6,867	10.0	-2.2	11	49
New York	160.9	4,477	4,845	5,226	8.2	7.8	20	23
New Jersey	224.3	4,428	4,943	5,220	11.6	5.6	4	33
Wyoming	222.5	4,022	4,488	4,809	11.5	7.1	5	27
District of Columbia	178.4	3,657	4,116	4,753	12.5	15.4	2	5
Connecticut	201.9	3,666	4,061	4,477	10.7	10.2	8	12
Delaware	219.4	3,524	3,735	4,155	5.9	11.2	35	9
Maryland	193.4	3,488	3,720	4,101	6.6	10.2	33	12
Rhode Island	220.3	3,389	3,720	4,097	9.7	10.1	13	15
Pennsylvania	182.4	3,385	3,725	4,002	10.0	7.4	11	24
Montana	216.1	3,442	3,631	3,968	5.4	9.2	37	18
Oregon	258.9	3,604	3,771	3,963	4.6	5.0	43	36
Massachusetts	168.4	2,958	3,176	3,889	7.3	22.4	32	2
Wisconsin	201.7	3,380	3,553	3,880	5.1	9.2	40	18
Vermont	128.1	3,102	3,148	3,783	1.4	20.1	50	3
Kansas	231.6	3,096	3,361	3,668	8.5	9.1	18	20
Hawaii	200.0	3,347	3,982	3,596	18.9	-9.6	1	51
Illinois	185.5	3,018	3,397	3,517	12.5	3.5	2	40
Washington	191.2	2,878	3,106	3,437	7.9	10.6	24	11
Michigan	214.8	3,243	3,498	3,434	7.8	-1.8	26	48
Florida	219.8	2,923	3,201	3,409	9.5	6.4	14	30
Iowa	197.7	3,064	3,239	3,409	5.7	5.2	36	34
Minnesota	172.2	3,136	3,376	3,408	7.6	0.9	29	44
Colorado	198.0	2,961	3,261	3,398	10.1	4.2	10	38
Ohio	194.2	2,784	3,090	3,315	10.9	7.2	7	26
California	137.1	2,735	2,912	3,291	6.4	13.0	34	6
Texas	173.7	2,547	2,670	3,287	4.8	23.1	42	1
New Mexico	239.3	2,843	2,921	3,278	2.7	12.2	49	8
Oklahoma	263.5	3,039	3,312	3,264	8.9	-1.4	15	46
North Dakota	259.0	3,055	3,307	3,249	8.2	-1.7	20	47
Nebraska	193.0	2,708	2,927	3,128	8.0	6.8	23	28
Virginia	191.2	2,737	2,967	3,043	8.4	2.5	19	42
Maine	214.1	2,624	2,829	3,038	7.8	7.3	26	25
Nevada	141.0	2,758	2,870	2,998	4.0	4.4	45	37
Missouri	191.3	2,513	2,714	2,993	7.9	10.2	24	12
New Hampshire	165.7	2,687	2,796	2,964	4.0	6.0	45	31
West Virginia	205.8	2,465	2,587	2,866	4.9	10.7	41	10
Louisiana	172.5	2,718	2,821	2,821	3.7	0.0	47	45
South Dakota	186.1	2,411	2,657	2,813	10.2	5.8	9	32
Arizona	167.5	2,512	2,738	2,801	8.9	2.3	15	43
Kentucky	213.3	2,368	2,550	2,792	7.6	9.4	29	17
Georgia	195.4	2,146	2,309	2,692	7.5	16.5	31	4
South Carolina	152.3	2,247	2,431	2,650	8.1	9.0	22	21
Indiana	204.0	2,532	2,730	2,638	7.8	-3.3	26	50
North Carolina	229.2	2,265	2,460	2,588	8.6	5.2	17	34
Tennessee	186.6	2,061	2,173	2,349	5.4	8.0	37	22
Arkansas	218.0	2,025	2,257	2,344	11.4	3.8	6	39
Idaho	200.0	2,106	2,219	2,290	5.3	3.1	39	41
Alabama	158.1	2,019	2,102	2,241	4.1	6.6	44	29
Mississippi	198.3	1,895	1,962	2,205	3.5	12.3	48	7
Utah	179.6	1,965	1,992	2,182	1.3	9.5	51	16

SOURCE: Compiled by the National Center for Education Information. Basic data from National Education Association, Estimates of School Statistics, selected years.

54

schools spent an average of $3,429 to educate each child enrolled in 1984-85. That was 8.0 percent more than the $3,173 spent the year before which was 7.7 percent more than the $2,944 spent in 1982-83.

One reason per pupil expenditures may have outdistanced inflation is that states have been effective in keeping their total budgets for education up, or at least stable, at a time when enrollments were falling steadily. This could all change as enrollments in most states start back up this fall when the first wave of six-year-olds from the baby boomlet of the late 1970s starts to school.

Since the per pupil expenditure amount is usually tied directly to a state's economy and enrollment patterns, changes in spending per student that have occurred in the last few years are more significant than how a state ranks in per pupil expenditures.

Besides, rank hasn't changed much. Eight of the top ten states in spending per student in 1982-83 made the top ten in 1984-85. Likewise, all but three of the states that ranked in the bottom ten in 1982-83 were in the bottom ten two years later (Table 34).

Texas brought itself from thirty-ninth in 1983-84 to twenty-seventh last year by increasing its per pupil expenditure by 23.1 percent in just one year. Texas also led all the states last year in the rate of increase in total school expenditures (27.8 percent) and in school revenue receipts (17.7 percent).

By comparison, per capita income and personal income in Texas increased only 8.1 percent and 9.9 percent, respectively, last year.

Three states that rank in the bottom ten in per pupil expenditures have made significant efforts to raise their spending per student in the last two years— Georgia, Mississippi, and Arkansas.

Georgia spent 16.5 percent more per student enrolled in its public schools last year than it did in 1983-84 taking its rank from forty-fifth to forty-second. Georgia's average salary for its teachers also increased 10.7 percent in the same year and ranked thirty-fourth in the nation in 1984-85 after ranking forty-first the year before.

Mississippi went from last in both 1982-83 and 1983-84 to second from the bottom in per pupil expenditures last year by raising the amount it spends per student by 12.3 percent—4.3 percentage points higher than the increase in national average (8.0 percent).

Arkansas increased its spending per student by 11.4 percent the year before last (between 1982-83 and 1983-84) taking it from forty-eighth to forty-six. That was also the year Arkansas raised its average salary for teachers 12.6 percent taking it from fiftieth to forty-ninth. Last year Arkansas continued the upward swing in salaries for teachers, raising the average another 11.8 percent and moving the state up to forty-sixth on the salary measure. Per pupil expenditures, on the other hand, increased 3.8 percent last year in Arkansas putting the state forty-seventh in spending per student in 1984-85.

In addition to these three states, nineteen states have increased their spending per student by more than 10 percent in either or both of the last two years. Joining Texas in raising per pupil expenditures more than 20 percent in the last year are Massachusetts (22.4 percent) and Vermont (20.1 percent).

Massachusetts took its per pupil expenditures from twenty-fourth in 1982-83 and in 1983-84 to thirteenth last year. Massachusetts' enrollment went down slightly (0.1 percent) and its revenue receipts for education rose 15.6 percent in 1984-85 over 1983-84. The state's per capita income increased 9.9 percent from 1983 to 1984.

Vermont's 20.1 percentage increase in spending per pupil took the state from twenty-fifth in 1983-84 to fifteenth last year. Revenue receipts for education increased 9.7 percent and per capita income by 7.3 percent in the state during the same year. Enrollment dropped slightly (0.1 percent).

Personal Income and Per Capita Income
Total personal income in the United States reached the $3 billion mark in 1984—up 9.7 percent over the year before which was up 6.3 percent from 1982. Personal income rose 17.8 percent, after adjusting for inflation, between 1972 and 1982 (Table 35).

Since total personal income in a state is tied to population, it is more relevant for purposes of this report to look at changes in each state's per capita income.

56

TABLE 35. Total personal income (in thousands)

State	Percent change 1972-1982	1982-83	1983-84	1984-85	Percent change '82-'83	'83-'84	Rank of percent change '82-'83	'83-'84	1984-85 Rank
United States	170.9	2,571,517	2,734,464	3,000,827	6.3	9.7			
Alabama	179.2	34,119	36,536	39,826	7.1	9.1	22	30	24
Alaska	285.6	7,358	8,243	8,574	12.0	4.0	2	50	45
Arizona	238.9	29,109	31,567	35,504	8.4	12.4	12	3	27
Arkansas	189.5	19,408	20,802	22,843	7.1	9.8	22	22	33
California	197.6	310,699	333,706	367,538	7.4	10.1	20	18	1
Colorado	226.0	37,400	40,088	43,672	7.2	8.9	21	33	23
Connecticut	157.3	43,366	46,890	51,632	8.1	10.3	16	17	20
Delaware	140.7	7,084	7,643	8,298	7.8	8.5	17	36	48
District of Columbia	114.8	9,542	9,766	10,492	2.3	7.4	47	43	43
Florida	239.7	114,356	123,812	137,774	8.2	11.3	13	7	6
Georgia	183.9	54,011	59,551	66,779	10.2	12.2	4	4	12
Hawaii	176.0	11,589	12,396	13,255	6.9	6.9	25	44	38
Idaho	199.8	8,713	9,429	10,181	8.2	7.9	13	40	44
Illinois	140.8	138,460	142,444	158,024	2.8	10.9	46	10	4
Indiana	141.2	54,840	57,916	64,872	5.6	12.2	33	4	14
Iowa	142.2	31,330	31,071	35,177	-0.8	13.2	50	1	28
Kansas	168.7	28,289	29,351	32,472	3.7	10.6	44	13	30
Kentucky	171.6	32,794	34,899	38,622	6.5	10.9	27	10	26
Louisiana	235.1	44,652	45,540	48,417	2.0	6.3	48	47	22
Maine	166.9	10,261	11,298	12,349	10.1	9.3	5	27	40
Maryland	157.3	52,243	56,159	61,374	7.5	9.3	19	27	15
Massachusetts	141.8	69,923	76,463	84,497	9.4	10.5	8	15	10
Michigan	132.6	99,747	104,071	113,600	4.3	9.1	43	30	9
Minnesota	167.1	46,213	49,321	55,014	6.7	11.6	26	6	19
Mississippi	180.5	19,833	21,098	23,010	6.3	9.0	30	32	32
Missouri	149.9	50,423	54,817	60,738	8.7	10.9	11	10	16
Montana	165.4	7,677	8,121	8,419	5.7	3.6	32	51	47
Nebraska	145.1	16,942	17,849	19,721	5.3	10.4	35	16	34
Nevada	267.6	10,548	11,087	12,038	5.1	8.5	38	36	42
New Hampshire	206.0	10,179	11,610	12,842	14.0	10.6	1	13	39
New Jersey	145.5	97,599	104,548	114,837	7.1	9.8	22	22	8
New Mexico	215.8	12,483	13,512	14,707	8.2	8.8	13	35	37
New York	125.5	217,230	229,922	250,433	5.8	8.9	31	33	2
North Carolina	169.2	54,433	59,628	66,322	9.6	11.3	7	7	13
North Dakota	162.3	7,290	7,937	8,553	8.8	7.7	10	41	46
Ohio	140.3	115,087	120,539	132,404	4.7	9.8	41	22	7
Oklahoma	241.5	36,121	36,238	38,735	0.3	6.9	49	44	25
Oregon	188.5	27,350	28,659	30,973	4.7	8.0	41	39	31
Pennsylvania	143.6	129,956	136,409	146,894	5.0	7.7	39	41	5
Rhode Island	137.8	10,254	11,173	12,245	8.9	9.5	9	25	41
South Carolina	154.2	27,228	29,923	33,248	9.8	11.1	6	9	29
South Dakota	154.2	6,676	6,894	7,799	3.2	13.1	45	2	49
Tennessee	174.7	41,406	44,580	49,055	7.7	10.1	18	18	21
Texas	269.6	174,528	183,753	202,031	5.3	9.9	35	21	3
Utah	220.6	13,790	14,575	16,052	5.6	10.1	33	18	36
Vermont	166.7	4,909	5,231	5,665	6.5	8.2	27	38	51
Virginia	186.2	60,576	67,271	73,637	11.1	9.5	3	25	11
Washington	216.6	49,111	52,301	55,356	6.5	5.8	27	48	18
West Virginia	168.3	17,142	17,999	19,223	4.9	6.8	40	46	35
Wisconsin	157.8	51,033	53,699	58,668	5.2	9.3	37	27	17
Wyoming	294.0	6,205	6,130	6,437	-1.2	5.0	51	49	50

SOURCE: Compiled by the National Center for Education Information. Basic data from National Education Association, _Estimates of School Statistics_, selected years.

57

Per capita income increased 8.7 percent in 1984 over 1983 and 5.2 percent between 1982 and 1983, having risen 145 percent (6.5 percent in real terms) in the decade from 1972 to 1982.

As was the case with per pupil expenditures, states with the highest per capita incomes now were also the ones with the highest last year, the year before and in 1972. Alaska still heads the list even though the state's income per capita decreased slightly last year. The nine states following Alaska plus the District of Columbia in descending order of per capita income amount in 1984 are: 2, District of Columbia; 3, Connecticut; 4, New Jersey; 5, Massachusetts; 6, California; 7, New York; 8, Maryland; 9, Colorado; 10, Illinois; and 11, Delaware (Table 36).

Only Wyoming dropped out of the top ten states in per capita income since 1982. Wyoming is now twenty-first having been eighth two years ago.

With the exception of North Carolina, the bottom ten states in per capita income in 1984 were the same ones in 1982. Montana dropped from thirty-fifth in 1982 to forty-fourth in 1984. Mississippi still ranks last. The states having the ten lowest per capita incomes in 1984 were: 51, Mississippi; 50, Utah; 49, Arkansas; 48, West Virginia; 47, Alabama; 46, South Carolina; 45, Idaho; 44, Montana; 43, New Mexico; and 42, Kentucky.

Per Pupil Expenditures as Percentage of Per Capita Income

Per pupil expenditures as a percentage of per capita income varied in 1984-85 from a high of 40 percent in Alaska to 22 percent in several states. The gap seems to be narrowing. The range was from nearly 44 percent in Alaska to 18 percent in Alabama just two years ago.

The average on this measure has not changed in the last two years. The average for both 1982-83 and for 1984-85 was 26 percent, having risen from 23 percent in 1972.

Public Elementary and Secondary School Revenue Receipts

Total revenue receipts for public elementary and secondary education in the United States in 1984-85 came to an estimated $137.6 billion—7.8 percent higher than the year before and $544 million less than the total expenditures for schools in the

TABLE 36. Per capita income

State	Percent change 1972-1982	1982-83	1983-84	1984-85	Percent change '82-'83	Percent change '83-'84	Rank of percent change '82-'83	Rank of percent change '83-'84
United States	144.9	11,100	11,687	12,707	5.2	8.7		
Alaska	187.5	15,200	17,225	17,155	13.3	-0.4	1	51
District of Columbia	153.0	15,064	15,673	16,845	4.0	7.4	41	37
Connecticut	150.5	13,810	14,945	16,369	8.2	9.5	9	15
New Jersey	142.1	13,169	14,000	15,282	6.3	9.1	19	17
Massachusetts	141.0	12,153	13,260	14,574	9.1	9.9	4	9
California	147.8	12,616	13,256	14,344	5.0	8.2	31	26
New York	134.4	12,389	13,014	14,121	5.0	8.5	31	24
Maryland	146.2	12,237	13,047	14,111	6.6	8.1	16	29
Colorado	157.5	12,202	12,771	13,742	4.6	7.6	37	34
Illinois	136.8	12,091	12,401	13,728	2.5	10.7	45	5
Delaware	129.4	11,810	12,615	13,545	6.8	7.3	14	39
Kansas	151.7	11,717	12,102	13,319	3.2	10.0	43	8
Minnesota	149.9	11,155	11,901	13,219	6.6	11.0	16	4
Nevada	128.2	12,022	12,441	13,216	3.4	6.2	42	45
New Hampshire	151.5	10,721	12,109	13,148	12.9	8.5	2	24
Virginia	151.6	11,056	12,122	13,067	9.6	7.7	3	33
Hawaii	127.1	11,614	12,115	12,761	4.3	5.3	39	48
Rhode Island	142.3	10,751	11,694	12,730	8.7	8.8	6	20
Washington	157.1	11,466	12,162	12,728	6.0	4.6	21	49
Texas	184.4	11,423	11,686	12,636	2.3	8.1	46	29
Wyoming	172.4	12,211	11,920	12,586	-2.3	5.5	50	47
Florida	145.3	10,907	11,593	12,553	6.2	8.2	20	26
Michigan	130.4	10,942	11,476	12,518	4.8	9.0	35	19
North Dakota	147.0	10,830	11,664	12,461	7.7	6.8	12	42
Pennsylvania	144.4	10,934	11,468	12,343	4.8	7.6	35	34
Ohio	139.4	10,667	11,218	12,314	5.1	9.7	30	13
Wisconsin	143.3	10,725	11,311	12,309	5.4	8.8	28	20
Nebraska	134.7	10,641	11,175	12,280	5.0	9.8	31	11
Missouri	139.9	10,188	11,029	12,129	8.2	9.9	9	9
Iowa	138.6	10,754	10,697	12,090	-0.5	13.0	49	1
Indiana	133.5	9,994	10,570	11,799	5.7	11.6	24	3
Oklahoma	185.7	11,247	10,988	11,745	-2.3	6.8	50	42
Arizona	138.1	10,067	10,653	11,629	5.8	9.1	23	17
Oregon	139.1	10,231	10,768	11,582	5.2	7.5	29	36
Georgia	142.0	9,573	10,389	11,441	8.5	10.1	7	7
South Dakota	144.2	9,582	9,851	11,049	2.8	12.1	44	2
Louisiana	189.0	10,211	10,262	10,850	0.4	5.7	48	46
North Carolina	138.4	9,048	9,805	10,758	8.3	9.7	8	13
Vermont	139.3	9,478	9,957	10,692	5.0	7.3	31	39
Maine	143.7	9,031	9,861	10,678	9.1	8.2	4	26
Tennessee	141.5	8,899	9,515	10,400	6.9	9.3	13	16
Kentucky	147.7	8,893	9,396	10,374	5.6	10.4	26	6
New Mexico	150.4	9,135	9,656	10,330	5.7	6.9	24	41
Montana	138.3	9,544	9,945	10,216	4.2	2.7	40	50
Idaho	137.0	8,937	9,534	10,174	6.6	6.7	16	44
South Carolina	142.6	8,475	9,168	10,075	8.1	9.8	11	11
Alabama	150.7	8,647	9,229	9,981	6.7	8.1	15	29
West Virginia	147.6	8,758	9,160	9,846	4.5	7.4	38	37
Arkansas	155.0	8,424	8,936	9,724	6.0	8.8	21	20
Utah	134.1	8,820	9,005	9,719	2.0	7.9	47	32
Mississippi	153.7	7,725	8,155	8,857	5.5	8.6	27	23

SOURCE: Compiled by the National Center for Education Information. Basic data from U.S. Department of
Commerce, U.S. Bureau of Economic Analysis, State Per Capita Personal Income, selected years.

59

TABLE 37. Total revenue receipts

State	Percent change 1972-1982	1982-83	1983-84	1984-85	Percent change '82-'83	Percent change '83-'84	Rank of percent change '82-'83	Rank of percent change '83-'84	1984-85 Rank
United States	121.8	120,432,748	127,597,482	137,572,617	5.9	7.8			
Alabama	123.9	1,523,949	1,532,344	1,632,119	0.5	6.5	49	29	29
Alaska	285.7	598,852	643,011	683,415	7.3	6.2	18	33	38
Arizona	193.9	1,435,300	1,529,670	1,529,000	6.5	0.0	23	45	30
Arkansas	201.9	876,724	969,447	1,072,386	10.5	10.6	5	14	33
California	54.9	12,050,000	12,835,080	14,815,175	6.5	15.4	23	3	1
Colorado	172.0	1,772,800	1,911,645	2,038,856	7.8	6.6	13	27	22
Connecticut	94.0	1,858,389	1,985,460	2,130,113	6.8	7.2	20	22	21
Delaware	93.4	340,671	346,500	392,660	1.7	13.3	46	6	47
District of Columbia	44.7	346,606	363,397	384,181	4.8	5.7	33	35	48
Florida	187.9	4,491,023	4,973,013	5,725,091	10.7	15.1	4	4	8
Georgia	194.3	2,415,291	2,481,559	2,843,996	2.7	14.6	43	5	13
Hawaii	115.2	551,100	634,700	580,100	15.1	-8.6	2	51	42
Idaho	197.7	428,550	468,000	502,000	9.2	7.2	8	22	43
Illinois	93.0	6,117,657	6,423,606	6,614,303	5.0	2.9	32	41	5
Indiana	115.2	2,557,939	2,557,939	2,855,000	0.0	11.6	50	10	12
Iowa	111.2	1,637,012	1,694,961	1,687,316	3.5	-0.4	39	46	28
Kansas	164.7	1,346,636	1,409,256	1,511,697	4.6	7.2	35	22	31
Kentucky	162.6	1,494,500	1,617,000	1,690,500	8.1	4.5	10	38	27
Louisiana	140.6	2,075,130	2,105,740	2,347,200	1.4	11.4	47	12	19
Maine	154.3	549,260	580,554	624,740	5.7	7.6	29	20	39
Maryland	76.9	2,380,831	2,486,755	2,683,004	4.4	7.8	36	19	16
Massachusetts	109.2	2,900,000	2,969,533	3,433,235	2.3	15.6	45	2	10
Michigan	135.6	6,035,268	6,270,000	6,009,744	3.8	-4.1	38	48	7
Minnesota	93.3	2,406,900	2,581,500	2,593,320	7.2	0.4	19	44	18
Mississippi	147.6	889,089	915,762	1,021,067	3.0	11.5	41	11	34
Missouri	111.1	2,065,000	2,207,379	2,339,454	6.8	5.9	20	34	20
Montana	199.2	565,700	603,000	615,690	6.6	2.1	22	42	40
Nebraska	126.6	744,000	790,000	825,000	6.1	4.4	25	39	37
Nevada	166.5	397,244	419,091	460,400	5.5	9.8	30	16	46
New Hampshire	153.0	427,295	440,277	493,200	3.0	12.0	41	8	45
New Jersey	120.8	4,968,900	5,372,700	5,722,400	8.1	6.5	10	29	9
New Mexico	204.5	838,242	833,048	893,175	-0.6	7.2	51	22	36
New York	77.3	11,121,000	11,794,235	12,583,325	6.0	6.6	26	27	2
North Carolina	146.4	2,503,835	2,654,169	2,787,900	6.0	5.0	26	37	14
North Dakota	149.6	340,500	378,002	352,000	11.0	-6.8	3	50	50
Ohio	115.4	5,310,000	5,790,000	6,100,000	9.0	5.3	9	36	6
Oklahoma	123.0	1,890,000	2,088,860	1,986,000	10.5	-4.9	5	49	23
Oregon	198.4	1,595,946	1,650,080	1,720,000	3.3	4.2	40	40	26
Pennsylvania	108.2	6,204,300	6,523,500	6,946,060	5.1	6.4	31	32	4
Rhode Island	121.1	447,699	469,564	500,293	4.8	6.5	33	29	44
South Carolina	158.0	1,489,700	1,630,802	1,743,738	9.4	6.9	7	26	25
South Dakota	133.0	344,000	371,300	364,500	7.9	-1.8	12	47	49
Tennessee	165.1	1,695,179	1,736,012	1,958,187	2.4	12.7	44	7	24
Texas	231.1	8,311,967	8,800,000	10,362,776	5.8	17.7	28	1	3
Utah	220.3	886,051	896,882	1,002,619	1.2	11.8	48	9	35
Vermont	104.2	287,443	309,084	339,183	7.5	9.7	16	17	51
Virginia	145.2	2,647,167	2,844,950	3,059,978	7.4	7.5	17	21	11
Washington	134.2	2,248,039	2,423,561	2,625,828	7.8	8.3	13	18	17
West Virginia	190.1	949,546	1,023,120	1,137,249	7.7	11.1	15	13	32
Wisconsin	122.7	2,609,889	2,724,554	2,761,444	4.3	1.3	37	43	15
Wyoming	286.8	464,000	537,060	592,000	15.7	10.2	1	15	41

SOURCE: Compiled by the National Center for Education Information. Basic data from National Education Association, Estimates of School Statistics, selected years.

60

same year. An additional $4 billion in non-revenue receipts--the amount received by local education agencies from the sale of bonds and real property and equipment, plus loans and proceeds from insurance adjustments--brought total receipts to $141.6 billion in 1984-85 (Table 37).

Six states had a decrease in school revenue receipts last year over the year before--Hawaii, Iowa, Michigan, North Dakota, Oklahoma, and South Dakota. Hawaii, North Dakota and Oklahoma had had a big jump in revenue receipts the year before (1983-84). These same three states--Hawaii, North Dakota, and Oklahoma--also had a decline in total and per pupil expenditures in 1984-85. Only Iowa had a drop in enrollment.

The four states continuing the downward spiral of declining enrollments (New Jersey, New Mexico, Tennessee and West Virginia) all increased their school revenue receipts, total school expenditures and spending per student in 1984-85 (Table 38).

Sources of Revenue for Public Elementary and Secondary Schools

Financing public education in this country varies greatly from state to state and within states. One of the most significant changes in the decade between 1972-73 and 1982-83 was the shift from local sources to state sources for financing public education. All but eight states showed a decrease in local share of education costs and an increase in state share in that decade.

The trend was reflected in the national averages. In 1972-73, states

TABLE 38. States continuing decreases in enrollments with changes in revenue receipts, school expenditures, per pupil expenditures, and numbers of teachers.

Percent Change from 1983-84 to 1984-85

State	Revenue receipts	School expenditures	Per pupil expenditures	Total enrollment	Number teachers
United States	7.8	8.8	8.0	0.3	1.3
New Jersey	6.5	3.7	5.6	-2.6	-0.5
New Mexico	7.2	2.3	12.2	-3.3	-8.5
Tennessee	12.7	9.5	8.0	-0.6	2.2
West Virginia	11.1	6.8	10.7	-2.2	0.6

SOURCE: Compiled by the National Center for Education Information. Basic data from the National Education Association, Estimates of School Statistics, selected years.

61

contributed 40.6 percent of public elementary and secondary revenue receipts. Local and "other" sources came up with 51.5 percent, and the federal government, 7.9 percent. By 1982-83, the proportion of total revenue receipts from states for public elementary and secondary schools had increased to 50.3 percent. From local sources, it had decreased to 42.3 percent. The federal share dropped to 7.4 percent in 1982-83.

However, this trend seems to be slowing. In both 1983-84 and 1984-85, the state share of revenue receipts for public elementary and secondary education dropped to 49.0 percent. The local share for these two years rose slightly from 42.3 percent in 1982-83 to 44.5 percent in 1983-84 and 44.8 percent in 1984-85.

Federal Share of Revenue Receipts for Public Elementary and Secondary Education

The most noticeable change in revenue receipts for education in the last couple of years has been the diminishing federal share. The federal contribution to total revenue receipts for public elementary and secondary education dropped from 7.9 percent in 1972-73 to 7.4 percent in 1982-83. The federal share dropped a whole percentage point in the following year. In 1983-84, the federal government contributed 6.4 percent of the total $127.6 billion in revenue receipts for public elementary and secondary education. The federal share dropped to 6.2 percent of the total $137.6 billion in 1984-85 (Table 39).

The federal share for education decreased in thirty-two states in the decade between 1972-73 and 1982-83 and has continued to drop in fifteen of them. Pennsylvania shows the most dramatic cut in federal share of its revenue receipts for public elementary and secondary education. After experiencing only a 0.3 percent drop in federal share for education in the decade between 1972-73 and 1982-83, Pennsylvania recorded a decrease in federal share from 7.5 percent in 1982-83 to 4.3 percent in 1983-84 to 3.2 percent in 1984-85--second lowest in the nation for that year.

Six states and the District of Columbia have received more than 10 percent of their revenue receipts for public elementary and secondary education from the federal government in each of the last three years. All of them are located in the South--Alabama, Arkansas, Kentucky, Mississippi, New Mexico, and North Carolina

TABLE 39. State federal revenue receipts as a percentage of revenue

State	Change in percent 1972-82	1982-83	1983-84	1984-85
United States	-0.5	7.4	6.4	6.2
Alabama	-2.2	14.8	13.1	11.9
Alaska	-9.5	5.7	1.3	2.9
Arizona	3.2	11.4	8.5	10.5
Arkansas	-2.0	13.3	12.5	11.0
California	-2.1	5.3	6.9	6.8
Colorado	-1.6	5.4	4.7	3.9
Connecticut	1.8	4.9	5.2	5.0
Delaware	3.7	11.2	9.4	7.8
District of Columbia	8.6	15.5	10.2	11.3
Florida	-2.7	7.1	8.2	7.2
Georgia	-2.3	10.2	9.3	9.5
Hawaii	1.4	9.9	9.0	8.9
Idaho	-5.2	6.9	7.1	6.8
Illinois	2.5	8.5	7.6	6.7
Indiana	1.2	6.3	5.7	4.2
Iowa	2.5	7.3	5.4	5.5
Kansas	-3.2	4.8	5.0	4.6
Kentucky	-4.2	10.7	10.5	10.1
Louisiana	-4.3	9.4	8.8	9.6
Maine	0.8	10.1	7.8	7.6
Maryland	-1.0	5.9	5.6	5.7
Massachusetts	-0.4	4.8	4.5	5.5
Michigan	4.3	8.1	4.3	4.2
Minnesota	0.0	4.7	4.4	4.1
Mississippi	-3.9	23.0	19.4	17.8
Missouri	0.1	8.1	7.2	6.2
Montana	0.0	8.5	9.1	9.0
Nebraska	-1.4	7.1	6.3	5.5
Nevada	0.9	0.6	5.2	4.0
New Hampshire	-0.9	3.9	3.7	3.2
New Jersey	-2.3	3.5	3.8	5.7
New Mexico	-10.3	10.2	10.8	11.0
New York	-1.4	4.0	3.8	4.0
North Carolina	2.6	16.1	11.4	10.3
North Dakota	-3.4	7.3	7.1	7.1
Ohio	-0.8	5.0	5.2	5.1
Oklahoma	0.5	10.3	7.3	7.4
Oregon	4.5	8.8	5.6	4.9
Pennsylvania	-0.3	7.5	4.3	3.2
Rhode Island	-3.0	4.7	4.6	4.1
South Carolina	-3.4	13.6	12.0	6.9
South Dakota	-3.2	8.7	8.1	10.6
Tennessee	-0.1	13.0	10.0	9.9
Texas	-2.0	10.0	6.8	7.8
Utah	-3.9	5.2	5.1	5.4
Vermont	0.9	7.0	5.7	6.2
Virginia	-3.8	6.6	6.6	6.9
Washington	-3.3	5.4	4.4	3.9
West Virginia	-3.9	9.0	9.2	9.1
Wisconsin	1.5	5.4	4.4	3.9
Wyoming	-5.3	4.0	2.6	3.7

SOURCE: Compiled by the National Center for Education Information. Basic data from the National Education Association, Estimates of School Statistics, selected years.

TABLE 40. State revenue receipts (percentages)

State	Change in percent 1972-82	1982-83	1983-84	1984-85
United States	9.7	50.3	49.0	49.0
Alabama	0.3	64.3	67.3	72.4
Alaska	10.5	78.3	83.1	73.4
Arizona	4.1	45.7	52.3	52.4
Arkansas	6.3	54.3	54.3	59.2
California	51.8	85.8	67.0	67.1
Colorado	10.0	36.9	42.0	40.2
Connecticut	13.9	37.0	38.2	40.0
Delaware	-2.0	67.6	67.6	69.4
District of Columbia	0.0	0.0	0 0	0.0
Florida	6.6	61.9	54.5	53.5
Georgia	2.2	55.6	58.6	50.3
Hawaii	1.3	89.8	90.7	90.8
Idaho	23.2	62.6	64.1	64.7
Illinois	1.1	38.0	37.7	37.6
Indiana	27.1	58.6	53.6	53.4
Iowa	7.5	42.1	41.0	42.0
Kansas	17.0	44.4	44.2	45.1
Kentucky	15.2	70.5	70.9	68.6
Louisiana	-0.1	55.9	59.4	53.4
Maine	15.2	49.7	50.9	51.0
Maryland	-7.6	40.2	39.6	40.4
Massachusetts	15.2	39.4	41.3	42.5
Michigan	-11.5	36.1	35.1	33.9
Minnesota	-9.1	48.9	54.1	51.9
Mississippi	4.3	53.3	55.3	56.7
Missouri	4.5	39.6	39.9	37.2
Montana	22.2	47.4	45.3	45.0
Nebraska	12.3	27.9	28.5	28.1
Nevada	22.8	60.6	42.4	39.5
New Hampshire	-0.7	6.9	7.1	8.0
New Jersey	13.8	40.0	39.3	40.0
New Mexico	17.8	77.8	77.7	77.4
New York	1.3	41.9	41.3	43.1
North Carolina	-2.6	61.5	61.7	61.5
North Dakota	22.7	51.5	56.4	59.5
Ohio	7.4	40.7	43.9	42.6
Oklahoma	17.3	60.2	66.7	61.4
Oregon	16.5	36.8	28.8	29.0
Pennsylvania	-5.4	45.2	45.4	45.4
Rhode Island	1.2	37.0	35.8	36.8
South Carolina	1.4	57.1	59.3	62.8
South Dakota	14.1	27.6	26.9	26.9
Tennessee	2.1	47.2	45.9	49.9
Texas	3.7	50.6	47.7	45.6
Utah	3.2	56.3	54.7	54.4
Vermont	2.2	35.2	33.8	33.4
Virginia	7.1	41.6	43.0	44.6
Washington	28.0	75.2	75.1	74.9
West Virginia	5.6	62.4	61.2	63.6
Wisconsin	6.8	37.4	37.9	39.5
Wyoming	0.9	34.7	29.6	28.7

SOURCE: Compiled by the National Center for Education Information. Basic data from the National Education Association, Estimates of School Statistics, selected years.

However, with the exception of New Mexico, the share contributed by the federal government has diminished steadily in the last three years in each of these states.

New Jersey and New Mexico are the only states that have had a steady increase in federal share of their revenue receipts for public elementary and secondary education in the last three years. However, eight states showed an increase from 1982-83 to 1983-84 followed by a drop in 1984-85--California, Colorado, Connecticut, Florida, Kansas, Montana, Ohio, and West Virginia. With the exception of Florida, the changes in share of revenue receipts for education contributed by the federal government in these states were ever so slight in the last three years.

States whose federal share of school revenue receipts went down from 1982-83 to 1983-84 but back up the following year are: Alaska, Arizona, Georgia, Iowa, Louisiana, Maryland, Massachusetts, Oklahoma, South Dakota, Texas, Utah, Vermont and Wyoming. The District of Columbia gets added to this list too. Again, only half of these states showed any appreciable increase in federal share of revenue receipts for public elementary and secondary schools--Arizona, the District of Columbia, Louisiana, Massachusetts, South Dakota, Texas, and Wyoming.

It is noteworthy that the state that pays its teachers the most and spends the greatest amount on each pupil enrolled in its schools receives the smallest share of revenue receipts from the federal government. Alaska got only 2.9 percent of its money for public elementary and secondary education from Uncle Sam in 1984-85, having received only 1.3 percent the year before. Alaska, on the other hand, did receive 15.2 percent in 1972-73 and 5.7 percent in 1982-83 from the federal government.

State Share of Revenue Receipts for Public Elementary and Secondary Education

The range of state share of revenue receipts for public elementary and secondary education is from a high of 90.8 percent in Hawaii to a low of 8.0 percent in New Hampshire (Tables 40 and 41).

TABLE 41. Local and other revenue receipts (percentage)

State	Change in percent 1972-82	1982-83	1983-84	1984-85
United States	-9.2	42.3	44.5	44.8
Alabama	2.0	21.0	19.6	15.6
Alaska	-1.0	16.0	15.7	23.6
Arizona	-7.4	42.9	39.2	37.1
Arkansas	-4.3	32.4	33.1	29.8
California	-49.7	8.9	26.1	26.1
Colorado	-8.4	57.7	53.3	55.9
Connecticut	-15.1	58.7	56.7	55.1
Delaware	-1.8	21.2	23.1	22.7
District of Columbia	-2.6	84.5	89.8	88.7
Florida	-3.9	31.0	37.4	39.3
Georgia	0.1	34.2	32.1	40.2
Hawaii	-2.7	0.3	0.3	0.3
Idaho	-18.1	30.4	28.8	28.5
Illinois	-3.7	53.4	54.6	55.7
Indiana	-28.4	35.1	40.7	42.4
Iowa	-10.0	50.6	53.7	52.6
Kansas	-13.8	50.8	50.8	50.4
Kentucky	-11.1	18.7	18.6	21.2
Louisiana	4.5	34.7	31.8	36.9
Maine	-16.0	40.2	41.3	41.4
Maryland	8.6	53.9	54.8	53.9
Massachusetts	-14.9	55.8	54.1	51.9
Michigan	7.2	55.8	60.6	61.9
Minnesota	9.1	46.3	41.5	44.0
Mississippi	-0.4	23.7	25.2	25.5
Missouri	-4.6	52.3	52.9	56.6
Montana	-22.1	44.2	45.6	46.0
Nebraska	-10.9	65.0	65.2	66.4
Nevada	-23.7	31.8	52.4	56.5
New Hampshire	1.7	89.2	89.2	88.8
New Jersey	-11.7	56.4	57.0	56.6
New Mexico	-7.6	12.0	11.5	11.6
New York	0.1	54.1	55.0	52.9
North Carolina	1.9	22.4	26.9	28.2
North Dakota	-19.4	41.1	36.4	33.4
Ohio	-6.6	54.3	50.9	52.3
Oklahoma	-17.8	29.5	26.0	31.2
Oregon	-21.1	54.4	65.6	66.1
Pennsylvania	5.8	47.4	50.3	51.4
Rhode Island	1.8	58.3	59.5	59.0
South Carolina	2.0	29.3	28.6	30.3
South Dakota	-10.9	63.7	65.0	62.6
Tennessee	-2.1	39.8	44.1	40.3
Texas	-1.7	39.5	45.5	46.6
Utah	-0.7	38.5	40.1	40.2
Vermont	-3.1	57.8	60.5	60.4
Virginia	-3.2	51.8	50.4	48.5
Washington	-24.6	19.4	19.2	19.4
West Virginia	-1.8	28.5	29.6	27.3
Wisconsin	-8.3	57.2	57.7	56.7
Wyoming	4.4	61.3	67.8	67.6

SOURCE: Compiled by the National Center for Education Information. Basic data from the National Education Association, Estimates of School Statistics, selected years.

Twenty-one states recorded a greater than 10 percent increase in state share of education revenue receipts between 1972-73 and 1982-83. Seven of them experienced a greater than 20 percent increase for the decade—California, Idaho, Indiana, Montana, Nevada, North Dakota, and Washington. Six of these seven states decreased their piece of the pie in both of the last two years. Idaho did not. Only five of the twenty states have continued to increase their share of total revenue receipts for public elementary and secondary education in the last two years, Idaho being one of them. The other four states are: Connecticut, Maine, Massachusetts, and North Dakota.

The move toward the states contributing an ever increasing share of revenue receipts for public elementary and secondary schools seemed to have peaked in 1983-84 for some states. Nine of the forty-two states that increased their share in the decade between 1972-73 and 1982-83 continued to do so the following year but pulled back on their share of revenue receipts for their public elementary and secondary schools last year—Alaska, Colorado, Georgia, Kentucky, Missouri, Nebraska, Ohio, Oklahoma, and South Carolina.

Twelve states have decreased their share of school revenue in both of the last two years. Only eight states recorded a decrease in their share of money for public education in the decade between 1972-73 and 1982-83.

Local and "Other" Sources of Revenue for Public Elementary and Secondary Education

The local and "other" contribution to revenue receipts for public elementary and secondary education is increasing again after a decade of getting smaller. The local and "other" share diminished from 51.5 percent in 1972-73 to 42.3 percent in 1982-83 and has increased to 44.5 percent in 1983-84 and on up to 44.8 percent in 1984-85.

The greatest contribution by local and "other" sources is in the state of New Hampshire (88.8 percent). The lowest is in Hawaii (0.3 percent).

The local share of total revenue receipts for public elementary and secondary education decreased in thirty-seven states, plus the District of Columbia, in the decade between 1972-73 and 1982-83, but has turned around and been increasing steadily the last two years in fourteen of those states.

Three of the thirteen states that recorded an increase in local share of revenue receipts for the decade from 1972-73 to 1982-83 continue to show an increase--Michigan, North Carolina, and Pennsylvania.

CHAPTER VII

Who Is Going into Teaching?

The news about who's been going into teaching the last several years has not been good. It is well known by now that the number of persons studying to become teachers has dropped steadily since the peak year 1972. That the academic caliber of persons intending to be teachers has been going down also has been widely publicized.

However, we may be seeing a turn-around in both of these trends. The data hasn't been collected in any hard way yet, but some college of education deans are saying their enrollments were up last fall after years of decline.

And, what could be even better news, the Scholastic Aptitude Test (SAT) scores of high school students who say they intend to major in education when they get to college are rising faster than the national average SAT scores. The gap between the national average and the intended education majors' average has narrowed from 80 points in 1982 to 70 points in 1985. Furthermore, the greatest increases in scores of students intending to major in education are occurring in states that project the biggest demand for new teachers—the South and West.

Numbers of Teacher Education Students

A survey conducted by the National Center for Education Information in spring and summer 1984 showed that the number of new teacher graduates dropped 53 percent from 1973 to 1983, that enrollment in teacher education programs decreased by a third, and that persons newly admitted into teacher education decreased 44 percent during this period.[23]

Data from the National Center for Education Statistics shows that the

108,309 bachelor's degrees conferred in education in 1980-81 were 44.2 percent fewer than the number conferred in 1972-73.[24]

NCES data further show that there was a 57.4 percent drop in the number of elementary education degrees granted from 1970-71 to 1980-81.[25] The demand for new teachers for the next few years is at the elementary school level. Demand is also high for science and mathematics. The number of persons getting a degree in mathematics education dropped from 2,217 in 1970-71 to 798 in 1980-81 (a 64 percent decline). The number of science education degrees conferred decreased from 891 to 597 (33 percent) for the period.

The proportion of first-time, full-time freshmen indicating teaching as a probable career occupation plummeted from 19.3 percent in fall 1970 to 4.7 percent in fall 1982.

NCES's High School and Beyond Studies and National Longitudinal Studies of High School Seniors of 1972 showed that the proportion of high school seniors who intended to major in education in college dropped from 12.0 percent in 1972 to 7.0 percent in 1980. The proportion of female high school seniors intending to major in education decreased from 20.1 percent to 11.0 percent for whites, from 9.3 percent to 5.6 percent for blacks, and 14.1 percent to 9.9 percent for Hispanics. For male high school seniors, the corresponding percentages by race are: white males, from

TABLE 42. Percent of first-time full-time freshmen indicating elementary/secondary teaching as probable career occupation: fall 1970 to 1982

Fall of Year	Total	Elementary Teaching	Secondary Teaching
		(Percent)	
1970	19.3	8.0	11.3
1971	15.4	6.8	8.6
1972	12.1	5.6	6.5
1973	8.8	4.2	4.6
1974	7.7	3.5	4.2
1975	6.5	3.0	3.5
1976	8.0	4.3	3.7
1977	6.9	4.0	2.9
1978	6.2	3.7	2.5
1979	6.4	3.8	2.6
1980	6.0	3.8	2.2
1981	5.5	3.5	2.0
1982	4.7	3.0	1.7

SOURCE: U.S. Department of Education: National Center for Education Statistics, The Condition of Education--1983, p. 218.

70

6.0 percent to 3.4 percent; black males, 4.7 percent to 3.9 percent; and Hispanic males, from 9.8 percent in 1972 to 3.0 percent in 1980 (Table 43).

These data are further substantiated by information produced by Scholastic Aptitude Test (SAT) takers. The proportion of SAT-takers who said they might major in education when they got to college decreased from 11.0 percent in 1972 to 4.6 percent in 1984.

Academic Caliber of Education Majors

Nothing raises the ire of people in the business of educating, certifying, and hiring teachers more than statements indicating that the academic caliber of persons going into teaching has been declining. The bottom line of this issue has yet to be written, because nobody to date has come up with hard data about the academic caliber of persons who pass through a teacher education program, get certified, and go on to become teachers.

The National Center for Education Information, in its survey last year of colleges and universities that have teacher education programs, attempted to collect data on SAT and ACT scores, high school grade point averages, class rank and high school courses taken in mathematics, science and foreign language for persons newly admitted into teacher education and for students who finish teacher education programs.

TABLE 43. College-bound seniors who intend to major in education, by sex and racial/ethnic group: spring 1972 and 1980

| Field | Total | Male | | | | Female | | | |
		Total	White Non-Hispanic	Black Non-Hispanic	Hispanic	Total	White Non-Hispanic	Black Non-Hispanic	Hispanic
1972 Seniors:									
Total	100.0	100.0	100.0	100.0	100.0	100.0	100.0	100.0	100.0
Education	12.0	6.0	6.0	4.7	9.8	18.8	20.1	9.3	14.1
Other field	88.0	94.0	94.0	95.3	90.0	81.2	79.9	90.7	85.9
Sample size	7,969	4,021	3,718	190	113	3,948	3,542	294	112
1980 Seniors:									
Total	100.0	100.0	100.0	100.0	100.0	100.0	100.0	100.0	100.0
Education	7.0	3.4	3.4	3.9	3.0	10.3	11.0	5.6	9.9
Other field	93.0	96.6	96.6	96.1	97.0	89.7	89.0	94.4	90.1
Sample size	11,259	5,367	4,253	608	506	5,892	4,329	905	658

SOURCE: The National Center for Education Statistics, The Condition of Education, 1983, p. 220.

Eighty-two percent of the NCEI respondents said they do not consider SAT or ACT scores when admitting students into teacher education. Most of the institutions preparing teachers don't keep any high school information about their teacher education students. They argue they don't accept students into teacher education programs until their sophomore or junior year of college. The average college grade point average required to get into a teacher education program in 1983 was 2.29 on a 4.0 scale.[26]

Some isolated institutions have come up with data that says their teacher education students have grade-point averages that are about the same as liberal arts majors in their universities. These data cannot be extrapolated to the universe of all teacher education students nor do they provide contrary evidence that the academic caliber of persons studying to be teachers is lower than it was fifteen years ago.

SAT Scores of High School Students Intending to Major in Education

It may be true that all of those high school students who take the SAT and check a box saying they intend to major in education when they get to college don't wind up doing so, much less become teachers. But many of them do, and their SAT scores tell us something about their academic aptitude in comparison with other students.

The SAT scores of intended education majors were lower than those of almost every other intended major in 1973 and continued to fall faster than the declining national average until 1983 when SAT scores started edging back up. In 1973, the average SAT score was 937 and, for intended education majors, 878--59 points lower. In 1982, the national average SAT score was 893 and the intended education majors' score was 813--80 points under. In 1985, the average SAT score rose to 906 for the nation and to 836 for intended majors in education, thus narrowing the gap slightly to 70 points.

For SAT-verbal scores, the gap between the national average and the average score for high school students who say they might major in education in college is even narrower. In 1985, the national average verbal score was 431, and for intended education majors, it was 404--27 points less. For math, the scores were: national average, 475 and intended education majors, 432—43 points lower.

Even though the gaps are narrowing, it's still a fact that, without exception in all fifty states and the District of Columbia, the SAT scores of those intending to major in education fall below the state's average SAT score (Tables 44, 45, and 46).

Thirteen states and the District of Columbia showed dramatic increases in SAT-verbal scores of those intending to major in education between 1982 and 1984: Arkansas (+47 points), the District of Columbia (+26 points), Idaho (+22 points), Michigan (+22 points), Mississippi (+57 points), Missouri (+13 points), Montana (+13 points), Nevada (+30), New Mexico (+23), South Dakota (+24), Tennessee (+12), Utah (+65), West Virginia (+28) and Wyoming (+80).

Ten states showed a significant positive turn-around, having had decreases in SAT-verbal scores between 1978 and 1982. It is noteworthy that all of these states are located in regions of the country that are experiencing the greatest demands for new teachers--in the South and West (Table 47).

Fifteen states also showed a big jump in SAT-math scores of their intended education majors between 1982 and 1984. Those states with their corresponding SAT-verbal score changes, state average math and verbal score changes and changes between 1978 and 1982 can be found in Table 47.

With the exception of Michigan, these states, too, are all located in the South and West.

Thirteen states showed a decrease in average SAT-math scores and thirteen had a decline in average SAT-verbal scores (not necessarily the same thirteen states), compared with seven states that showed a decrease in SAT-math scores and eight a decline in SAT-verbal scores for intended education majors.

The states that had a decline in both average SAT-verbal and average SAT-math scores between 1982 and 1984 were: Alaska, Arizona, Georgia, Idaho, Minnesota, North Dakota, and Washington. Of these states, only Alaska and Arizona showed a decrease in scores of intended education majors, and those were only for the math portion.

The five other states that had a decline in SAT-math scores for students intending to major in education were: Montana, Nebraska, North Carolina, South

TABLE 44. SAT math scores

State	Score change '72 to '82	1982	1983	1984	Percent change 82–83	Percent change 83–84	Rank of percent change 82–83	Rank of percent change 83–84	1984 Rank
United States	−17.0	467	468	471	0.2	0.6			
Alabama	60.0	501	508	531	1.3	4.5	2	2	12
Alaska	−16.0	477	468	471	−1.8	0.6	50	20	33
Arizona	22.0	511	505	509	−1.1	0.7	49	15	24
Arkansas	8.0	519	518	544	−0.1	5.0	33	1	7
California	−19.0	474	474	476	0.0	0.4	25	27	30
Colorado	−7.0	515	520	514	0.9	−1.1	6	50	19
Connecticut	−20.0	464	465	468	0.2	0.6	18	20	37
Delaware	−20.0	465	467	469	0.4	0.4	11	27	36
District of Columbia	12.0	423	427	426	0.9	−0.2	6	42	49
Florida	20.0	463	464	467	0.2	0.6	18	20	39
Georgia	0.0	429	428	412	−0.2	−3.7	34	51	51
Hawaii	−23.0	465	471	474	1.2	0.6	3	20	31
Idaho	−3.0	513	513	512	0.0	−0.1	25	40	20
Illinois	8.0	515	517	518	0.3	0.1	15	36	16
Indiana	−18.0	453	454	454	0.2	0.0	18	38	46
Iowa	−7.0	572	573	570	0.1	−0.5	24	46	1
Kansas	3.0	545	540	549	−0.9	1.6	46	5	4
Kentucky	−1.0	510	513	518	0.5	0.9	9	10	16
Louisiana	−21.0	505	502	508	−0.5	1.1	40	8	25
Maine	−17.0	463	464	463	0.2	−0.2	18	42	42
Maryland	−18.0	464	466	468	0.4	0.4	11	27	37
Massachusetts	−17.0	463	463	467	0.0	0.8	25	13	39
Michigan	21.0	514	511	515	−0.5	0.7	40	15	18
Minnesota	−4.0	543	538	539	−0.9	0.1	46	36	10
Mississippi	71.0	509	507	512	−0.3	0.9	38	10	20
Missouri	−2.0	510	510	512	0.0	0.3	25	32	20
Montana	−3.0	546	535	544	−2.0	1.6	51	5	7
Nebraska	50.0	552	546	548	−1.0	0.3	48	32	5
Nevada	−30.0	481	480	489	−0.2	1.8	34	4	28
New Hampshire	−21.0	482	481	483	−0.2	0.4	34	27	29
New Jersey	−17.0	453	455	458	0.4	0.6	11	20	45
New Mexico	−6.0	517	519	527	0.3	1.5	15	7	13
New York	−28.0	467	466	470	−0.2	0.8	34	13	34
North Carolina	−7.0	431	431	432	0.0	0.2	25	34	48
North Dakota	−3.0	563	560	554	−0.5	−1.0	40	49	3
Ohio	−7.0	502	504	508	0.3	0.7	15	15	25
Oklahoma	−4.0	518	521	525	0.5	0.7	9	15	14
Oregon	−10.0	473	469	472	−0.8	0.6	45	20	32
Pennsylvania	−17.0	461	461	462	0.0	0.2	25	34	43
Rhode Island	−19.0	457	459	461	0.4	0.4	11	27	44
South Carolina	−12.0	412	415	419	0.7	0.9	8	10	50
South Dakota	7.0	553	560	566	1.2	1.0	3	9	2
Tennessee	11.0	519	519	523	0.0	0.7	25	15	15
Texas	−23.0	453	453	453	0.0	0.0	25	38	47
Utah	−26.0	528	545	542	3.2	−0.5	1	46	9
Vermont	−11.0	471	472	470	0.2	−0.4	18	45	34
Virginia	−13.0	462	463	466	0.2	0.6	18	20	41
Washington	−7.0	514	510	505	−0.7	−0.9	44	48	27
West Virginia	7.0	506	512	510	1.1	−0.3	5	44	23
Wisconsin	−8.0	535	533	532	−0.3	−0.1	38	40	11
Wyoming	−17.0	533	530	545	−0.5	2.8	40	3	6

SOURCE: Compiled by the National Center for Education Information. Basic data from the College Entrance Examination Board, state reports on College Bound Seniors, 1972, 1982, 1983, and 1984 (New York: College Entrance Examination Board, 1972, 1982, 1983, 1984).

TABLE 44. SAT verbal scores

State	Score change '72 to '82	1982	1983	1984	Percent change 82-83	Percent change 83-84	Rank of percent change 82-83	Rank of percent change 83-84	1984 Rank
United States	-27.0	426	425	426	-0.2	0.2			
Alabama	44.0	463	466	467	0.6	0.2	10	26	22
Alaska	-28.0	446	437	443	-2.0	1.3	51	2	29
Arizona	-37.0	470	465	469	-1.0	0.8	45	5	19
Arkansas	-6.0	480	482	482	0.4	0.0	12	34	12
California	-39.0	425	421	421	-0.9	0.0	43	34	43
Colorado	-24.0	468	469	468	0.2	-0.2	18	44	21
Connecticut	-29.0	432	433	436	0.2	0.6	18	8	32
Delaware	-26.0	432	433	433	0.2	0.0	18	34	34
District of Columbia	6.0	398	399	397	0.2	-0.5	18	47	47
Florida	-32.0	426	423	423	-0.7	0.0	41	34	42
Georgia	-11.0	394	390	392	-1.0	0.5	45	16	50
Hawaii	-41.0	392	393	395	0.2	0.5	18	16	48
Idaho	-13.0	482	479	480	-0.6	0.2	37	26	14
Illinois	-13.0	462	462	463	0.0	0.2	29	26	24
Indiana	-28.0	407	410	410	0.7	0.0	8	34	46
Iowa	-10.0	516	520	519	0.7	-0.1	8	43	2
Kansas	-7.0	500	498	502	-0.4	0.8	35	5	4
Kentucky	-2.0	475	475	479	0.0	0.8	29	5	16
Louisiana	-14.0	470	469	472	-0.2	0.6	33	8	18
Maine	-24.0	427	427	429	0.0	0.4	29	19	35
Maryland	-29.0	425	427	429	0.4	0.4	12	19	35
Massachusetts	-28.0	425	427	429	0.4	0.4	12	19	35
Michigan	1.0	459	458	461	-0.2	0.6	33	8	26
Minnesota	-24.0	485	482	481	-0.6	-0.2	37	44	13
Mississippi	66.0	479	474	480	-1.0	1.2	45	3	14
Missouri	-18.0	465	466	469	0.2	0.6	18	8	19
Montana	-25.0	487	480	490	-1.4	2.0	49	1	7
Nebraska	39.0	493	494	493	0.2	-0.2	18	44	6
Nevada	49.0	436	441	442	1.1	0.2	5	26	30
New Hampshire	-26.0	443	444	448	0.2	0.9	18	4	28
New Jersey	-30.0	416	418	418	0.4	0.0	12	34	44
New Mexico	-12.0	480	484	487	0.8	0.6	6	8	9
New York	-31.0	429	422	424	-1.6	0.4	50	19	40
North Carolina	-15.0	396	394	395	-0.5	0.2	36	26	48
North Dakota	-20.0	505	505	500	0.0	-0.9	29	49	5
Ohio	-5.0	456	458	460	0.4	0.4	12	19	27
Oklahoma	-12.0	483	489	484	1.2	-1.0	4	51	11
Oregon	-20.0	435	432	435	-0.6	0.6	37	8	33
Pennsylvania	-24.0	424	425	425	0.2	0.0	18	34	39
Rhode Island	-31.0	420	422	424	0.4	0.4	12	19	40
South Carolina	-21.0	378	383	384	1.3	0.2	3	26	51
South Dakota	9.0	522	517	520	-0.9	0.5	43	16	1
Tennessee	1.0	480	483	486	0.6	0.6	10	8	10
Texas	-30.0	415	412	413	-0.7	0.2	41	26	45
Utah	-31.0	494	508	503	2.8	-0.9	1	49	3
Vermont	-20.0	433	434	437	0.2	0.6	18	8	31
Virginia	-18.0	426	427	428	0.2	0.2	18	26	38
Washington	-22.0	468	463	463	-1.0	0.0	45	34	24
West Virginia	-7.0	462	466	466	0.8	0.0	6	34	23
Wisconsin	-26.0	476	473	475	-0.6	0.4	37	19	17
Wyoming	-27.0	484	492	489	1.6	-0.6	2	48	8

SOURCE: Compiled by the National Center for Education Information. Basic data from the College Entrance Examination Board, state reports on College Bound Seniors, 1972, 1982, 1983, and 1984 (New York: College Entrance Examination Board, 1972, 1982, 1983, 1984).

TABLE 45. SAT math scores of intended education majors

State	Score change '78 to '82	1982	1983	1984	Percent change 82-83	Percent change 83-84	Rank of percent change 82-83	Rank of percent change 83-84	1984 Rank
United States	-3.0	419	418	425	-0.2	1.6			
Alabama	31.0	428	453	466	5.8	2.8	7	12	13
Alaska	-9.0	437	417	429	-4.5	2.8	49	12	32
Arizona	-27.0	449	442	445	-1.5	0.6	44	34	26
Arkansas	-11.0	445	439	485	-1.3	10.4	42	2	6
California	0.0	424	421	431	-0.7	2.3	37	15	31
Colorado	-5.0	460	454	461	-1.3	1.5	42	25	17
Connecticut	-14.0	408	409	416	0.2	1.7	20	21	41
Delaware	-7.0	409	407	414	-0.4	1.7	28	21	43
District of Columbia	-23.0	367	378	396	2.9	4.7	10	7	49
Florida	2.0	414	415	424	0.2	2.1	20	18	38
Georgia	1.0	393	392	401	-0.2	2.2	26	17	48
Hawaii	-12.0	418	414	429	-0.9	3.6	39	10	32
Idaho	9.0	450	478	463	6.2	-3.1	4	49	16
Illinois	-4.0	455	452	459	-0.6	1.5	33	25	19
Indiana	-5.0	419	420	426	0.2	1.4	20	27	37
Iowa	-8.0	478	514	545	7.5	6.0	2	5	1
Kansas	-9.0	471	500	506	6.1	1.2	6	29	4
Kentucky	12.0	450	441	449	-2.0	1.8	45	20	24
Louisiana	30.0	446	449	451	0.6	0.4	19	37	23
Maine	-12.0	417	415	428	-0.4	3.1	28	11	34
Maryland	-2.0	415	419	421	0.9	0.4	16	37	40
Massachusetts	-12.0	407	407	414	0.0	1.7	23	21	43
Michigan	-9.0	451	450	474	-0.2	5.3	26	6	12
Minnesota	-10.0	475	489	475	2.9	-2.8	10	47	10
Mississippi	-74.0	406	452	449	11.3	-0.6	1	42	24
Missouri	8.0	453	457	460	0.8	0.6	17	34	18
Montana	-24.0	476	489	475	2.7	-2.8	12	47	10
Nebraska	14.0	489	464	465	-5.1	0.2	50	39	14
Nevada	5.0	420	423	439	0.7	3.7	18	9	27
New Hampshire	-10.0	424	420	427	-0.9	1.6	39	24	36
New Jersey	-4.0	405	403	411	-0.4	1.9	28	19	45
New Mexico	-23.0	445	425	464	-4.4	9.1	48	3	15
New York	-7.0	433	430	436	-0.6	1.3	33	28	28
North Carolina	11.0	393	389	392	-1.0	0.7	41	33	50
North Dakota	0.0	0	509	502	-0.1	-1.3	25	45	5
Ohio	3.0	454	452	457	-0.4	1.1	28	30	20
Oklahoma	-23.0	448	456	453	1.7	-0.6	15	42	22
Oregon	-8.0	420	428	433	1.9	1.1	14	30	30
Pennsylvania	-6.0	422	419	424	-0.7	1.1	37	30	38
Rhode Island	-13.0	415	406	416	-2.1	2.4	46	14	41
South Carolina	6.0	384	382	383	-0.5	0.2	32	39	51
South Dakota	25.0	531	564	539	6.2	-4.4	4	51	2
Tennessee	-1.0	475	463	481	-2.5	3.8	47	8	8
Texas	-8.0	406	406	406	0.0	0.0	23	41	47
Utah	-30.0	463	480	513	3.6	6.8	8	4	3
Vermont	0.0	430	427	409	-0.6	-4.2	33	50	46
Virginia	-8.0	408	418	428	2.4	2.3	13	15	34
Washington	-13.0	454	451	454	-0.6	0.6	33	34	21
West Virginia	-26.0	411	440	435	7.0	-1.1	3	44	29
Wisconsin	-14.0	471	486	476	3.1	-2.0	9	46	9
Wyoming	-20.0	453	420	485	-7.2	15.4	51	1	6

SOURCE: Compiled by the National Center for Education Information. Basic data from the College Entrance Examination Board, state reports on College Bound Seniors, 1972, 1982, 1983, and 1984 (New York: College Entrance Examination Board, 1972, 1982, 1983, 1984).

TABLE 45. SAT verbal scores of intended education majors

State	Score change '78 to '82	1982	1983	1984	Percent change 82-83	83-84	Rank of percent change 82-83	83-84	1984 Rank
United States	-2.0	394	394	398	0.0	1.0			
Alabama	30.0	400	436	441	9.0	1.1	2	28	15
Alaska	-12.0	413	405	414	-1.9	2.2	45	15	28
Arizona	-2.0	440	430	445	-2.2	3.4	48	12	12
Arkansas	-27.0	420	432	467	2.8	8.1	9	4	6
California	0.0	399	397	400	-0.5	0.7	36	32	36
Colorado	-10.0	433	428	436	-1.1	1.8	40	20	20
Connecticut	-8.0	395	395	401	0.0	1.5	27	22	34
Delaware	-1.0	389	389	389	0.0	0.0	27	37	44
District of Columbia	18.0	348	375	374	7.7	-0.2	4	39	47
Florida	1.0	394	391	393	-0.7	0.5	38	34	42
Georgia	-3.0	366	367	374	0.2	1.9	25	18	47
Hawaii	-16.0	365	359	466	-1.6	1.9	44	18	50
Idaho	-10.0	426	474	448	11.2	-5.4	1	50	11
Illinois	1.0	423	420	424	-0.7	0.9	38	31	26
Indiana	-4.0	386	387	394	0.2	1.8	25	20	41
Iowa	19.0	473	487	477	2.9	-2.0	8	46	5
Kansas	8.0	455	453	459	-0.4	1.3	35	23	9
Kentucky	34.0	444	431	431	-2.9	0.0	50	37	22
Louisiana	39.0	432	423	419	-2.0	-0.9	47	44	27
Maine	-9.0	389	387	400	-0.5	3.3	36	13	36
Maryland	-2.0	394	403	400	2.2	-0.7	11	43	36
Massachusetts	-7.0	388	388	391	0.0	0.7	27	32	43
Michigan	-5.0	423	425	445	0.4	4.7	23	7	12
Minnesota	1.0	443	445	440	0.4	-1.1	23	45	16
Mississippi	-67.0	404	432	461	6.9	6.7	5	5	8
Missouri	-2.0	426	433	439	1.6	1.3	15	23	17
Montana	-26.0	431	435	444	0.9	2.0	19	17	14
Nebraska	10.0	444	447	412	0.6	-7.8	20	51	29
Nevada	-22.0	398	409	428	2.7	4.6	10	8	23
New Hampshire	-2.0	408	400	405	-1.9	1.2	45	25	31
New Jersey	-3.0	384	384	388	0.0	1.0	27	29	45
New Mexico	3.0	439	421	462	-4.1	9.7	51	2	7
New York	-3.0	405	400	404	-1.2	1.0	41	29	32
North Carolina	10.0	365	360	368	-1.3	2.2	42	15	49
North Dakota	0.0	0	445	484	-0.1	8.7	33	3	3
Ohio	0.0	423	429	426	1.4	-0.6	16	42	24
Oklahoma	-5.0	442	452	438	2.2	-3.0	11	47	19
Oregon	-11.0	401	406	411	1.2	1.2	17	25	30
Pennsylvania	-1.0	398	400	402	0.5	0.5	21	34	33
Rhode Island	-8.0	393	384	398	-2.2	3.6	48	11	39
South Carolina	4.0	356	358	356	0.5	-0.5	21	41	51
South Dakota	1.0	490	495	514	1.0	3.8	18	10	1
Tennessee	4.0	446	439	458	-1.5	4.3	43	9	10
Texas	-10.0	385	385	384	0.0	-0.2	27	39	46
Utah	-68.0	430	468	495	8.8	5.7	3	6	2
Vermont	-8.0	399	408	395	2.2	-3.1	11	48	40
Virginia	0.0	388	396	401	2.0	1.2	14	25	34
Washington	-11.0	431	431	433	0.0	0.4	27	36	21
West Virginia	-17.0	397	412	425	3.7	3.1	7	14	25
Wisconsin	-9.0	430	454	439	5.5	-3.3	6	49	17
Wyoming	-17.0	402	401	482	-0.2	20.1	34	1	4

SOURCE: Compiled by the National Center for Education Information. Basic data from the College Entrance Examination Board, state reports on College Bound Seniors, 1972, 1982, 1983, and 1984 (New York: College Entrance Examination Board, 1972, 1982, 1983, 1984).

TABLE 46. Profile of high school seniors taking the SAT: 1984

State	Number taking SAT	Percent of all grads	Percent from non-public schools	Percent minority	Percent women	Percent intended majors
United States	964,739	31.1	19.8	19.7	51.8	4.6
Alabama	2,804	4.6	28.4	21.6	48.9	2.8
Alaska	1,908	33.2	2.5	16.6	53.6	8.0
Arizona	4,054	12.2	19.0	14.2	48.9	3.2
Arkansas	1,425	4.5	16.4	10.2	48.3	3.1
California	102,358	34.8	18.5	34.9	52.3	3.6
Colorado	6,933	18.6	11.8	11.0	50.3	3.8
Connecticut	29,669	63.4	25.1	10.0	51.9	4.4
Delaware	4,354	46.4	36.0	14.6	52.3	3.2
District of Columbia	3,097	40.2	48.5	68.1	50.5	1.7
Florida	37,907	35.9	19.6	17.7	52.6	4.0
Georgia	33,027	48.3	13.6	24.7	54.0	5.8
Hawaii	6,459	41.0	36.2	77.8	55.3	4.7
Idaho	1,073	8.1	7.3	5.7	47.5	3.8
Illinois	21,766	13.3	26.4	14.2	49.5	3.9
Indiana	33,940	46.9	10.5	9.4	53.4	6.4
Iowa	1,370	3.2	14.8	6.2	49.1	3.5
Kansas	1,933	6.4	13.1	9.6	46.9	3.6
Kentucky	3,308	6.3	26.0	6.5	48.4	2.8
Louisiana	2,971	3.6	53.1	20.0	49.5	3.9
Maine	7,854	47.9	15.2	3.0	52.3	8.2
Maryland	29,477	48.2	19.5	24.2	53.9	3.7
Massachusetts	52,534	62.0	21.1	8.8	51.6	3.8
Michigan	14,014	10.1	18.3	19.9	50.6	1.9
Minnesota	6,623	9.6	21.9	5.4	48.0	3.5
Mississippi	913	2.2	38.0	19.6	49.9	2.1
Missouri	7,265	9.1	34.9	14.1	50.0	3.4
Montana	1,091	9.2	6.9	4.2	51.2	2.5
Nebraska	1,466	6.5	17.5	6.5	48.1	3.1
Nevada	1,814	17.9	10.4	13.4	50.3	3.4
New Hampshire	7,759	55.6	21.7	4.1	50.8	5.3
New Jersey	65,290	59.5	20.5	18.0	50.9	4.3
New Mexico	1,623	8.0	24.5	22.2	47.9	2.7
New York	132,728	62.6	20.6	20.2	52.3	4.3
North Carolina	33,223	45.4	7.6	22.0	54.7	5.6
North Dakota	320	3.4	11.8	4.2	45.9	5.9
Ohio	25,391	14.5	28.5	9.7	48.5	4.1
Oklahoma	1,999	4.5	22.9	10.9	48.7	2.3
Oregon	12,981	43.9	8.3	8.7	52.0	7.5
Pennsylvania	83,291	50.6	22.1	9.7	51.6	5.4
Rhode Island	6,415	48.8	22.1	6.7	54.4	4.6
South Carolina	18,029	44.1	12.1	26.5	55.7	6.4
South Dakota	278	3.0	12.0	6.3	50.7	4.6
Tennessee	4,715	6.3	36.3	9.9	49.4	2.5
Texas	58,110	32.8	8.4	25.9	52.9	6.1
Utah	753	2.9	24.5	8.9	45.9	2.1
Vermont	3,865	53.5	15.5	3.6	52.0	6.5
Virginia	35,064	50.5	11.5	18.9	52.8	5.1
Washington	12,024	23.5	11.1	13.1	51.6	5.4
West Virginia	1,856	7.3	12.3	7.7	48.0	3.9
Wisconsin	8,543	10.5	25.7	7.1	49.0	3.8
Wyoming	366	6.2	4.5	5.6	47.3	6.4

SOURCE: Compiled by the National Center for Education Information. Basic data from the College Entrance Examination Board, state reports on College Bound Seniors, 1984 (New York: College Entrance Examination Board, 1984); and the National Education Association, Estimates of School Statistics 1983-84, 1984.

TABLE 47. SAT score changes for intended education majors and for states having largest gains in SAT-verbal and math scores for intended education majors: 1982 to 1984 and 1978 to 1982

State	1982-84 INTENDED EDUCATION MAJORS		1982-84 STATE AVERAGE		1978-82 INTENDED EDUCATION MAJORS	
	SAT verbal score change	SAT math score change	SAT verbal score change	SAT math score change	SAT verbal score change	SAT math score change
Wyoming	+80	+32	+5	+12	-17.0	-20.0
Utah	+65	+50	+9	+14	-68.0	-30.0
Mississippi	+57	+43	+1	+3	-67.0	-74.0
Arkansas	+47	+40	+2	+25	-27.0	-11.0
Alabama	+41	+38	+4	+30	30.0	31.0
Nevada	+30	+19	+6	+8	-22.0	5.0
W. Virginia	+28	+24	+4	+4	-17.0	-26.0
District of Columbia	+26	+29	-1	+3	0.0	0.0
South Dakota	+24	+8	-2	+13	1.0	25.0
New Mexico	+23	+19	+7	+10	3.0	-23.0
Idaho	+22	+13	-2	-1	-10.0	9.0
Michigan	+22	+23	+2	+1	-5.0	-9.0
Missouri	+13	+7	+4	+2	-2.0	8.0
Montana	+13	-1	+3	-2	-26.0	-24.0
Virginia	+13	+20	+2	+4	0.0	-8.0
Tennessee	+12	+6	+6	+4	4.0	-1.0
Oregon	+10	+13	0	-1	-11.0	-8.0
Iowa	+4	+67	+3	-2	19.0	-8.0
Kansas	-4	+35	+2	+4	8.0	-9.0

SOURCE: Compiled by the National Center for Education Information. Selected data from The College Entrance Examination Board (New York: College Entrance Examination Board, 1978, 1982, 1984)

Carolina and Vermont. Of these, Montana, Nebraska and Vermont had state averages in math that dropped too.

The eight states that showed a drop in SAT-verbal scores for intended education majors in 1984 over 1982 were: Kentucky, Louisiana, Minnesota, Nebraska, New Hampshire, New York, Oklahoma and Texas. Minnesota's and New York's average SAT-verbal scores also declined between these two years.

CHAPTER VIII

Teacher Education and Certification

Nothing about teaching causes more concern than the ways teachers are educated and certified in this country. The diversity of requirements alone defies imagination. There are some 1,287 institutions of higher education now in the business of educating teachers—115 more than there were a decade ago when there were 33 percent more students enrolled in teacher education programs and 53 percent more prospective teachers graduating from them (Table 48).

The National Center for Education Information survey of teacher education programs last summer revealed that more education courses are required to complete teacher education programs now than were required a decade ago for prospective elementary, secondary and special education teachers. In 1983, colleges and universities required their teacher candidates to have, on the average, five more semester hours of clinical experience (student teaching/practicum, classroom observation) than they required in 1973. They are demanding that students take an additional four semester hours of education courses.[27]

Currently, a person studying to be a elementary school teacher has to take an average of sixty-two semester hours of general studies, thirty-six hours of professional studies and seventeen semester hours of clinical experience. A prospective secondary school teacher is required to take an average of sixty-four semester hours of general studies, twenty-five hours of professional education courses and fifteen hours of clinical experience (Table 49).

Only 47 percent of the respondents to the NCEI survey last year said they required passage of an exit test of any kind for completion of their teacher education programs. Only 5 percent demand that prospective teachers completing their programs pass a content-area test.[28]

Changes are occurring rapidly in testing teachers, so it is highly likely that, by now, many more institutions are requiring passage of one or more types of tests

TABLE 48. Numbers of institutions of higher education (IHE's) that have teacher education programs, numbers of teacher education graduates, numbers of new teaching certificates issued, percent who got new jobs: 1984

State	No. IHE's with teacher ed program	Percent of total 4-yr IHE's with teacher ed	No. grads of teacher ed programs	Total certified	Estimated percent certified in '84 who got jobs
Alabama	30	100	1,900	7,050	60
Alaska	5	83	184	NA	40
Arizona	5	56	NA	9,520	NA
Arkansas	16	84	1,926	2,383	80
California	79	52	6,500	7,500	70
Colorado	14	54	2,505	8,000	NA
Connecticut	14	50	2,491	2,951	27
Delaware	3	60	255	NA	80-85
District of Columbia	8	35	700	2,075	10
Florida	27	50	2,170	5,777	95
Georgia	33	79	2,856	4,976	95
Hawaii	4	57	261	275	65
Idaho	6	100	NA	NA	NA
Illinois	58	62	6,174	11,724	NA
Indiana	39	82	3,750	NA	NA
Iowa	29	76	2,398	NA	55
Kansas	24	86	2,036	4,187	NA
Kentucky	23	72	NA	NA	NA
Louisiana	21	79	1,820	1,964	NA
Maine	11	55	NA	1,000	25
Maryland	20	61	1,316	NA	NA
Massachusetts	49	60	NA	NA	NA
Michigan	31	53	5,000	6,000	NA
Minnesota	27	60	2,434	NA	50
Mississippi	15	65	1,689	2,250	26
Missouri	36	57	5,900	6,500	NA
Montana	8	67	NA	NA	NA
Nebraska	15	71	2,253	2,249	67
Nevada	2	67	NA	3,000	NA
New Hampshire	13	100	693	1,687	70
New Jersey	26	62	7,000	10,500	10
New Mexico	9	82	NA	NA	NA
New York	96	46	NA	NA	27
North Carolina	44	90	4,500	6,400	NA
North Dakota	9	90	683	775	80
Ohio	48	60	5,829	9,800	21
Oklahoma	20	74	NA	1,980	NA
Oregon	15	50	1,700	2,700	40
Pennsylvania	88	66	7,200	9,800	38
Rhode Island	9	82	NA	NA	NA
South Carolina	28	88	1,282	3,172	60
South Dakota	13	81	NA	1,328	95
Tennessee	37	74	4,000	5,500	20
Texas	64	71	7,830	9,830	NA
Utah	6	100	1,842	2,442	69
Vermont	13	72	425	675	25
Virginia	34	76	5,295	NA	100
Washington	16	68	2,138	3,758	48
West Virginia	18	85	2,017	3,387	NA
Wisconsin	31	72	2,819	NA	NA
Wyoming	1	100	300	300	25

SOURCE: National Center for Education Information, Teacher Certification Surveys, 1984 and 1985, unpublished data.

82

before a person exits from a teacher education program with their stamp of approval.

Certification of Teachers

The process of certifying teachers in the United States is like a moving target. Each state has its own rules. Certification requirements within states are ever-changing and vary widely from state to state.

A person certified to teach United States government in one state would not be certified to teach American history in that state, but that same teacher could not only teach American history but also political science in another state. A person could meet all the requirements for a license to teach every elementary grade in one state and only certain grades in another state. Some states give broad certificates that allow a person to teach several different grades and subjects. Other states give certificates that are very specific concerning which grades and what subjects one can teach. And, as a matter of fact, most states permit people to teach who don't meet all the requirements anyway by giving them emergency credentials.[29]

TABLE 49. Average number college semester hours required to complete the teacher
education program by field of study

Field of Study	Academic year 1983			Academic year 1973		
	Elem.	Sec.	Sp. Ed.	Elem.	Sec.	Sp. Ed.
General Studies	62	64	55	62	59	51
Professional Studies	36	25	38	32	22	34
Clinical Experience	17	15	19	12	10	14
Total	115	104	112	106	91	99

Definitions: Elementary includes general elementary, early childhood, preschool, and/or kindergarten. Secondary includes all subject specialities in junior or senior high or middle school. Exclude--physical, fine arts, occupational/ vocational education and support personnel.

General Studies--include liberal arts courses; exclude SCDE courses.

Professional Studies--include SCDE courses; exclude student teaching/practicum.

Clinical Experience--include student teaching/practicum, classroom observation.

SOURCE: National Center for Education Information, The Making of a Teacher: A Report on Teacher Education and Certification, 1984, p. 27.

TABLE 50. States' semester hour course requirements for teacher certification

State	Elementary General	Professional	Clinical	Secondary General	Professional	Clinical	Special Education General	Professional	Clinical
Alabama	60		- 72 -	60		- 80 -	60		- 75 -
Alaska					approved program				
Arizona	45		- 24 -	45		- 22 -	45		- 18 -
Arkansas	48-50	18	6	48	18	6	48-50	18	6
California	84	12	12	varies	12	12	varies by specialty		
Colorado					approved program				
Connecticut	75	24	6	45	12	6	NS	NS	NS
Delaware	60	45	6	60	15	6	60	39	6
District of Columbia	NS	NS	6	NS	NS	6	NS	NS	6
Florida	21	14	6	12-30	14	6	15-32	12	6
Georgia	38	12	9	38	12	9	38	12	9
Hawaii					approved program				
Idaho	42	24	6	20	50	6	NS	30	6
Illinois					not available				
Indiana	70	21	9	40	49-65	9	40	65	9
Iowa					not specified				
Kansas				approved program--transcript analysis					
Kentucky	45	32	a	45	25	a	45	42	*
Louisiana	46	30	9	46	27	9	46	27	9
Maine	60	24	6	60	12	6	60	18	6
Maryland	80	26	8	24	18	6	NA	33	6
Massachusetts	b	21	300C	b	21	300C	b	33	150C
Michigan					approved program				
Minnesota				approved program--full-time student teaching					
Mississippi	42	54	6	42	21	6	42	21	6
Missouri	60	50	10	60	55	10	60	60	15
Montana					24				
Nebraska	c								
Nevada	88	21	15	36	87	14	50	77	NA
New Hampshire					competency-based				
New Jersey	30	200C	1yr	30	200C	1yr	18	15	8*
New Mexico					66				
New York	0	24	NS	0	12	NS	0	24	NS
North Carolina				does not use course/hour requirements					
North Dakota	-	20	9	-	20	9	-	20	9
Ohio					not available				
Oklahoma	50	18-20	10-12	50	18-20	10-12	50	18-20	10-12
Oregon	40	24	10	40	24	10	40	30	10
Pennsylvania				does not count course hours					
Rhode Island					not available				
South Carolina					not specified				
South Dakota	50	72	6	AP	18	6	AP	AP	6
Tennessee	27	20	6	40	20	4	40	40	6-8
Texas					not available				
Utah	32	28	8	28	27	8	32	18	8
Vermont					competency-based				
Virginia	48	12	6	48	12	6	48	12	6
Washington	d	d	8wks	d	d	8wks	d	d	8wks
West Virginia	40	20	4wks	40	20	4wks	40	20	4wks
Wisconsin	40-44	26	5	40-44	18	5	40-44	38	5
Wyoming					not available				

NS--not specified   NA--not available   AP--approved program   C--clock hours

a Kentucky requires 150 clock hours clinical experience plus 12 weeks student teaching for elementary and secondary candidates and 200 clock hours clinical experience plus 12 weeks student teaching for special education candidates

b Massachusetts requires a "sound arts and sciences program" in general studies

c Nebraska requires of all teaching candidates that general studies comprise one-fourth to one-half of the total B.A. program and that professional studies comprise one-sixth. The clinical experience requirement is 240 clock hours.

d Washington requires of all teaching candidates that general and professional studies meet the "minimum generic standard" and requires eight weeks of student teaching.

SOURCE: National Center for Education Information, Teacher Certification Survey, 1985, unpublished data.

Forty-eight states use what is called the "approved program" route for certifying teachers. This simply means that a person who graduates from a college or university teacher education program that was approved by the state automatically qualifies for a teaching certificate.

Some states offer an alternative to the approved program route. They all require a baccalaureate degree, but the credit hours demanded in general studies, professional education courses and clinical experience vary from state to state.

Initial teaching certificates last longer in some states than in others. The range is all the way from one year in Oklahoma and Tennessee to "life" in Massachusetts, Missouri, New Jersey and Texas. The requirements for getting a teaching certificate renewed are also quite specific and quite different from state to state. Renewals are also valid for different periods of time.

Simplification of certification requirements and procedures could be long in coming. "Each state has the exclusive responsibility for the quality and content of its own professional preparation/certification programs in that state. This responsibility may be vested in or shared by the State Education Agency, a State Standards Commission, or a State Board of Education. Regardless of title, the state agency is the only legally accountable agency in matters concerning approval/accreditation of programs. The individual state cannot abrogate its legal responsibility; nor should any state ignore its obligation to protect the 'public interest' and the independence and integrity of the state and its institutions."[30]

Certification Requirements State by State

The National Center for Education Information conducted a survey of state directors of teacher education and certification in both the summers of 1984 and 1985 to determine what is going on in the states regarding certification of teachers. In addition, the NCEI survey collected data on numbers of institutions of higher education that have teacher education programs in each state, how many prospective teachers graduated from them in the last two years, projected shortages by grade level and subject area, numbers of emergency certificates being issued, and changes in the offing for certifying teachers.

The results confirm the widely held view that the hoops one has to jump through to become a teacher aren't particularly threatening but may be just too bothersome, thus turning off potential candidates for teaching who simply don't see the point of it all.

The range in number of college credits required in general studies, professional education courses and clinical experience varies widely from state to state for each type of teaching certificate. To get a certificate to teach in elementary schools in California, for example, one must take about eighty-four semester hours in general studies, twelve in education courses and acquire twelve hours in clinical experiences. In Mississippi, on the other hand, to qualify for an elementary teaching certificate, one must have forty-two hours of general studies, fifty-four hours of professional education courses and six hours of clinical experiences (Table 50).

Changes in Certification Requirements in the Last Two Years

All but twenty-one states changed their requirements for teacher certification within the last two years. Most of the changes were intended to make standards more rigorous. Ten states introduced some sort of testing for teacher certification, and for nine of these, the testing includes a fundamental basic skills test. These nine states are: California, Colorada, Connecticut, Indiana, Kansas, Nebraska (effective 1986, BST), New Hampshire, and Pennsylvania. The tenth, New Jersey, requires the National Teacher Examination (NTE) General Test Core Battery of elementary teaching candidates and the NTE Speciality Tests of its secondary teaching candidates (Table 51).

New Jersey also introduced the most radical and most widely publicized change in certifying teachers in the last year. It passed a law that allows a person to get a teaching certificate without ever having gone through a teacher education program. What New Jersey's alternative to the traditional approved-program route for teacher certification does is allow a person who has a baccalaureate degree to become certified after a year of supervised practical experience in the classroom and passage of the NTE general test for elementary teachers and an NTE subject specialization test for secondary teachers.

86

TABLE 51. States requiring specific tests for certification as of summer 1985*

National Teachers Examination (NTE)	Standardized Basic Skills Test (SBST)	State-Developed Basic Skills Test (SDBST)	Standardized Content Area Test (SCAT)	State-Developed Content Area Test (SDCAT)	Other test
Arkansas	Colorado	Arizona	North Carolina	Alabama	Alabama
Indiana	Connecticut	California	West Virginia	Georgia	Arizona
Kentucky	Delaware	Florida		Oklahoma	Florida
Louisiana	Massachusetts	Pennsylvania		Pennsylvania	Kansas
Mississppi	West Virginia	South Carolina		South Carolina	
New Mexico		Texas		West Virginia	
North Carolina		Washington			
South Carolina					
Tennessee					
Virginia					

Definitions: NTE -- National Teacher Examination
            SBST -- standardized basic skills test
            SDBST -- state-developed basic skills test
            SCAT -- standardized content area test
            SDCAT -- state-developed content area test
            OT -- other test

* Some states require more than one type of test

SOURCE: National Center for Education Information, Teacher Certification Surveys, 1984 and 1985, unpublished data.

TABLE 52. Tests required for certification: 1985 and projected within the next three years, by state.

State	NTE	SBST	SDBST	SCAT	SDCAT	OT	NTE	SBST	SDBST	SCAT	SDCAT	OT
			1985						Projected			
Alabama					X	X						
Alaska							----------considering----------					
Arizona			X									
Arkansas	X								X			
California			X									
Colorado		X										
Connecticut		X							X		X	X
Delaware		X					X			X		
D.C.			X							X	X	
Florida											X	
Georgia					X		X	X				
Hawaii												
Idaho							----------considering----------					
Illinois							X					
Indiana												
Iowa							----------considering----------					
Kansas										X		
Kentucky	X											
Louisiana	X						X	X	X			
Maine							X					
Maryland							X					
Massachusetts					X							X
Michigan												
Minnesota												
Mississippi	X											
Missouri							X			X		
Montana									X	X		
Nebraska									X	X		
Nevada							X					
New Hampshire												
New Jersey							X					
New Mexico	X						X					
New York												
No. Carolina	X			X								
North Dakota												
Ohio							----------considering----------					
Oklahoma					X		X					
Oregon								X				
Pennsylvania			X		X							
Rhode Island							----------considering----------					
So. Carolina	X		X		X							
South Dakota												
Tennessee	X						X			X	X	
Texas						X	X					
Utah							X					
Vermont							X					
Virginia	X											
Washington			X									
West Virginia		X		X	X	X						
Wisconsin											X	X
Wyoming												

NTE--National Teacher Examination; SBST--Standardized Basic Skills Test;
SDBST--State-developed Basic Skills Test; SCAT--Standardized Content Area Test;
SDCAT--State-developed Content Area Test; OT--Other Test

SOURCE: National Center for Education Information, Teacher Certification Surveys, 1984 and 1985, unpublished data.

New Jersey had over 1,000 applicants for the alternative program in 1984-85. Thirty-six had been hired by the end of July 1985. New Jersey anticipates hiring more but could not say how many as of July 30, 1985.

Only Colorado and Oklahoma reported changing their teacher certification requirements within the last two years to include more experience in the classroom prior to getting a license to teach.

Teacher Testing

Testing teachers has become one of the most controversial issues surrounding teaching. There are those who would like to see passage of a national proficiency examination similar to the bar examination for lawyers and the CPA examination for accountants, a requirement for certification to teach. There are others who would like to see each state develop its own test.

While there is disagreement on what should be tested and who should administer the test, there is unprecedented agreement that teachers should be tested before they enter the profession. The public is in favor of it, the teachers themselves are in favor of competency testing for teachers, and probably most important of all, the unions that represent teachers (the National Education Association and the American Federation of Teachers) are stepping into the forefront to carry the banner for teacher testing.

A real proficiency test for teachers would be a far cry from the basic skills tests being introduced in many states. It would go beyond testing fundamental literacy to assessing knowledge of subjects to be taught and pedagogical knowledge.

As of summer 1985, twenty-four states require passage of some kind of paper-pencil test for teacher certification. Twelve of these states require that their prospective teachers pass a simple basic skills test (Table 52).

Emergency Certification

The availability of emergency certificates has been the boondoggle in raising standards for teacher certification. Every time a state faces a shortage of teachers, it simply issues emergency certificates to people who want to teach.

TABLE 53. Substandard, limited or emergency certificates issued in 1983, by state

State	Issue S,L or E. Cred.	Avail. With Less Than Bachelor's	Authorization	Renewal Requirements
Alabama	Yes	Yes	specific	none
Alaska	Yes	No	specific	6 semester units
Arizona	Yes	No	specific	6 semester units
Arkansas	Yes	No	specific	6 semester units
California	Yes	Yes	broad	6 semester units
Colorado	Yes	Yes	broad	none
Connecticut	Yes	No	broad	6 semester units
Delaware	Yes	Yes	silent	
Dist. of Col.	Yes	Yes	broad	6 semester units
Florida	Yes	Yes	specific	none
Georgia	Yes	No	specific	Test & 10 qtr. units
Hawaii	Yes	Yes	broad	none
Idaho	No	Yes	broad	cannot be renewed
Illinois	Yes	Yes	specific	
Indiana	Yes	Yes	silent	6 semester units
Iowa	Yes	No	silent	2 courses
Kansas	Yes	Yes	broad	none
Kentucky	Yes	Yes	broad	none
Louisiana	Yes	No	specific	6 semester units
Maine	Yes	No	broad	none
Maryland	Yes	Yes	specific	6 semester units
Massachusetts	No	-------	-------	-------
Michigan	Yes	Yes	broad	6 semester units
Minnesota	Yes	No	silent	8 quarter units
Mississippi	Yes	No	specific	6 semester units
Missouri	Yes	No	broad	8 semester units
Montana	Yes	Yes	specific	12 quarter units
Nebraska	Yes	Yes	specific	will not issue 2nd
Nevada	Yes	Yes	silent	will not issue
New Hampshire	Yes	No	silent	must show progress
New Jersey	Yes	Yes	specific	6 semester units
New Mexico	Yes	No	broad	varies by certificate
New York	Yes	Yes	broad	6 semester units
North Carolina	Yes	Yes	silent	6 semester units
North Dakota	Yes	No	broad	12 quarter units
Ohio	Yes	Yes	broad	none
Oklahoma	Yes	Yes	broad	8 semester units
Oregon	Yes	Yes	broad	6 semester units
Pennsylvania	Yes	Yes	broad	10 semester units
Rhode Island	Yes	Yes	silent	6 semester units
South Carolina	Yes	No	specific	6 semester units
South Dakota	Yes	Yes	broad	show progress
Tennessee	Yes	No	broad	9 quarter units
Texas	Yes	Yes	silent	6 semester units
Utah	Yes	No	broad	1 course per qtr.
Vermont	No	-------	-------	-------
Virginia	No	-------	-------	-------
Washington	Yes	No	broad	very rarely given twice
West Virginia	Yes	No	broad	6 semester units
Wisconsin	Yes	No	broad	
Wyoming	Yes	No	specific	non-renewable

SOURCE: National Center for Education Information, The Making of a Teacher, 1984, p. 40.

TABLE 54. Teachers' credentials: 1984

State	No. teachers certified in 1984-85	Total No. teachers in 1984-85	No. teachers on emergency credential	Estimated % total certified teachers in 1984-85	Estimated % total teachers on emergency credential
Alabama	7,050	36,099	74	20	0.20
Alaska	4,734	6,090	4	78	0.07
Arizona	9,520	25,920	NA	37	NA
Arkansas	2,383	24,085	6	10	0.02
California	8,000	175,135	5,738	5	3.30
Colorado	8,000	28,822	1,631	28	5.70
Connecticut	2,951	32,467	62	9	0.20
Delaware	NA	5,516	294	NA	5.33
District of Columbia	2,075	5,792	<1%	36	<1.00
Florida	5,777	86,223	10,000	7	11.60
Georgia	4,976	56,321	9,900	9	17.58
Hawaii	275	8,141	10	3	0.12
Idaho	NA	10,160	21	NA	0.21
Illinois	10,192	100,497	NA	10	NA
Indiana	11,724	49,646	487	24	0.81
Iowa	NA	30,336	400	NA	1.32
Kansas	4,187	26,260	NA	16	NA
Kentucky	NA	32,400	15	NA	0.05
Louisiana	1,964	46,840	315	4	0.67
Maine	1,000	12,510	400	8	3.26
Maryland	NA	37,694	250	NA	0.66
Massachusetts	NA	56,333	125	NA	0.22
Michigan	6,000	79,900	74	8	0.10
Minnesota	NA	39,400	92	NA	0.23
Mississippi	2,250	24,772	1,031	9	4.16
Missouri	6,500	47,240	2,200	14	4.66
Montana	NA	9,756	1,500	NA	15.38
Nebraska	2,249	17,513	244	13	1.40
Nevada	3,000	7,496	375	40	5.00
New Hampshire	1,687	10,104	130	17	1.30
New Jersey	10,500	72,858	2,000	14	2.75
New Mexico	NA	14,200	800	NA	5.63
New York	12,565	164,900	4,000	8	2.42
North Carolina	6,400	56,084	10	12	0.02
North Dakota	775	7,300	6	11	0.08
Ohio	9,800	94,429	3,733	10	3.95
Oklahoma	1,982	35,000	600	6	1.70
Oregon	2,700	24,413	200	11	0.82
Pennsylvania	9,800	101,150	23	10	0.02
Rhode Island	NA	7,548	17	NA	0.22
South Carolina	3,172	33,340	1,252	10	3.76
South Dakota	1,328	8,022	100	17	1.25
Tennessee	5,500	40,008	NA	14	NA
Texas	9,830	172,639	4,330	6	2.51
Utah	2,442	16,188	150	15	0.93
Vermont	675	6,200	11	11	0.18
Virginia	NA	56,863	0	NA	0.00
Washington	3,758	35,155	80	11	0.23
West Virginia	3,385	22,557	1,325	15	5.90
Wisconsin	NA	45,350	1,100	NA	2.43
Wyoming	300	6,990	0	4	0.00

SOURCE: National Center for Education Information, <u>Teacher Certification Surveys</u>, 1984 and 1985, unpublished data.

These emergency, substandard or limited certificates, as they are variously called, usually carry with them a stipulation that the person take education courses and do a variety of other things, such as pass a test, in order to become fully certified someday (Table 53).

All but two states issue substandard, limited or emergency credentials to people who don't meet all of the criteria for a real bonafide teaching certificate. Half of the states will give a substandard credential to people who have less than a bachelor's degree. Wyoming and Virginia do not issue any type of substandard credential. In Idaho, a non-certified person can teach with a letter of authorization. Massachusetts lets non-certified people teach on a one-year waiver.

Respondents to the NCEI survey of state teacher education and certification directors indicate a wide range in numbers of people teaching without full certification. It is no surprise that the majority of states reporting the largest numbers of noncredentialed teachers are states in the South and West where enrollments are surging and in states with large urban areas where discipline problems are greatest and people are not anxious to teach (Table 54).

Interestingly, very few states reported having any people teaching in their states who did not have any kind of teaching credential. Thirty-nine states said they didn't have anybody teaching without a credential; seven reported 1 percent or fewer; two said they didn't know, and three states reported from 2 percent in Massachusetts to 10 percent in Montana to nearly 16 percent in Louisiana. We really don't know how many teachers are working without certification.

CHAPTER IX

Summary and Conclusions

Seldom before in American education, if ever, has more attention been paid to teachers. And rightly so. The quality of our educational system is determined, to a very large extent, by the people who choose to teach.

Many reports in the last three years have shown that both the quality and quantity of those becoming teachers have been on the decline. Numerous critics have objected that publishing such "negative" information would only make matters worse, and even heighten the difficulty of attracting the best qualified minds into teaching. Others, especially those of us producing the disturbing data, felt these studies would bring to the attention of the public--and to all who might be thinking about teaching as a career--the realities of what has been going on in this noble occupation, and would dramatize that we had better be doing something about attacking the problem before it becomes monumental.

An analysis of the data in the last two years, over a wide range of teacher-related issues, dramatically demonstrates that all the brouhaha over teaching is paying off in slow, but steady, progress.

o <u>Salaries of teachers have outstripped the rate of inflation in each of the last two years</u>. After losing in purchasing power by 12.2 percent between 1972 and 1982, teachers' salaries rose 6.9 percent in 1984-85 and 6.2 percent in 1983-84. The inflation rate in 1983 was 3.2 percent and in 1984 was 4.3 percent. The average salary for teachers increased 13.7 percent in the last two years--from $20,715 in 1982-83 to $23,546 in 1984-85. The median household income for teachers is the same as that for all college graduates. Both had a median income of about $30,000 in 1983. Four percent of the current teaching force (about 85,000 teachers) has a household income of $15,000 or less, compared with 16 percent of the working public. Thirteen percent of teachers (about 275,000), compared with 20 percent of the working public, are in a household earning $50,000 or more. Teachers' salaries are higher than those of state and local government employees, and both are outstripping the inflation rate. Yet, a smaller and smaller portion of ever-increasing school spending goes for teachers' salaries.

o The SAT scores of prospective teachers are edging up faster than the national averages. The gap between the SAT scores of high school students who say they are going to major in education when they get to college and the national average SAT score narrowed from 80 points in 1982 to 70 points in 1985. While the average SAT score rose from 893 in 1982 to 906 in 1985, the average score for intended education majors climbed from 813 to 836 in the three years. The biggest gains in SAT scores of prospective teachers occurred in states in the South and West where there is the greatest demand for new teachers. While the gaps are narrowing, it is still a fact that, without exception in all fifty states and the District of Columbia, the SAT scores of high school students who say they might go into education fall considerably below the state's average SAT score.

o More people seem to be going into teaching than was predicted. Estimates of a pending teacher shortage have been grim. The National Center for Education Statistics' latest projections call for 1.65 million additional teachers between fall 1985 and fall 1993. That's two-thirds of the 2.40 million public and private elementary and secondary school teachers in classrooms today. Sixty-eight percent of the 1,651,000 additional teachers needed will be elementary school teachers. NCES projects we will need an additional 1,118,000 elementary teachers and 533,000 secondary school teachers by 1993. These figures represent 139 percent of the elementary school teachers and 27 percent of the secondary school teachers currently employed. An analysis of NCES projections and numbers of teachers in 1984-85 showed that states actually employed more teachers than NCES estimated they would need that year. The number of teacher graduates in 1983 was smaller than the estimated number of additional teachers needed in 1984-85. The additional teachers being hired are coming from a "reserve pool" of certified teachers, accumulated in the years when supply exceeded demand, and/or from issuing an emergency certificate to anybody who wants to teach. In any event, classrooms were filled with teachers last year even though demand was expected to exceed supply.

o New Demands Are Being Made on Teachers. The changing demographics of school-age children is such that teachers will be facing far greater numbers of poor children and children from many different racial and ethnic backgrounds in the next few years. Today, 13 million of the 62 million children under eighteen years old live in poverty, compared with 10 million of the 69 million children in 1970. Minority children made up 14.8 percent of all children under eighteen in 1970. They now comprise 18.3 percent of all children. Minority enrollment in public elementary and secondary schools nationwide rose from 21.7 percent in 1972 to 26.7 percent in 1981. It is expected to reach a third by the mid-90s.

o Most states have made numerous changes in how they educate and certify teachers, but in many cases, these changes have failed to produce necessary reform. It is no secret that adding more education courses, as many states have done, does not get to the heart of the problem of getting quality teachers into classrooms. Nor does requiring passage of a basic skills test insure that a teacher is competent to teach. The biggest problem in teacher education and certification may be that the process is too cumbersome and cries out for simplification.

SUMMARY TABLES SOURCES

National Center for Education Information. Basic data from The National Education Association "Estimates of School Statistics," 1972-73, 1982-83, 1983-84, and 1984-85; U.S. Bureau of Economic Analysis "State Per Capita Income," selected years; U.S. Bureau of the Census Statistical Abstract of the U.S., 1984 and 1985, and "State Population Estimates, by Age and Components of Change, 1980 to 1984"; The College Entrance Examination Board State Reports on College Bound Seniors, 1972, 1978, 1982, 1984; the National Center for Education Statistics, published and unpublished data; U.S. Bureau of Labor Statistics "NEWS" May 1980, 1984, and 1985.

	Percent change 1972-73 to 1982-83	1982-83	1983-84	1984-85	Percent change 1982-83 to 1983-84	Percent change 1983-84 to 1984-85
Public Elementary School Enrollment	-11.1	23,671,666	23,443,766	23,770,897	-0.9	1.3
Public Secondary School Enrollment	-17.9	16,027,167	15,780,075	15,602,579	-1.5	-1.1
Public Elementary and Secondary Enrollment	-14.0	39,698,833	39,223,841	39,373,476	-1.1	0.3
Numbers of Public Elementary Teachers	3.0	1,179,282	1,171,053	1,184,337	-0.6	1.1
Numbers of Public Secondary School Teachers	-0.4	956,229	946,004	961,205	-1.0	1.6
Numbers of Public Elementary and Secondary Teachers	1.4	2,135,511	2,117,057	2,145,542	-0.8	1.3
Elementary Teachers' Salaries	102.9	20,205	21,452	23,092	6.1	7.6
Secondary Teachers' Salaries	101.0	21,380	22,667	24,276	6.0	7.0
Total Teachers' Salaries	102.0	20,715	22,019	23,546	6.2	6.9
Per Pupil Expenditures in ADA	181.8	2,944	3,173	3,429	7.7	8.0
Total Current Expenditures (in thousands)	126.3	119,093,398	126,883,778	138,117,496	6.5	8.8
Total Revenue Receipts (in thousands)	121.8	120,432,748	127,597,582	137,572,617	5.9	7.8

	Change in percent 1972-73 to 1982-83	Percent share 1982-83	1983-84	1984-85
Federal Revenue Receipts	-0.5	7.4	6.4	6.2
State Revenue Receipts	9.7	50.3	49.0	49.0
Local and Other Revenue Receipts	-9.2	42.3	44.5	44.8

	Percent change 1972 to 1982	1982	1983	1984	Percent change 1982 to 1983	Percent change 1983 to 1984
Total Personal Income (in millions)	170.9	2,571,517	2,734,464	3,000,827	6.3	9.7
Per Capita Income	144.9	11,100	11,687	12,707	5.2	8.7
Population (in thousands)	10.6	231,786	233,975	236,158	0.9	0.9
Population Under Age 5	2.3	17,372,000	17,826,000	17,816,000	2.6	0.0

	Score change 1972 to 1982	Average score 1982	1983	1984	Percent change 1982 to 1983	Percent change 1983 to 1984
SAT Verbal Scores	-27.0	426	425	426	-0.2	0.2
SAT Math Scores	-17.0	467	468	471	0.2	0.6

	Score change 1978 to 1982	Average score 1982	1983	1984	Percent change 1982 to 1983	Percent change 1983 to 1984
SAT Verbal Scores of Intended Education Majors	-2.0	394	394	398	0.0	1.0
SAT Math Scores of Intended Education Majors	-3.0	419	418	425	-0.2	1.6

	Change in percent 1972 to 1981	Percent minority enrollment 1972	1976	1981
Percentage of Minority Enrollment	5.0	21.7	24.0	26.7

	Change in percent 1965 to 1980	Percent of all students enrolled in private schools 1965	1970	1980
Percentage of Private School Enrollment	-2.2	13.0	11.9	10.8

	Change in percent 1971 to 1983	1971-72	1980-81	1983-84
Graduation Rates	-3.9	77.8	71.9	73.9

	Change in percent 1980 to 1985	Percent unemployed 1980	1984	1985
Unemployment Rates	0.9	6.6	8.1	7.5

97

SUMMARY TABLE 2. Alabama

	Percent change 1972-73 to 1982-83	1982-83	1983-84	1984-85	Percent change 1982-83 to 1983-84	Percent change 1983-84 to 1984-85	State's rank in percent change 1982-83 to 1983-84	State's rank in percent change 1983-84 to 1984-85	State's Rank 1982	1983	1984
Public Elementary School Enrollment	-5.1	386,828	385,291	392,304	-0.3	1.8	16	12	22	22	22
Public Secondary School Enrollment	-10.2	337,209	336,610	335,263	-0.1	-0.4	16	33	16	15	17
Public Elementary and Secondary Enrollment	-7.6	724,037	721,901	727,567	-0.2	0.7	11	15	20	20	20
Numbers of Public Elementary Teachers	17.7	19,862	19,950	18,634	0.4	-6.5	13	51	21	21	25
Numbers of Public Secondary School Teachers	12.5	19,222	19,250	17,465	0.1	-9.2	19	49	19	19	19
Numbers of Public Elementary and Secondary Teachers	15.0	39,084	39,200	36,099	0.2	-7.9	17	50	20	18	21
Elementary Teachers' Salaries	116.8	17,400	18,000	20,209	3.4	12.2	41	7	38	40	34
Secondary Teachers' Salaries	121.4	18,000	18,000	20,209	0.0	12.2	50	4	40	46	41
Total Teachers' Salaries	120.2	17,850	18,000	20,209	0.8	12.2	50	4	37	42	36
Per Pupil Expenditures in ADA	158.1	2,019	2,102	2,241	4.1	6.6	44	29	49	49	49
Total Current Expenditures (in thousands)	133.8	1,561,110	1,569,844	1,708,000	0.5	8.8	51	19	26	29	28
Total Revenue Receipts (in thousands)	123.9	1,523,949	1,532,344	1,632,119	0.5	6.5	49	29	27	29	29

	Change in percent 1972-73 to 1982-83	Percent share 1982-83	1983-84	1984-85
Federal Revenue Receipts	-2.2	14.8	13.1	11.9
State Revenue Receipts	0.3	64.3	67.3	72.4
Local and Other Revenue Receipts	2.0	21.0	19.6	15.6

	Percent change 1972 to 1982	1982	1983	1984	Percent change 1982 to 1983	Percent change 1983 to 1984	State's rank in percent change 1982 to 1983	State's rank in percent change 1983 to 1984	Rank 1982	1983	1984
Total Personal Income (in millions)	179.2	34,119	36,536	39,826	7.1	9.1	22	30	25	24	24
Per Capita Income	150.7	8,647	9,229	9,981	6.7	8.1	15	29	48	46	47
Population (in thousands)	11.4	3,941	3,959	3,990	0.4	0.7	37	26	22	22	22
Population Under Age 5	-0.7	302,000	302,000	296,000	0.0	-1.9	43	41	21	21	22

	Score change 1972 to 1982	Average score 1982	1983	1984	Percent change 1982 to 1983	Percent change 1983 to 1984	State's rank in percent change 1982 to 1983	State's rank in percent change 1983 to 1984	1982 score	1983 score	1984 score
SAT Verbal Scores	44.0	463	466	467	0.6	0.2	10	26	23	20	22
SAT Math Scores	60.0	501	508	531	1.3	4.5	2	2	27	23	12

	Score change 1978 to 1982	Average score 1982	1983	1984	Percent change 1982 to 1983	Percent change 1983 to 1984	State's rank in percent change 1982 to 1983	State's rank in percent change 1983 to 1984	1982 score	1983 score	1984 score
SAT Verbal Scores of Intended Education Majors	30.0	400	436	441	9.0	1.1	2	28	29	12	15
SAT Math Scores of Intended Education Majors	31.0	428	453	466	5.8	2.8	7	12	27	15	13

	Change in percent 1972 to 1981	Percent minority enrollment 1972	1976	1981
Percentage of Minority Enrollment	-0.9	34.5	34.2	33.6

	Change in percent 1965 to 1980	Percent of all students enrolled in private schools 1965	1970	1980
Percentage of Private School Enrollment	4.1	3.5	6.9	7.6

	Change in percent 1971 to 1983	1971-72	1980-81	1983-84
Graduation Rates	1.0	66.4	66.1	67.4

	Change in percent 1980 to 1985	Percent unemployed 1980	1984	1985
Unemployment Rates	2.9	7.8	11.5	10.7

98

SUMMARY TABLE 3. Alaska

	Percent change 1972-73 to 1982-83	1982-83	1983-84	1984-85	Percent change 1982-83 to 1983-84	Percent change 1983-84 to 1984-85	State's rank in percent change 1982-83 to 1983-84	State's rank in percent change 1983-84 to 1984-85	State's Rank 1982	State's Rank 1983	State's Rank 1984
Public Elementary School Enrollment	-5.3	49,256	50,200	52,000	1.9	3.6	1	4	49	49	48
Public Secondary School Enrollment	14.1	40,068	39,317	41,990	-1.8	6.8	31	1	49	48	48
Public Elementary and Secondary Enrollment	2.4	89,324	89,517	93,990	0.2	5.0	7	1	51	50	48
Numbers of Public Elementary Teachers	32.7	2,793	3,214	3,800	15.0	18.2	1	1	50	49	47
Numbers of Public Secondary School Teachers	40.1	3,234	3,173	2,290	-1.8	-27.8	39	51	45	45	49
Numbers of Public Elementary and Secondary Teachers	35.9	6,027	6,387	6,090	5.9	-4.6	2	48	49	48	49
Elementary Teachers' Salaries	129.0	33,784	36,292	39,520	7.6	8.9	14	13	1	1	1
Secondary Teachers' Salaries	134.7	34,154	36,841	39,900	7.9	8.4	9	16	1	1	1
Total Teachers' Salaries	131.3	33,983	36,564	39,751	7.8	8.8	12	15	1	1	1
Per Pupil Expenditures in ADA	320.0	6,383	7,026	6,867	10.0	-2.2	11	49	1	1	1
Total Current Expenditures (in thousands)	264.2	602,174	658,207	690,000	9.3	4.8	10	36	38	38	38
Total Revenue Receipts (in thousands)	285.7	598,852	643,011	683,415	7.3	6.2	18	33	38	38	38

	Change in percent 1972-73 to 1982-83	Percent share 1982-83	1983-84	1984-85
Federal Revenue Receipts	-9.5	5.7	1.3	2.9
State Revenue Receipts	10.5	78.3	83.1	73.4
Local and Other Revenue Receipts	-1.0	16.0	15.7	23.6

	Percent change 1972 to 1982	1982	1983	1984	Percent change 1982 to 1983	1983 to 1984	State's rank in percent change 1982 to 1983	1983 to 1984	Rank 1982	1983	1984
Total Personal Income (in millions)	285.6	7,358	8,243	8,574	12.0	4.0	2	50	46	45	45
Per Capita Income	187.5	15,200	17,225	17,155	13.3	-0.4	1	51	1	1	1
Population (in thousands)	34.4	444	479	500	7.8	4.3	1	1	51	51	51
Population Under Age 5	31.4	46,000	52,000	56,000	13.0	7.6	1	1	48	48	47

	Score change 1972 to 1982	Average score 1982	1983	1984	Percent change 1982 to 1983	1983 to 1984	State's rank in percent change 1982 to 1983	1983 to 1984	1982 score	1983 score	1984 score
SAT Verbal Scores	-28.0	446	437	443	-2.0	1.3	51	2	28	30	29
SAT Math Scores	-16.0	477	468	471	-1.8	0.6	50	20	30	34	33

	Score change 1978 to 1982	Average score 1982	1983	1984	Percent change 1982 to 1983	1983 to 1984	State's rank in percent change 1982 to 1983	1983 to 1984	1982 score	1983 score	1984 score
SAT Verbal Scores of Intended Education Majors	-12.0	413	405	414	-1.9	2.2	45	15	23	30	28
SAT Math Scores of Intended Education Majors	-9.0	437	417	429	-4.5	2.8	49	12	24	38	32

	Change in percent 1972 to 1981	Percent minority enrollment 1972	1976	1981
Percentage of Minority Enrollment	12.1	16.3	25.8	28.4

	Change in percent 1965 to 1980	Percent of all students enrolled in private schools 1965	1970	1980
Percentage of Private School Enrollment	0.2	4.0	2.5	4.2

	Change in percent 1971 to 1983	1971-72	1980-81	1983-84
Graduation Rates	-1.5	79.3	68.9	77.8

	Change in percent 1980 to 1985	Percent unemployed 1980	1984	1985
Unemployment Rates	-1.0	11.2	11.9	10.2

	Percent change 1972-73 to 1982-83	1982-83	1983-84	1984-85	Percent change 1982-83 to 1983-84	Percent change 1983-84 to 1984-85	State's rank in percent change 1982-83 to 1983-84	State's rank in percent change 1983-84 to 1984-85	State's Rank 1982	State's Rank 1983	State's Rank 1984
Public Elementary School Enrollment	2.2	388,873	387,175	401,000	-0.4	3.5	19	5	21	21	21
Public Secondary School Enrollment	10.1	163,552	158,585	166,000	-3.0	4.6	43	4	32	32	31
Public Elementary and Secondary Enrollment	4.4	552,425	545,760	567,000	-1.2	3.8	30	2	26	26	26
Numbers of Public Elementary Teachers	32.0	18,488	18,343	18,700	-0.7	1.9	30	24	24	25	24
Numbers of Public Secondary School Teachers	41.5	7,265	7,319	7,220	0.7	-1.3	16	37	35	36	35
Numbers of Public Elementary and Secondary Teachers	34.8	25,753	25,662	25,920	-0.3	1.0	23	26	30	30	30
Elementary Teachers' Salaries	96.2	19,860	21,546	23,247	8.4	7.8	10	19	22	21	20
Secondary Teachers' Salaries	82.2	20,220	21,753	23,683	7.5	8.8	12	15	28	25	21
Total Teachers' Salaries	87.6	19,962	21,605	23,380	8.2	8.2	10	19	25	21	20
Per Pupil Expenditures in ADA	167.5	2,512	2,738	2,801	8.9	2.3	15	43	39	36	40
Total Current Expenditures (in thousands)	204.7	1,333,600	1,434,753	1,490,000	7.5	3.8	18	39	30	30	31
Total Revenue Receipts (in thousands)	193.9	1,435,300	1,529,670	1,529,000	6.5	0.0	23	45	30	30	30

	Change in percent 1972-73 to 1982-83	Percent share 1982-83	1983-84	1984-85
Federal Revenue Receipts	3.2	11.4	8.5	10.5
State Revenue Receipts	4.1	45.7	52.3	52.4
Local and Other Revenue Receipts	-7.4	42.9	39.2	37.1

	Percent change 1972 to 1982	1982	1983	1984	Percent change 1982 to 1983	Percent change 1983 to 1984	State's rank in percent change 1982 to 1983	State's rank in percent change 1983 to 1984	Rank 1982	Rank 1983	Rank 1984
Total Personal Income (in millions)	238.9	29,109	31,567	35,504	8.4	12.4	12	3	28	27	27
Per Capita Income	138.1	10,067	10,653	11,629	5.8	9.1	23	17	34	33	33
Population (in thousands)	42.4	2,892	2,963	3,053	2.4	3.0	5	2	29	28	28
Population Under Age 5	34.3	239,000	254,000	261,000	6.2	2.7	5	3	27	26	26

	Score change 1972 to 1982	Average score 1982	1983	1984	Percent change 1982 to 1983	Percent change 1983 to 1984	State's rank in percent change 1982 to 1983	State's rank in percent change 1983 to 1984	1982 score	1983 score	1984 score
SAT Verbal Scores	-37.0	470	465	469	-1.0	0.8	45	5	18	23	19
SAT Math Scores	22.0	511	505	509	-1.1	0.7	49	15	20	25	24

	Score change 1978 to 1982	Average score 1982	1983	1984	Percent change 1982 to 1983	Percent change 1983 to 1984	State's rank in percent change 1982 to 1983	State's rank in percent change 1983 to 1984	1982 score	1983 score	1984 score
SAT Verbal Scores of Intended Education Majors	-2.0	440	430	445	-2.2	3.4	48	12	9	19	12
SAT Math Scores of Intended Education Majors	-27.0	449	442	445	-1.5	0.6	44	34	19	22	26

	Change in percent 1972 to 1981	Percent minority enrollment 1972	1976	1981
Percentage of Minority Enrollment	6.5	27.2	31.4	33.7

	Change in percent 1965 to 1980	Percent of all students enrolled in private schools 1965	1970	1980
Percentage of Private School Enrollment	-1.2	8.5	8.6	7.3

	Change in percent 1971 to 1983	1971-72	1980-81	1983-84
Graduation Rates	-15.2	83.6	68.9	68.4

	Change in percent 1980 to 1985	Percent unemployed 1980	1984	1985
Unemployment Rates	-0.4	6.1	5.3	5.7

	Percent change 1972-73 to 1982-83	1982-83	1983-84	1984-85	Percent change 1982-83 to 1983-84	Percent change 1983-84 to 1984-85	State's rank in percent change 1982-83 to 1983-84	State's rank in percent change 1983-84 to 1984-85	State's Rank 1982	State's Rank 1983	State's Rank 1984
Public Elementary School Enrollment	-1.7	233,645	232,536	232,337	-0.4	0.0	19	26	33	33	34
Public Secondary School Enrollment	-7.6	198,920	193,827	200,331	-2.5	3.3	38	7	28	28	28
Public Elementary and Secondary Enrollment	-4.5	432,565	426,363	432,668	-1.4	1.4	35	12	32	32	32
Numbers of Public Elementary Teachers	15.3	11,589	11,657	11,773	0.5	0.9	11	30	34	34	34
Numbers of Public Secondary School Teachers	12.8	12,123	12,240	12,312	0.9	0.5	13	22	27	27	27
Numbers of Public Elementary and Secondary Teachers	14.0	23,712	23,897	24,085	0.7	0.7	14	29	33	33	33
Elementary Teachers' Salaries	105.1	14,579	16,436	18,382	12.7	11.8	1	9	50	49	47
Secondary Teachers' Salaries	108.7	15,459	17,396	19,456	12.5	11.8	1	7	50	48	46
Total Teachers' Salaries	107.2	15,029	16,929	18,933	12.6	11.8	1	7	50	49	46
Per Pupil Expenditures in ADA	218.0	2,025	2,257	2,344	11.4	3.8	6	39	48	46	47
Total Current Expenditures (in thousands)	217.9	906,628	992,574	1,022,194	9.4	2.9	9	43	33	33	35
Total Revenue Receipts (in thousands)	201.9	876,723	969,447	1,072,386	10.5	10.6	5	14	35	33	33

	Change in percent 1972-73 to 1982-83	Percent share 1982-83	Percent share 1983-84	Percent share 1984-85
Federal Revenue Receipts	-2.0	13.3	12.5	11.0
State Revenue Receipts	6.3	54.3	54.3	59.2
Local and Other Revenue Receipts	-4.3	32.4	33.1	29.8

	Percent change 1972 to 1982	1982	1983	1984	Percent change 1982 to 1983	Percent change 1983 to 1984	State's rank in percent change 1982 to 1983	State's rank in percent change 1983 to 1984	Rank 1982	Rank 1983	Rank 1984
Total Personal Income (in millions)	189.5	19,408	20,802	22,843	7.1	9.8	22	22	33	33	33
Per Capita Income	155.0	8,424	8,936	9,724	6.0	8.8	21	20	50	50	49
Population (in thousands)	13.5	2,307	2,328	2,349	0.9	0.9	22	20	33	33	33
Population Under Age 5	7.9	177,000	179,000	177,000	1.1	-1.1	37	30	34	34	34

	Score change 1972 to 1982	Average score 1982	Average score 1983	Average score 1984	Percent change 1982 to 1983	Percent change 1983 to 1984	State's rank in percent change 1982 to 1983	State's rank in percent change 1983 to 1984	1982 score	1983 score	1984 score
SAT Verbal Scores	-6.0	480	482	482	0.4	0.0	12	34	12	11	12
SAT Math Scores	8.0	519	518	544	-0.1	5.0	33	1	11	15	7

	Score change 1978 to 1982	Average score 1982	Average score 1983	Average score 1984	Percent change 1982 to 1983	Percent change 1983 to 1984	State's rank in percent change 1982 to 1983	State's rank in percent change 1983 to 1984	1982 score	1983 score	1984 score
SAT Verbal Scores of Intended Education Majors	-27.0	420	432	467	2.8	8.1	9	4	22	15	6
SAT Math Scores of Intended Education Majors	-11.0	445	439	485	-1.3	10.4	42	2	22	25	6

	Change in percent 1972 to 1981	Percent minority enrollment 1972	Percent minority enrollment 1976	Percent minority enrollment 1981
Percentage of Minority Enrollment	-5.9	29.4	23.2	23.5

	Change in percent 1965 to 1980	Percent of all students enrolled in private schools 1965	Percent of all students enrolled in private schools 1970	Percent of all students enrolled in private schools 1980
Percentage of Private School Enrollment	1.1	2.9	4.5	4.0

	Change in percent 1971 to 1983	1971-72	1980-81	1983-84
Graduation Rates	6.1	70.1	73.2	76.2

	Change in percent 1980 to 1985	Percent unemployed 1980	Percent unemployed 1984	Percent unemployed 1985
Unemployment Rates	2.0	6.8	9.3	8.8

101

	Percent change 1972-73 to 1982-83	1982-83	1983-84	1984-85	Percent change 1982-83 to 1983-84	1983-84 to 1984-85	State's rank in percent change 1982-83 to 1983-84	1983-84 to 1984-85	State's Rank 1982	1983	1984
Public Elementary School Enrollment	-1.2	2,801,818	2,835,050	2,855,780	1.1	0.7	4	21	1	1	1
Public Secondary School Enrollment	-29.0	1,263,668	1,252,936	1,294,650	-0.8	3.3	25	7	3	3	3
Public Elementary and Secondary Enrollment	-12.0	4,065,486	4,087,986	4,150,430	0.5	1.5	4	11	1	1	1
Numbers of Public Elementary Teachers	-7.6	108,756	108,496	107,040	-0.2	-1.3	21	42	1	1	1
Numbers of Public Secondary School Teachers	-11.5	64,514	61,939	68,095	-4.0	10.0	47	2	3	3	3
Numbers of Public Elementary and Secondary Teachers	-9.1	173,270	170,435	175,135	-1.6	2.7	39	10	1	2	1
Elementary Teachers' Salaries	99.2	23,465	25,492	26,170	8.6	2.6	9	45	7	6	7
Secondary Teachers' Salaries	93.4	25,331	27,232	27,890	7.5	2.4	12	46	5	5	6
Total Teachers' Salaries	95.1	24,035	26,403	26,300	9.8	-0.3	6	48	6	5	7
Per Pupil Expenditures in ADA	137.1	2,735	2,912	3,291	6.4	13.0	34	6	31	31	26
Total Current Expenditures (in thousands)	64.5	12,180,000	13,070,000	14,787,179	7.3	13.1	19	3	1	1	1
Total Revenue Receipts (in thousands)	54.9	12,050,000	12,835,080	14,815,175	6.5	15.4	23	3	1	1	1

	Change in percent 1972-73 to 1982-83	Percent share 1982-83	1983-84	1984-85
Federal Revenue Receipts	-2.1	5.3	6.9	6.8
State Revenue Receipts	51.8	85.8	67.0	67.1
Local and Other Revenue Receipts	-49.7	8.9	26.1	26.1

	Percent change 1972 to 1982	1982	1983	1984	Percent change 1982 to 1983	1983 to 1984	State's rank in percent change 1982 to 1983	1983 to 1984	Rank 1982	1983	1984
Total Personal Income (in millions)	197.6	310,699	333,706	367,538	7.4	10.1	20	18	1	1	1
Per Capita Income	147.8	12,616	13,256	14,344	5.0	8.2	31	26	5.	6	6
Population (in thousands)	20.1	24,697	25,174	25,622	1.9	1.7	10	8	1	1	1
Population Under Age 5	18.3	1,917,000	2,008,000	2,063,000	4.7	2.7	12	3	1	1	1

	Score change 1972 to 1982	Average score 1982	1983	1984	Percent change 1982 to 1983	1983 to 1984	State's rank in percent change 1982 to 1983	1983 to 1984	1982 score	1983 score	1984 score
SAT Verbal Scores	-39.0	425	421	421	-0.9	0.0	43	34	39	43	43
SAT Math Scores	-19.0	474	474	476	0.0	0.4	25	27	31	30	30

	Score change 1978 to 1982	Average score 1982	1983	1984	Percent change 1982 to 1983	1983 to 1984	State's rank in percent change 1982 to 1983	1983 to 1984	1982 score	1983 score	1984 score
SAT Verbal Scores of Intended Education Majors	0.0	399	397	400	-0.5	0.7	36	32	30	36	36
SAT Math Scores of Intended Education Majors	0.0	424	421	431	-0.7	2.3	37	15	28	31	31

	Change in percent 1972 to 1981	Percent minority enrollment 1972	1976	1981
Percentage of Minority Enrollment	15.3	27.6	34.9	42.9

	Change in percent 1965 to 1980	Percent of all students enrolled in private schools 1965	1970	1980
Percentage of Private School Enrollment	1.5	9.6	8.5	11.1

	Change in percent 1971 to 1983	1971-72	1980-81	1983-84
Graduation Rates	-5.3	80.4	68.2	75.1

	Change in percent 1980 to 1985	Percent unemployed 1980	1984	1985
Unemployment Rates	1.0	6.3	8.6	7.3

102

	Percent change 1972-73 to 1982-83	1982-83	1983-84	1984-85	Percent change 1982-83 to 1983-84	Percent change 1983-84 to 1984-85	State's rank in percent change 1982-83 to 1983-84	State's rank in percent change 1983-84 to 1984-85	State's Rank 1982	1983	1984
Public Elementary School Enrollment	-0.5	320,798	319,064	322,416	-0.5	1.0	21	18	28	28	27
Public Secondary School Enrollment	-10.6	224,411	223,111	223,011	-0.5	0.0	22	22	24	24	24
Public Elementary and Secondary Enrollment	-5.1	545,209	542,175	545,427	-0.5	0.6	16	16	27	27	27
Numbers of Public Elementary Teachers	21.2	15,434	15,287	15,283	-0.9	0.0	34	33	28	28	28
Numbers of Public Secondary School Teachers	11.9	13,941	14,160	13,539	1.5	-4.3	9	45	26	25	26
Numbers of Public Elementary and Secondary Teachers	16.6	29,375	29,447	28,822	0.2	-2.1	17	47	28	28	28
Elementary Teachers' Salaries	112.0	21,066	22,452	24,150	6.5	7.5	26	20	18	15	18
Secondary Teachers' Salaries	119.5	22,291	23,789	24,800	6.7	4.2	23	39	14	12	16
Total Teachers' Salaries	122.4	21,470	22,895	24,456	6.6	6.8	24	29	17	16	17
Per Pupil Expenditures in ADA	198.0	2,961	3,261	3,398	10.1	4.2	10	38	23	21	24
Total Current Expenditures (in thousands)	157.7	1,636,181	1,788,412	1,877,796	9.3	4.9	10	35	24	24	24
Total Revenue Receipts (in thousands)	172.0	1,772,800	1,911,645	2,038,856	7.8	6.6	13	27	23	23	22

	Change in percent 1972-73 to 1982-83	Percent share 1982-83	1983-84	1984-85
Federal Revenue Receipts	-1.6	5.4	4.7	3.9
State Revenue Receipts	10.0	36.9	42.0	40.2
Local and Other Revenue Receipts	-8.4	57.7	53.3	55.9

	Percent change 1972 to 1982	1982	1983	1984	Percent change 1982 to 1983	Percent change 1983 to 1984	State's rank in percent change 1982 to 1983	State's rank in percent change 1983 to 1984	Rank 1982	1983	1984
Total Personal Income (in millions)	226.0	37,400	40,088	43,672	7.2	8.9	21	33	23	23	23
Per Capita Income	157.5	12,202	12,771	13,742	4.6	7.6	37	34	9	9	9
Population (in thousands)	26.6	3,071	3,139	3,178	2.2	1.2	7	14	27	26	26
Population Under Age 5	21.5	243,000	259,000	264,000	6.5	1.9	3	6	26	25	25

	Score change 1972 to 1982	Average score 1982	1983	1984	Percent change 1982 to 1983	Percent change 1983 to 1984	State's rank in percent change 1982 to 1983	State's rank in percent change 1983 to 1984	1982 score	1983 score	1984 score
SAT Verbal Scores	-24.0	468	469	468	0.2	-0.2	18	44	20	18	21
SAT Math Scores	-7.0	515	520	514	0.9	-1.1	6	50	15	12	19

	Score change 1978 to 1982	Average score 1982	1983	1984	Percent change 1982 to 1983	Percent change 1983 to 1984	State's rank in percent change 1982 to 1983	State's rank in percent change 1983 to 1984	1982 score	1983 score	1984 score
SAT Verbal Scores of Intended Education Majors	-10.0	433	428	436	-1.1	1.8	40	20	11	21	20
SAT Math Scores of Intended Education Majors	-5.0	460	454	461	-1.3	1.5	42	25	10	14	17

	Change in percent 1972 to 1981	Percent minority enrollment 1972	1976	1981
Percentage of Minority Enrollment	3.7	18.4	20.3	22.1

	Change in percent 1965 to 1980	Percent of all students enrolled in private schools 1965	1970	1980
Percentage of Private School Enrollment	-2.4	8.5	7.3	6.1

	Change in percent 1971 to 1983	1971-72	1980-81	1983-84
Graduation Rates	-4.7	83.9	80.0	79.2

	Change in percent 1980 to 1985	Percent unemployed 1980	1984	1985
Unemployment Rates	1.3	5.4	6.2	6.7

103

	Percent change 1972-73 to 1982-83	1982-83	1983-84	1984-85	Percent change 1982-83 to 1983-84	1983-84 to 1984-85	State's rank in percent change 1982-83 to 1983-84	1983-84 to 1984-85	State's Rank 1982	1983	1984
Public Elementary School Enrollment	-29.5	337,299	325,936	315,794	-3.3	-3.1	49	50	27	27	28
Public Secondary School Enrollment	-13.8	167,851	161,464	162,218	-3.8	0.4	47	19	31	31	32
Public Elementary and Secondary Enrollment	-25.0	505,150	487,400	478,012	-3.5	-1.9	49	47	29	29	29
Numbers of Public Elementary Teachers	-1.3	19,214	18,902	18,907	-1.6	0.0	39	33	22	22	22
Numbers of Public Secondary School Teachers	-15.0	13,996	13,813	13,560	-1.3	-1.8	33	40	25	26	25
Numbers of Public Elementary and Secondary Teachers	-7.2	33,210	32,715	32,467	-1.5	-0.7	37	41	24	24	25
Elementary Teachers' Salaries	101.0	20,405	22,384	24,250	9.6	8.3	6	16	20	16	16
Secondary Teachers' Salaries	89.1	21,250	23,031	24,940	8.3	8.2	7	17	19	17	15
Total Teachers' Salaries	91.5	20,731	22,624	24,520	9.1	8.3	8	18	20	19	16
Per Pupil Expenditures in ADA	201.9	3,666	4,061	4,477	10.7	10.2	8	12	5	6	6
Total Current Expenditures (in thousands)	117.2	1,858,683	1,985,760	2,130,513	6.8	7.2	23	27	22	22	21
Total Revenue Receipts (in thousands)	94.0	1,858,389	1,985,460	2,130,113	6.8	7.2	20	22	22	22	21

	Change in percent 1972-73 to 1982-83	Percent share 1982-83	1983-84	1984-85
Federal Revenue Receipts	1.8	4.9	5.2	5.0
State Revenue Receipts	13.9	37.0	38.2	40.0
Local and Other Revenue Receipts	-15.1	58.7	56.7	55.1

	Percent change 1972 to 1982	1982	1983	1984	Percent change 1982 to 1983	1983 to 1984	State's rank in percent change 1982 to 1983	1983 to 1984	Rank 1982	1983	1984
Total Personal Income (in millions)	157.3	43,366	46,890	51,632	8.1	10.3	16	17	21	20	20
Per Capita Income	150.5	13,810	14,945	16,369	8.2	9.5	9	15	3	3	3
Population (in thousands)	2.7	3,126	3,138	3,154	0.3	0.5	38	31	26	27	27
Population Under Age 5	-17.2	193,000	193,000	195,000	0.0	1.0	43	10	33	33	33

	Score change 1972 to 1982	Average score 1982	1983	1984	Percent change 1982 to 1983	1983 to 1984	State's rank in percent change 1982 to 1983	1983 to 1984	1982 score	1983 score	1984 score
SAT Verbal Scores	-29.0	432	433	436	0.2	0.6	18	8	33	32	32
SAT Math Scores	-20.0	464	465	468	0.2	0.6	18	20	37	38	37

	Score change 1978 to 1982	Average score 1982	1983	1984	Percent change 1982 to 1983	1983 to 1984	State's rank in percent change 1982 to 1983	1983 to 1984	1982 score	1983 score	1984 score
SAT Verbal Scores of Intended Education Majors	-8.0	395	395	401	0.0	1.5	27	22	35	38	34
SAT Math Scores of Intended Education Majors	-14.0	408	409	416	0.2	1.7	20	21	41	42	41

	Change in percent 1972 to 1981	Percent minority enrollment 1972	1976	1981
Percentage of Minority Enrollment	4.0	13.0	15.4	17.0

	Change in percent 1965 to 1980	Percent of all students enrolled in private schools 1965	1970	1980
Percentage of Private School Enrollment	-3.5	17.8	13.3	14.3

	Change in percent 1971 to 1983	1971-72	1980-81	1983-84
Graduation Rates	-2.2	80.1	70.6	77.9

	Change in percent 1980 to 1985	Percent unemployed 1980	1984	1985
Unemployment Rates	-0.7	5.5	5.1	4.8

104

SUMMARY TABLE 9. Delaware

	Percent change 1972-73 to 1982-83	1982-83	1983-84	1984-85	Percent change 1982-83 to 1983-84	Percent change 1983-84 to 1984-85	State's rank in percent change 1982-83 to 1983-84	State's rank in percent change 1983-84 to 1984-85	State's Rank 1982	State's Rank 1983	State's Rank 1984
Public Elementary School Enrollment	-33.6	45,963	45,545	46,901	-0.9	3.0	27	6	51	51	51
Public Secondary School Enrollment	-28.0	46,683	45,861	44,866	-1.7	-2.2	30	44	44	44	45
Public Elementary and Secondary Enrollment	-31.0	92,646	91,406	91,767	-1.3	0.3	34	20	48	48	49
Numbers of Public Elementary Teachers	-9.1	2,439	2,451	2,600	0.4	6.0	13	5	51	51	51
Numbers of Public Secondary School Teachers	-18.0	2,970	2,985	2,916	0.5	-2.3	17	42	47	47	46
Numbers of Public Elementary and Secondary Teachers	-14.1	5,409	5,436	5,516	0.4	1.4	16	21	50	51	51
Elementary Teachers' Salaries	92.1	20,078	20,378	22,712	1.4	11.4	48	10	21	24	21
Secondary Teachers' Salaries	97.6	21,075	21,375	23,788	1.4	11.2	48	8	22	27	20
Total Teachers' Salaries	95.1	20,625	20,925	23,300	1.4	11.3	46	8	21	24	21
Per Pupil Expenditures in ADA	219.4	3,524	3,735	4,155	5.9	11.2	35	9	8	9	7
Total Current Expenditures (in thousands)	77.7	325,146	331,500	376,000	1.9	13.4	49	2	48	50	49
Total Revenue Receipts (in thousands)	93.4	340,671	346,500	392,660	1.7	13.3	46	6	49	50	47

	Change in percent 1972-73 to 1982-83	Percent share 1982-83	1983-84	1984-85
Federal Revenue Receipts	3.7	11.2	9.4	7.8
State Revenue Receipts	-2.0	67.6	67.6	69.4
Local and Other Revenue Receipts	-1.8	21.2	23.1	22.7

	Percent change 1972 to 1982	1982	1983	1984	Percent change 1982 to 1983	1983 to 1984	State's rank in percent change 1982 to 1983	1983 to 1984	Rank 1982	1983	1984
Total Personal Income (in millions)	140.7	7,084	7,643	8,298	7.8	8.5	17	36	48	48	48
Per Capita Income	129.4	11,810	12,615	13,545	6.8	7.3	14	39	13	10	11
Population (in thousands)	4.9	600	606	613	1.0	1.1	20	16	48	48	48
Population Under Age 5	-10.4	43,000	43,000	43,000	0.0	0.0	43	16	49	49	49

	Score change 1972 to 1982	Average score 1982	1983	1984	Percent change 1982 to 1983	1983 to 1984	State's rank in percent change 1982 to 1983	1983 to 1984	1982 score	1983 score	1984 score
SAT Verbal Scores	-26.0	432	433	433	0.2	0.0	18	34	33	32	34
SAT Math Scores	-20.0	465	467	469	0.4	0.4	11	27	35	35	36

	Score change 1978 to 1982	Average score 1982	1983	1984	Percent change 1982 to 1983	1983 to 1984	State's rank in percent change 1982 to 1983	1983 to 1984	1982 score	1983 score	1984 score
SAT Verbal Scores of Intended Education Majors	-1.0	389	389	389	0.0	0.0	27	37	39	40	44
SAT Math Scores of Intended Education Majors	-7.0	409	407	414	-0.4	1.7	28	21	40	43	43

	Change in percent 1972 to 1981	Percent minority enrollment 1972	1976	1981
Percentage of Minority Enrollment	7.5	21.3	24.3	28.8

	Change in percent 1965 to 1980	Percent of all students enrolled in private schools 1965	1970	1980
Percentage of Private School Enrollment	3.1	15.9	13.4	19.0

	Change in percent 1971 to 1983	1971-72	1980-81	1983-84
Graduation Rates	10.2	78.7	72.2	88.9

	Change in percent 1980 to 1985	Percent unemployed 1980	1984	1985
Unemployment Rates	-1.6	7.6	6.9	6.0

	Percent change 1972-73 to 1982-83	1982-83	1983-84	1984-85	Percent change 1982-83 to 1983-84	1983-84 to 1984-85	State's rank in percent change 1982-83 to 1983-84	1983-84 to 1984-85	State's Rank 1982	1983	1984
Public Elementary School Enrollment	-41.8	50,921	50,251	49,787	-1.3	-0.9	35	39	48	48	49
Public Secondary School Enrollment	-30.8	40,184	38,592	37,610	-3.9	-2.5	48	47	48	49	49
Public Elementary and Secondary Enrollment	-37.4	91,105	88,843	87,397	-2.4	-1.6	45	46	50	51	51
Numbers of Public Elementary Teachers	-23.9	3,154	3,355	3,526	6.3	5.0	2	11	48	48	49
Numbers of Public Secondary School Teachers	-26.1	2,190	2,293	2,266	4.7	-1.1	3	35	50	51	51
Numbers of Public Elementary and Secondary Teachers	-24.8	5,344	5,648	5,792	5.6	2.5	3	13	51	50	50
Elementary Teachers' Salaries	0.0	25,610	27,659	28,582	8.0	3.3	11	43	3	3	2
Secondary Teachers' Salaries	0.0	25,610	27,659	28,679	8.0	3.6	8	41	4	3	4
Total Teachers' Salaries		25,610	27,659	28,621	8.0	3.4	11	41	3	3	3
Per Pupil Expenditures in ADA	178.4	3,657	4,116	4,753	12.5	15.4	2	5	6	5	5
Total Current Expenditures (in thousands)	45.5	306,258	349,461	380,600	14.1	8.9	3	17	50	48	48
Total Revenue Receipts (in thousands)	44.7	346,606	363,397	384,181	4.8	5.7	33	35	47	49	48

	Change in percent 1972-73 to 1982-83	Percent share 1982-83	1983-84	1984-85
Federal Revenue Receipts	8.6	15.5	10.2	11.3
State Revenue Receipts	0.0	0.0	0.0	0.0
Local and Other Revenue Receipts	-2.6	84.5	89.8	88.7

	Percent change 1972 to 1982	1982	1983	1984	Percent change 1982 to 1983	1983 to 1984	State's rank in percent change 1982 to 1983	1983 to 1984	Rank 1982	1983	1984
Total Personal Income (in millions)	114.8	9,542	9,766	10,492	2.3	7.4	47	43	43	43	43
Per Capita Income	153.0	15,064	15,673	16,845	4.0	7.4	41	37	2	2	2
Population (in thousands)	-15.2	626	623	623	-0.4	0.0	50	45	47	47	47
Population Under Age 5	-33.9	39,000	41,000	42,000	5.1	2.4	10	5	50	50	50

	Score change 1972 to 1982	Average score 1982	1983	1984	Percent change 1982 to 1983	1983 to 1984	State's rank in percent change 1982 to 1983	1983 to 1984	1982 score	1983 score	1984 score
SAT Verbal Scores	6.0	398	399	397	0.2	-0.5	18	47	47	47	47
SAT Math Scores	12.0	423	427	426	0.9	-0.2	6	42	50	50	49

	Score change 1978 to 1982	Average score 1982	1983	1984	Percent change 1982 to 1983	1983 to 1984	State's rank in percent change 1982 to 1983	1983 to 1984	1982 score	1983 score	1984 score
SAT Verbal Scores of Intended Education Majors	18.0	348	375	374	7.7	-0.2	4	39	50	47	47
SAT Math Scores of Intended Education Majors	-23.0	367	378	396	2.9	4.7	10	7	50	51	49

	Change in percent 1972 to 1981	Percent minority enrollment 1972	1976	1981
Percentage of Minority Enrollment	0.9	95.5	96.5	96.4

	Change in percent 1965 to 1980	Percent of all students enrolled in private schools 1965	1970	1980
Percentage of Private School Enrollment	3.7	13.8	10.3	17.5

	Change in percent 1971 to 1983	1971-72	1980-81	1983-84
Graduation Rates	3.5	54.9	51.4	58.4

	Change in percent 1980 to 1985	Percent unemployed 1980	1984	1985
Unemployment Rates	0.8	7.4	9.6	8.2

SUMMARY TABLE 11. Florida

	Percent change 1972-73 to 1982-83	1982-83	1983-84	1984-85	Percent change 1982-83 to 1983-84	Percent change 1983-84 to 1984-85	State's rank in percent change 1982-83 to 1983-84	State's rank in percent change 1983-84 to 1984-85	State's Rank 1982	State's Rank 1983	State's Rank 1984
Public Elementary School Enrollment	-10.2	783,685	778,909	795,797	-0.6	2.1	23	10	8	8	8
Public Secondary School Enrollment	-10.8	701,232	716,796	728,127	2.2	1.5	4	14	6	5	5
Public Elementary and Secondary Enrollment	-10.4	1,484,917	1,495,705	1,523,924	0.7	1.8	3	10	8	8	8
Numbers of Public Elementary Teachers	38.8	46,030	46,435	48,186	0.8	3.8	10	16	7	7	6
Numbers of Public Secondary School Teachers	6.8	35,978	36,639	38,037	1.8	3.8	6	6	7	6	6
Numbers of Public Elementary and Secondary Teachers	22.8	82,008	83,074	86,223	1.3	3.7	10	8	7	7	7
Elementary Teachers' Salaries	105.7	18,633	19,928	21,442	6.9	7.5	23	20	29	27	26
Secondary Teachers' Salaries	92.8	18,058	19,156	20,569	6.0	7.3	27	20	38	38	37
Total Teachers' Salaries	99.8	18,275	19,545	21,057	6.9	7.7	22	21	34	34	31
Per Pupil Expenditures in ADA	219.8	2,923	3,201	3,409	9.5	6.4	14	30	25	23	21
Total Current Expenditures (in thousands)	188.9	4,421,307	4,855,811	5,312,743	9.8	9.4	7	11	9	9	9
Total Revenue Receipts (in thousands)	187.9	4,491,023	4,973,013	5,725,091	10.7	15.1	4	4	9	9	8

	Change in percent 1972-73 to 1982-83	Percent share 1982-83	Percent share 1983-84	Percent share 1984-85
Federal Revenue Receipts	-2.7	7.1	8.2	7.2
State Revenue Receipts	6.6	61.9	54.5	53.5
Local and Other Revenue Receipts	-3.9	31.0	37.4	39.3

	Percent change 1972 to 1982	1982	1983	1984	Percent change 1982 to 1983	Percent change 1983 to 1984	State's rank in percent change 1982 to 1983	State's rank in percent change 1983 to 1984	Rank 1982	Rank 1983	Rank 1984
Total Personal Income (in millions)	239.7	114,356	123,812	137,774	8.2	11.3	13	7	7	6	6
Per Capita Income	145.3	10,907	11,593	12,553	6.2	8.2	20	26	23	23	22
Population (in thousands)	38.5	10,466	10,680	10,976	2.0	2.7	9	3	7	7	6
Population Under Age 5	20.1	651,000	691,000	720,000	6.1	4.1	6	2	8	7	7

	Score change 1972 to 1982	Average score 1982	Average score 1983	Average score 1984	Percent change 1982 to 1983	Percent change 1983 to 1984	State's rank in percent change 1982 to 1983	State's rank in percent change 1983 to 1984	1982 score	1983 score	1984 score
SAT Verbal Scores	-32.0	426	423	423	-0.7	0.0	41	34	37	40	42
SAT Math Scores	20.0	463	464	467	0.2	0.6	18	20	39	39	39

	Score change 1978 to 1982	Average score 1982	Average score 1983	Average score 1984	Percent change 1982 to 1983	Percent change 1983 to 1984	State's rank in percent change 1982 to 1983	State's rank in percent change 1983 to 1984	1982 score	1983 score	1984 score
SAT Verbal Scores of Intended Education Majors	1.0	394	391	393	-0.7	0.5	38	34	36	39	42
SAT Math Scores of Intended Education Majors	2.0	414	415	424	0.2	2.1	20	18	38	39	38

	Change in percent 1972 to 1981	Percent minority enrollment 1972	Percent minority enrollment 1976	Percent minority enrollment 1981
Percentage of Minority Enrollment	4.2	28.0	29.1	32.2

	Change in percent 1965 to 1980	Percent of all students enrolled in private schools 1965	1970	1980
Percentage of Private School Enrollment	4.8	7.2	10.5	12.0

	Change in percent 1971 to 1983	1971-72	1980-81	1983-84
Graduation Rates	-4.8	70.3	63.6	65.5

	Change in percent 1980 to 1985	Percent unemployed 1980	1984	1985
Unemployment Rates	1.0	4.9	5.4	5.9

107

	Percent change 1972-73 to 1982-83	1982-83	1983-84	1984-85	Percent change 1982-83 to 1983-84	1983-84 to 1984-85	State's rank in percent change 1982-83 to 1983-84	1983-84 to 1984-85	State's Rank 1982	1983	1984
Public Elementary School Enrollment	-5.3	652,900	648,500	648,970	-0.6	0.0	23	26	11	11	11
Public Secondary School Enrollment	-0.4	400,800	402,400	400,730	0.4	-0.4	7	33	11	11	11
Public Elementary and Secondary Enrollment	-3.6	1,053,700	1,050,900	1,049,700	-0.2	-0.1	11	30	11	11	11
Numbers of Public Elementary Teachers	17.6	33,916	33,660	34,420	-0.7	2.3	30	23	10	10	10
Numbers of Public Secondary School Teachers	13.8	22,604	22,610	21,901	0.0	-3.1	21	43	14	14	15
Numbers of Public Elementary and Secondary Teachers	16.1	56,520	56,270	56,321	-0.4	0.0	24	36	10	10	12
Elementary Teachers' Salaries	116.2	17,111	18,184	21,370	6.2	17.5	28	1	40	39	27
Secondary Teachers' Salaries	107.2	17,847	18,948	20,960	6.1	10.6	26	10	41	40	34
Total Teachers' Salaries	112.2	17,412	18,505	20,494	6.2	10.7	27	10	41	39	34
Per Pupil Expenditures in ADA	195.4	2,146	2,309	2,692	7.5	16.5	31	4	45	45	42
Total Current Expenditures (in thousands)	192.7	2,437,020	2,613,777	2,911,622	7.2	11.3	20	5	15	14	13
Total Revenue Receipts (in thousands)	194.3	2,415,291	2,481,559	2,843,996	2.7	14.6	43	5	15	17	13

	Change in percent 1972-73 to 1982-83	Percent share 1982-83	1983-84	1984-85
Federal Revenue Receipts	-2.3	10.2	9.3	9.5
State Revenue Receipts	2.2	55.6	58.6	50.3
Local and Other Revenue Receipts	0.1	34.2	32.1	40.2

	Percent change 1972 to 1982	1982	1983	1984	Percent change 1982 to 1983	1983 to 1984	State's rank in percent change 1982 to 1983	1983 to 1984	Rank 1982	1983	1984
Total Personal Income (in millions)	183.9	54,011	59,551	66,779	10.2	12.2	4	4	14	13	12
Per Capita Income	142.0	9,573	10,389	11,441	8.5	10.1	7	7	37	35	35
Population (in thousands)	17.3	5,648	5,732	5,837	1.4	1.8	12	6	12	12	11
Population Under Age 5	1.2	438,000	446,000	443,000	1.8	-0.6	28	27	10	10	10

	Score change 1972 to 1982	Average score 1982	1983	1984	Percent change 1982 to 1983	1983 to 1984	State's rank in percent change 1982 to 1983	1983 to 1984	1982 score	1983 score	1984 score
SAT Verbal Scores	-11.0	394	390	392	-1.0	0.5	45	16	49	50	50
SAT Math Scores	0.0	429	428	412	-0.2	-3.7	34	51	49	49	51

	Score change 1978 to 1982	Average score 1982	1983	1984	Percent change 1982 to 1983	1983 to 1984	State's rank in percent change 1982 to 1983	1983 to 1984	1982 score	1983 score	1984 score
SAT Verbal Scores of Intended Education Majors	-3.0	366	367	374	0.2	1.9	25	18	46	48	47
SAT Math Scores of Intended Education Majors	1.0	393	392	401	-0.2	2.2	26	17	47	48	48

	Change in percent 1972 to 1981	Percent minority enrollment 1972	1976	1981
Percentage of Minority Enrollment	0.6	33.7	35.2	34.3

	Change in percent 1965 to 1980	Percent of all students enrolled in private schools 1965	1970	1980
Percentage of Private School Enrollment	4.5	2.7	5.5	7.2

	Change in percent 1971 to 1983	1971-72	1980-81	1983-84
Graduation Rates	1.1	64.8	62.8	65.9

	Change in percent 1980 to 1985	Percent unemployed 1980	1984	1985
Unemployment Rates	0.2	5.8	6.3	6.0

	Percent change 1972–73 to 1982–83	1982–83	1983–84	1984–85	Percent change 1982–83 to 1983–84	Percent change 1983–84 to 1984–85	State's rank in percent change 1982–83 to 1983–84	State's rank in percent change 1983–84 to 1984–85	State's Rank 1982	State's Rank 1983	State's Rank 1984
Public Elementary School Enrollment	-10.1	86,925	86,920	88,813	0.0	2.2	12	9	42	42	42
Public Secondary School Enrollment	-7.8	74,949	75,012	74,551	0.0	-0.6	13	36	39	39	39
Public Elementary and Secondary Enrollment	-9.0	161,874	161,932	163,364	0.0	0.8	9	13	40	40	40
Numbers of Public Elementary Teachers	23.4	4,499	4,400	4,459	-2.2	1.3	46	26	45	45	45
Numbers of Public Secondary School Teachers	7.2	3,727	3,673	3,682	-1.4	0.2	34	27	42	42	42
Numbers of Public Elementary and Secondary Teachers	16.6	8,226	8,073	8,141	-1.8	0.8	42	28	42	42	42
Elementary Teachers' Salaries	138.2	25,335	25,300	24,628	-0.1	-2.6	50	50	4	7	12
Secondary Teachers' Salaries	131.2	24,024	24,000	24,628	0.0	2.6	50	44	8	11	17
Total Teachers' Salaries	135.4	24,796	24,357	24,628	-1.7	1.1	51	46	5	10	15
Per Pupil Expenditures in ADA	200.0	3,347	3,982	3,596	18.9	-9.6	1	51	14	7	17
Total Current Expenditures (in thousands)	135.7	541,100	621,200	578,400	14.8	-6.8	2	51	40	39	42
Total Revenue Receipts (in thousands)	115.2	551,100	634,700	580,100	15.1	-8.6	2	51	40	39	42

	Change in percent 1972–73 to 1982–83	Percent share 1982–83	Percent share 1983–84	Percent share 1984–85
Federal Revenue Receipts	1.4	9.9	9.0	8.9
State Revenue Receipts	1.3	89.8	90.7	90.8
Local and Other Revenue Receipts	-2.7	0.3	0.3	0.3

	Percent change 1972 to 1982	1982	1983	1984	Percent change 1982 to 1983	Percent change 1983 to 1984	State's rank in percent change 1982 to 1983	State's rank in percent change 1983 to 1984	Rank 1982	Rank 1983	Rank 1984
Total Personal Income (in millions)	176.0	11,589	12,396	13,255	6.9	6.9	25	44	38	38	38
Per Capita Income	127.1	11,614	12,115	12,761	4.3	5.3	39	48	15	15	17
Population (in thousands)	20.0	997	1,023	1,039	2.6	1.5	3	11	39	39	39
Population Under Age 5	13.5	84,000	89,000	90,000	5.9	1.1	8	9	39	39	39

	Score change 1972 to 1982	Average score 1982	Average score 1983	Average score 1984	Percent change 1982 to 1983	Percent change 1983 to 1984	State's rank in percent change 1982 to 1983	State's rank in percent change 1983 to 1984	1982 score	1983 score	1984 score
SAT Verbal Scores	-41.0	392	393	395	0.2	0.5	18	16	50	49	48
SAT Math Scores	-23.0	465	471	474	1.2	0.6	3	20	35	32	31

	Score change 1978 to 1982	Average score 1982	Average score 1983	Average score 1984	Percent change 1982 to 1983	Percent change 1983 to 1984	State's rank in percent change 1982 to 1983	State's rank in percent change 1983 to 1984	1982 score	1983 score	1984 score
SAT Verbal Scores of Intended Education Majors	-16.0	365	359	366	-1.6	1.9	44	18	47	50	50
SAT Math Scores of Intended Education Majors	-12.0	418	414	429	-0.9	3.6	39	10	34	41	32

	Change in percent 1972 to 1981	Percent minority enrollment 1972	Percent minority enrollment 1976	Percent minority enrollment 1981
Percentage of Minority Enrollment	0.0	0.0	79.5	75.2

	Change in percent 1965 to 1980	Percent of all students enrolled in private schools 1965	Percent of all students enrolled in private schools 1970	Percent of all students enrolled in private schools 1980
Percentage of Private School Enrollment	2.8	15.6	10.9	18.4

	Change in percent 1971 to 1983	1971–72	1980–81	1983–84
Graduation Rates	-5.7	87.9	81.5	82.2

	Change in percent 1980 to 1985	Percent unemployed 1980	Percent unemployed 1984	Percent unemployed 1985
Unemployment Rates	-0.1	4.6	5.6	4.5

109

SUMMARY TABLE 14. Idaho

	Percent change 1972-73 to 1982-83	1982-83	1983-84	1984-85	Percent change 1982-83 to 1983-84	1983-84 to 1984-85	State's rank in percent change 1982-83 to 1983-84	1983-84 to 1984-85	State's Rank 1982	1983	1984
Public Elementary School Enrollment	28.7	115,237	115,550	118,647	0.2	2.6	8	8	39	39	39
Public Secondary School Enrollment	-6.5	90,587	90,792	92,053	0.2	1.4	10	15	38	38	38
Public Elementary and Secondary Enrollment	11.0	205,824	206,342	210,700	0.2	2.1	7	8	39	39	38
Numbers of Public Elementary Teachers	41.0	5,090	5,120	5,315	0.5	3.8	11	16	42	41	42
Numbers of Public Secondary School Teachers	10.6	4,720	4,780	4,845	1.2	1.3	11	18	38	38	38
Numbers of Public Elementary and Secondary Teachers	24.8	9,810	9,900	10,160	0.9	2.6	12	12	39	39	39
Elementary Teachers' Salaries	125.5	16,920	17,925	18,970	5.9	5.8	29	35	43	42	44
Secondary Teachers' Salaries	133.9	18,300	19,400	20,500	6.0	5.6	27	33	36	37	38
Total Teachers' Salaries	129.2	17,585	18,640	19,700	5.9	5.6	28	36	38	38	42
Per Pupil Expenditures in ADA	200.0	2,106	2,219	2,290	5.3	3.1	39	41	46	47	48
Total Current Expenditures (in thousands)	197.9	450,000	475,140	499,130	5.5	5.0	32	34	43	43	44
Total Revenue Receipts (in thousands)	197.7	428,550	468,000	502,000	9.2	7.2	8	22	44	44	43

	Change in percent 1972-73 to 1982-83	Percent share 1982-83	1983-84	1984-85
Federal Revenue Receipts	-5.2	6.9	7.1	6.8
State Revenue Receipts	23.2	62.6	64.1	64.7
Local and Other Revenue Receipts	-18.1	30.4	28.8	28.5

	Percent change 1972 to 1982	1982	1983	1984	Percent change 1982 to 1983	1983 to 1984	State's rank in percent change 1982 to 1983	1983 to 1984	1982	Rank 1983	1984
Total Personal Income (in millions)	199.8	8,713	9,429	10,181	8.2	7.9	13	40	44	44	44
Per Capita Income	137.0	8,937	9,534	10,174	6.6	6.7	16	44	43	43	45
Population (in thousands)	26.5	977	989	1,001	1.2	1.2	14	14	40	40	40
Population Under Age 5	41.2	96,000	99,000	96,000	3.1	-3.0	17	49	38	38	38

	Score change 1972 to 1982	Average score 1982	1983	1984	Percent change 1982 to 1983	1983 to 1984	State's rank in percent change 1982 to 1983	1983 to 1984	1982 score	1983 score	1984 score
SAT Verbal Scores	-13.0	482	479	480	-0.6	0.2	37	26	11	14	14
SAT Math Scores	-3.0	513	513	512	0.0	-0.1	25	40	19	17	20

	Score change 1978 to 1982	Average score 1982	1983	1984	Percent change 1982 to 1983	1983 to 1984	State's rank in percent change 1982 to 1983	1983 to 1984	1982 score	1983 score	1984 score
SAT Verbal Scores of Intended Education Majors	-10.0	426	474	448	11.2	-5.4	1	50	17	3	11
SAT Math Scores of Intended Education Majors	9.0	450	478	463	6.2	-3.1	4	49	17	9	16

	Change in percent 1972 to 1981	Percent minority enrollment 1972	1976	1981
Percentage of Minority Enrollment	3.7	4.5	5.7	8.2

	Change in percent 1965 to 1980	Percent of all students enrolled in private schools 1965	1970	1980
Percentage of Private School Enrollment	-2.3	5.1	6.1	2.8

	Change in percent 1971 to 1983	1971-72	1980-81	1983-84
Graduation Rates	06.1	84.0	76.6	77.9

	Change in percent 1980 to 1985	Percent unemployed 1980	1984	1985
Unemployment Rates	1.3	8.2	8.4	9.5

110

	Percent change 1972-73 to 1982-83	1982-83	1983-84	1984-85	Percent change 1982-83 to 1983-84	1983-84 to 1984-85	State's rank in percent change 1982-83 to 1983-84	1983-84 to 1984-85	State's Rank 1982	1983	1984
Public Elementary School Enrollment	-12.5	1,286,858	1,271,447	1,266,937	-1.1	-0.3	32	34	4	4	4
Public Secondary School Enrollment	-33.5	588,912	572,261	570,121	-2.8	-0.3	41	31	8	8	8
Public Elementary and Secondary Enrollment	-20.3	1,875,770	1,843,708	1,837,058	-1.7	-0.3	40	36	4	4	4
Numbers of Public Elementary Teachers	7.8	67,627	66,374	65,620	-1.8	-1.1	42	41	4	4	4
Numbers of Public Secondary School Teachers	22.3	35,959	34,682	34,877	-3.6	0.5	44	22	8	8	9
Numbers of Public Elementary and Secondary Teachers	-5.1	103,586	101,056	100,497	-2.4	-0.5	45	38	5	5	5
Elementary Teachers' Salaries	102.4	21,400	22,324	25,759	4.3	15.3	40	3	13	18	8
Secondary Teachers' Salaries	99.6	24,036	25,297	27,842	5.2	10.0	33	11	7	6	7
Total Teachers' Salaries	102.0	22,315	23,345	25,829	4.6	10.6	37	11	11	12	10
Per Pupil Expenditures in ADA	185.5	3,018	3,397	3,517	12.5	3.5	2	40	22	16	18
Total Current Expenditures (in thousands)	104.6	5,356,892	5,892,580	6,011,380	10.0	2.0	6	46	6	6	6
Total Revenue Receipts (in thousands)	93.0	6,117,657	6,423,606	6,614,303	5.0	2.9	32	41	5	5	5

	Change in percent 1972-73 to 1982-83	Percent share 1982-83	1983-84	1984-85
Federal Revenue Receipts	2.5	8.5	7.6	6.7
State Revenue Receipts	1.1	38.0	37.7	37.6
Local and Other Revenue Receipts	-3.7	53.4	54.6	55.7

	Percent change 1972 to 1982	1982	1983	1984	Percent change 1982 to 1983	1983 to 1984	State's rank in percent change 1982 to 1983	1983 to 1984	Rank 1982	1983	1984
Total Personal Income (in millions)	140.8	138,460	142,444	158,024	2.8	10.9	46	10	4	4	4
Per Capita Income	136.8	12,091	12,401	13,728	2.5	10.7	45	5	11	12	10
Population (in thousands)	1.7	11,466	11,486	11,511	0.1	0.2	43	42	5	5	5
Population Under Age 5	-3.7	881,000	896,000	885,000	1.7	-1.2	29	32	4	4	4

	Score change 1972 to 1982	Average score 1982	1983	1984	Percent change 1982 to 1983	1983 to 1984	State's rank in percent change 1982 to 1983	1983 to 1984	1982 score	1983 score	1984 score
SAT Verbal Scores	-13.0	462	462	463	0.0	0.2	29	26	24	25	24
SAT Math Scores	8.0	515	517	518	0.3	0.1	15	36	15	16	16

	Score change 1978 to 1982	Average score 1982	1983	1984	Percent change 1982 to 1983	1983 to 1984	State's rank in percent change 1982 to 1983	1983 to 1984	1982 score	1983 score	1984 score
SAT Verbal Scores of Intended Education Majors	1.0	423	420	424	-0.7	0.9	38	31	19	25	26
SAT Math Scores of Intended Education Majors	-4.0	455	452	459	-0.6	1.5	33	25	11	16	19

	Change in percent 1972 to 1981	Percent minority enrollment 1972	1976	1981
Percentage of Minority Enrollment	3.7	24.9	25.4	28.6

	Change in percent 1965 to 1980	Percent of all students enrolled in private schools 1965	1970	1980
Percentage of Private School Enrollment	-5.9	20.9	17.1	15.0

	Change in percent 1971 to 1983	1971-72	1980-81	1983-84
Graduation Rates	0.2	76.9	71.3	77.1

	Change in percent 1980 to 1985	Percent unemployed 1980	1984	1985
Unemployment Rates	0.8	7.3	10.6	8.1

	Percent change 1972-73 to 1982-83	1982-83	1983-84	1984-85	Percent change 1982-83 to 1983-84	1983-84 to 1984-85	State's rank in percent change 1982-83 to 1983-84	1983-84 to 1984-85	State's Rank 1982	1983	1984
Public Elementary School Enrollment	-19.3	523,733	515,914	505,758	-1.4	-1.9	36	44	17	17	17
Public Secondary School Enrollment	-15.7	475,809	468,176	468,100	-1.6	0.0	29	22	9	9	9
Public Elementary and Secondary Enrollment	-17.6	999,542	984,090	973,858	-1.5	-1.0	37	42	12	12	12
Numbers of Public Elementary Teachers	-3.1	25,251	24,813	24,811	-1.7	0.0	41	33	15	15	16
Numbers of Public Secondary School Teachers	-3.1	25,191	24,643	24,835	-2.1	0.7	40	20	11	11	11
Numbers of Public Elementary and Secondary Teachers	-3.1	50,442	49,456	49,646	-1.9	0.3	43	34	14	13	14
Elementary Teachers' Salaries	101.1	19,693	21,147	22,652	7.3	7.1	17	27	24	22	22
Secondary Teachers' Salaries	98.4	20,554	22,031	23,544	7.1	6.8	17	25	25	22	22
Total Teachers' Salaries	99.7	20,123	21,587	23,089	7.2	6.9	17	27	23	22	22
Per Pupil Expenditures in ADA	204.0	2,532	2,730	2,638	7.8	-3.3	26	50	37	37	44
Total Current Expenditures (in thousands)	131.7	2,554,628	2,702,700	2,702,700	5.7	0.0	30	48	13	13	16
Total Revenue Receipts (in thousands)	115.2	2,557,939	2,557,939	2,855,000	0.0	11.6	50	10	13	15	12

	Change in percent 1972-73 to 1982-83	Percent share 1982-83	1983-84	1984-85
Federal Revenue Receipts	1.2	6.3	5.7	4.2
State Revenue Receipts	27.1	58.6	53.6	53.4
Local and Other Revenue Receipts	-28.4	35.1	40.7	42.4

	Percent change 1972 to 1982	1982	1983	1984	Percent change 1982 to 1983	1983 to 1984	State's rank in percent change 1982 to 1983	1983 to 1984	1982	Rank 1983	1984
Total Personal Income (in millions)	141.2	54,840	57,916	64,872	5.6	12.2	33	4	12	14	14
Per Capita Income	133.5	9,994	10,570	11,799	5.7	11.6	24	3	35	34	31
Population (in thousands)	3.3	5,482	5,479	5,498	0.0	0.3	45	40	14	14	14
Population Under Age 5	6.5	420,000	420,000	409,000	0.0	-2.6	43	46	11	12	12

	Score change 1972 to 1982	Average score 1982	1983	1984	Percent change 1982 to 1983	1983 to 1984	State's rank in percent change 1982 to 1983	1983 to 1984	1982 score	1983 score	1984 score
SAT Verbal Scores	-28.0	407	410	410	0.7	0.0	8	34	46	46	46
SAT Math Scores	-18.0	453	454	454	0.2	0.0	18	38	45	46	46

	Score change 1978 to 1982	Average score 1982	1983	1984	Percent change 1982 to 1983	1983 to 1984	State's rank in percent change 1982 to 1983	1983 to 1984	1982 score	1983 score	1984 score
SAT Verbal Scores of Intended Education Majors	-4.0	386	387	394	0.2	1.8	25	20	43	42	41
SAT Math Scores of Intended Education Majors	-5.0	419	420	426	0.2	1.4	20	27	33	32	37

	Change in percent 1972 to 1981	Percent minority enrollment 1972	1976	1981
Percentage of Minority Enrollment	0.7	11.3	11.4	12.0

	Change in percent 1965 to 1980	Percent of all students enrolled in private schools 1965	1970	1980
Percentage of Private School Enrollment	-2.5	11.2	10.2	8.7

	Change in percent 1971 to 1983	1971-72	1980-81	1983-84
Graduation Rates	2.7	75.6	74.0	78.3

	Change in percent 1980 to 1985	Percent unemployed 1980	1984	1985
Unemployment Rates	1.1	8.6	9.2	9.7

	Percent change 1972-73 to 1982-83	1982-83	1983-84	1984-85	Percent change 1982-83 to 1983-84	1983-84 to 1984-85	State's rank in percent change 1982-83 to 1983-84	1983-84 to 1984-85	State's Rank 1982	1983	1984
Public Elementary School Enrollment	-26.4	268,213	262,581	262,733	-2.1	0.0	45	26	30	30	30
Public Secondary School Enrollment	-19.3	237,389	232,385	227,669	-2.1	-2.0	35	42	23	23	23
Public Elementary and Secondary Enrollment	-23.2	505,582	494,966	490,402	-2.1	-0.9	41	40	28	28	28
Numbers of Public Elementary Teachers	-4.2	14,452	14,264	14,002	-1.3	-1.8	37	45	30	30	31
Numbers of Public Secondary School Teachers	4.6	16,362	16,422	16,334	0.3	-0.5	18	31	21	21	21
Numbers of Public Elementary and Secondary Teachers	0.2	30,814	30,686	30,336	-0.4	-1.1	24	44	27	27	27
Elementary Teachers' Salaries	96.7	18,542	19,366	20,135	4.4	3.9	39	40	30	33	35
Secondary Teachers' Salaries	92.9	19,892	20,808	21,629	4.6	3.9	37	40	29	30	30
Total Teachers' Salaries	94.9	19,257	20,140	20,934	4.5	3.9	38	40	29	29	32
Per Pupil Expenditures in ADA	197.7	3,064	3,239	3,409	5.7	5.2	36	34	19	22	21
Total Current Expenditures (in thousands)	122.4	1,548,288	1,602,882	1,666,376	3.5	3.9	43	38	27	27	29
Total Revenue Receipts (in thousands)	111.2	1,637,012	1,694,961	1,687,316	3.5	-0.4	39	46	25	25	28

	Change in percent 1972-73 to 1982-83	Percent share 1982-83	1983-84	1984-85
Federal Revenue Receipts	2.5	7.3	5.4	5.5
State Revenue Receipts	7.5	42.1	41.0	42.0
Local and Other Revenue Receipts	-10.0	50.6	53.7	52.6

	Percent change 1972 to 1982	1982	1983	1984	Percent change 1982 to 1983	1983 to 1984	State's rank in percent change 1982 to 1983	1983 to 1984	Rank 1982	1983	1984
Total Personal Income (in millions)	142.2	31,330	31,071	35,177	-0.8	13.2	50	1	27	28	28
Per Capita Income	138.6	10,754	10,697	12,090	-0.5	13.0	49	1	25	32	30
Population (in thousands)	1.5	2,906	2,905	2,910	0.0	0.1	45	44	28	29	29
Population Under Age 5	1.8	227,000	226,000	220,000	-0.4	-2.6	50	46	28	28	29

	Score change 1972 to 1982	Average score 1982	1983	1984	Percent change 1982 to 1983	1983 to 1984	State's rank in percent change 1982 to 1983	1983 to 1984	State's rank in 1982 score	1983 score	1984 score
SAT Verbal Scores	-10.0	516	520	519	0.7	-0.1	8	43	2	1	2
SAT Math Scores	-7.0	572	573	570	0.1	-0.5	24	46	1	1	1

	Score change 1978 to 1982	Average score 1982	1983	1984	Percent change 1982 to 1983	1983 to 1984	State's rank in percent change 1982 to 1983	1983 to 1984	State's rank in 1982 score	1983 score	1984 score
SAT Verbal Scores of Intended Education Majors	19.0	473	487	477	2.9	-2.0	8	46	2	2	5
SAT Math Scores of Intended Education Majors	-8.0	478	514	545	7.5	6.0	2	5	3	2	1

	Change in percent 1972 to 1981	Percent minority enrollment 1972	1976	1981
Percentage of Minority Enrollment	1.3	2.8	3.2	4.1

	Change in percent 1965 to 1980	Percent of all students enrolled in private schools 1965	1970	1980
Percentage of Private School Enrollment	-4.4	3.8	10.3	9.4

	Change in percent 1971 to 1983	1971-72	1980-81	1983-84
Graduation Rates	-1.0	89.0	83.8	88.0

	Change in percent 1980 to 1985	Percent unemployed 1980	1984	1985
Unemployment Rates	4.1	5.1	8.3	9.2

	Percent change 1972-73 to 1982-83	1982-83	1983-84	1984-85	Percent change 1982-83 to 1983-84	Percent change 1983-84 to 1984-85	State's rank in percent change 1982-83 to 1983-84	State's rank in percent change 1983-84 to 1984-85	State's Rank 1982	1983	1984
Public Elementary School Enrollment	-11.5	248,496	249,000	253,789	0.2	1.9	8	11	32	32	32
Public Secondary School Enrollment	-25.0	158,578	155,500	152,033	-1.9	-2.2	33	44	33	33	34
Public Elementary and Secondary Enrollment	-17.4	407,074	404,500	405,822	-0.6	0.3	20	20	33	33	33
Numbers of Public Elementary Teachers	11.6	14,375	14,320	14,723	-0.3	2.8	24	22	31	29	29
Numbers of Public Secondary School Teachers	-7.6	11,677	11,482	11,537	-1.6	0.4	36	26	28	29	29
Numbers of Public Elementary and Secondary Teachers	2.1	26,052	25,802	26,260	-0.9	1.7	33	19	29	29	29
Elementary Teachers' Salaries	118.5	18,146	19,507	21,110	7.5	8.2	16	18	31	28	29
Secondary Teachers' Salaries	115.1	18,317	19,690	21,290	7.4	8.1	14	18	35	34	31
Total Teachers' Salaries	-6.5	18,231	19,598	21,208	7.4	8.2	16	19	36	33	30
Per Pupil Expenditures in ADA	231.6	3,096	3,361	3,668	8.5	9.1	18	20	18	18	16
Total Current Expenditures (in thousands)	162.1	1,297,833	1,396,455	1,532,211	7.6	9.7	17	9	31	31	30
Total Revenue Receipts (in thousands)	164.7	1,346,636	1,409,256	1,511,697	4.6	7.2	35	22	31	31	31

	Change in percent 1972-73 to 1982-83	Percent share 1982-83	1983-84	1984-85
Federal Revenue Receipts	-3.2	4.8	5.0	4.6
State Revenue Receipts	17.0	44.4	44.2	45.1
Local and Other Revenue Receipts	-13.8	50.8	50.8	50.4

	Percent change 1972 to 1982	1982	1983	1984	Percent change 1982 to 1983	Percent change 1983 to 1984	State's rank in percent change 1982 to 1983	State's rank in percent change 1983 to 1984	Rank 1982	1983	1984
Total Personal Income (in millions)	168.7	28,289	29,351	32,472	3.7	10.6	44	13	29	30	30
Per Capita Income	151.7	11,717	12,102	13,319	3.2	10.0	43	8	14	17	12
Population (in thousands)	6.7	2,408	2,425	2,438	0.7	0.5	27	31	32	32	32
Population Under Age 5	13.4	195,000	199,000	199,000	2.0	0.0	27	16	32	32	32

	Score change 1972 to 1982	Average score 1982	1983	1984	Percent change 1982 to 1983	Percent change 1983 to 1984	State's rank in percent change 1982 to 1983	State's rank in percent change 1983 to 1984	1982 score	1983 score	1984 score
SAT Verbal Scores	-7.0	500	498	502	-0.4	0.8	35	5	4	5	4
SAT Math Scores	3.0	545	540	549	-0.9	1.6	46	5	6	6	4

	Score change 1978 to 1982	Average score 1982	1983	1984	Percent change 1982 to 1983	Percent change 1983 to 1984	State's rank in percent change 1982 to 1983	State's rank in percent change 1983 to 1984	1982 score	1983 score	1984 score
SAT Verbal Scores of Intended Education Majors	8.0	455	453	459	-0.4	1.3	35	23	3	6	9
SAT Math Scores of Intended Education Majors	-9.0	471	500	506	6.1	1.2	6	29	7	4	4

	Change in percent 1972 to 1981	Percent minority enrollment 1972	1976	1981
Percentage of Minority Enrollment	2.4	10.3	10.7	12.7

	Change in percent 1965 to 1980	Percent of all students enrolled in private schools 1965	1970	1980
Percentage of Private School Enrollment	-1.7	9.2	7.4	7.5

	Change in percent 1971 to 1983	1971-72	1980-81	1983-84
Graduation Rates	0.0	82.5	80.0	82.5

	Change in percent 1980 to 1985	Percent unemployed 1980	1984	1985
Unemployment Rates	1.0	4.0	5.5	5.0

114

	Percent change 1972-73 to 1982-83	1982-83	1983-84	1984-85	Percent change 1982-83 to 1983-84	1983-84 to 1984-85	State's rank in percent change 1982-83 to 1983-84	1983-84 to 1984-85	State's Rank 1982	1983	1984
Public Elementary School Enrollment	-3.9	434,426	431,243	427,966	-0.7	-0.7	25	38	19	19	19
Public Secondary School Enrollment	-17.0	215,942	216,171	216,455	0.1	0.1	11	21	26	25	25
Public Elementary and Secondary Enrollment	-8.8	650,368	647,414	644,421	-0.4	-0.4	14	37	23	23	23
Numbers of Public Elementary Teachers	7.9	20,931	20,778	21,000	-0.7	1.0	30	29	19	18	20
Numbers of Public Secondary School Teachers	-0.6	11,306	11,222	11,400	-0.7	1.5	29	16	31	31	30
Numbers of Public Elementary and Secondary Teachers	2.5	32,237	32,000	32,400	-0.7	1.2	30	23	25	26	26
Elementary Teachers' Salaries	134.5	17,929	19,340	20,095	7.8	3.9	13	40	33	34	36
Secondary Teachers' Salaries	136.5	19,270	20,680	20,110	7.3	-2.7	15	50	31	32	43
Total Teachers' Salaries	136.1	18,385	19,780	20,100	7.5	1.6	15	45	33	32	38
Per Pupil Expenditures in ADA	213.3	2,368	2,550	2,792	7.6	9.4	29	17	42	42	41
Total Current Expenditures (in thousands)	175.4	1,508,400	1,618,300	1,756,220	7.2	8.5	20	21	28	26	25
Total Revenue Receipts (in thousands)	162.6	1,494,500	1,617,000	1,690,500	8.1	4.5	10	38	28	28	27

	Change in percent 1972-73 to 1982-83	Percent share 1982-83	1983-84	1984-85
Federal Revenue Receipts	-4.2	10.7	10.5	10.1
State Revenue Receipts	15.2	70.5	70.9	68.6
Local and Other Revenue Receipts	-11.1	18.7	18.6	21.2

	Percent change 1972 to 1982	1982	1983	1984	Percent change 1982 to 1983	1983 to 1984	State's rank in percent change 1982 to 1983	1983 to 1984	Rank 1982	1983	1984
Total Personal Income (in millions)	171.6	32,794	34,899	38,622	6.5	10.9	27	10	26	26	26
Per Capita Income	147.7	8,893	9,396	10,374	5.6	10.4	26	6	45	45	42
Population (in thousands)	9.9	3,692	3,714	3,723	0.5	0.2	31	42	23	23	23
Population Under Age 5	2.5	284,000	286,000	277,000	0.7	-3.1	40	50	23	23	24

	Score change 1972 to 1982	Average score 1982	1983	1984	Percent change 1982 to 1983	1983 to 1984	State's rank in percent change 1982 to 1983	1983 to 1984	1982 score	1983 score	1984 score
SAT Verbal Scores	-2.0	475	475	479	0.0	0.8	29	5	17	15	16
SAT Math Scores	-1.0	510	513	518	0.5	0.9	9	10	21	17	16

	Score change 1978 to 1982	Average score 1982	1983	1984	Percent change 1982 to 1983	1983 to 1984	State's rank in percent change 1982 to 1983	1983 to 1984	1982 score	1983 score	1984 score
SAT Verbal Scores of Intended Education Majors	34.0	444	431	431	-2.9	0/0	50	37	5	17	22
SAT Math Scores of Intended Education Majors	12.0	450	441	449	-2.0	1.8	45	20	17	23	24

	Change in percent 1972 to 1981	Percent minority enrollment 1972	1976	1981
Percentage of Minority Enrollment	-0.4	9.5	10.1	9.1

	Change in percent 1965 to 1980	Percent of all students enrolled in private schools 1965	1970	1980
Percentage of Private School Enrollment	-2.9	12.3	10.4	9.4

	Change in percent 1971 to 1983	1971-72	1980-81	1983-84
Graduation Rates	-0.6	69.0	66.7	68.4

	Change in percent 1980 to 1985	Percent unemployed 1980	1984	1985
Unemployment Rates	0.9	7.5	10.4	8.4

115

SUMMARY TABLE 20. Louisiana

	Percent change 1972-73 to 1982-83	1982-83	1983-84	1984-85	Percent change 1982-83 to 1983-84	Percent change 1983-84 to 1984-85	State's rank in percent change 1982-83 to 1983-84	State's rank in percent change 1983-84 to 1984-85	State's Rank 1982	1983	1984
Public Elementary School Enrollment	7.6	556,000	555,390	579,900	-0.1	4.4	14	1	15	15	14
Public Secondary School Enrollment	-33.1	219,700	213,060	215,900	-3.0	1.3	43	16	25	26	26
Public Elementary and Secondary Enrollment	-8.5	775,700	768,450	795,800	-0.9	3.5	24	3	18	18	16
Numbers of Public Elementary Teachers	10.6	26,480	26,510	27,580	0.1	4.0	16	14	14	13	13
Numbers of Public Secondary School Teachers	1.2	15,980	15,110	14,140	-5.4	-6.4	49	47	22	23	24
Numbers of Public Elementary and Secondary Teachers	6.2	42,460	41,620	41,720	-2.0	0.2	44	35	17	17	17
Elementary Teachers' Salaries	118.1	18,120	18,700	19,400	3.2	3.7	43	42	32	37	41
Secondary Teachers' Salaries	116.7	18,915	19,615	20,210	3.7	3.0	40	43	33	35	40
Total Teachers' Salaries	118.0	18,420	19,100	19,690	3.6	3.0	40	43	31	36	43
Per Pupil Expenditures in ADA	172.5	2,718	2,821	2,821	3.7	0.0	47	45	32	34	38
Total Current Expenditures (in thousands)	142.3	2,078,800	2,130,900	2,213,500	2.5	3.8	48	39	19	19	20
Total Revenue Receipts (in thousands)	140.6	2,075,130	2,105,740	2,347,200	1.4	11.4	47	12	19	20	19

	Change in percent 1972-73 to 1982-83	Percent share 1982-83	1983-84	1984-85
Federal Revenue Receipts	-4.3	9.4	8.8	9.6
State Revenue Receipts	-0.1	55.9	59.4	53.4
Local and Other Revenue Receipts	4.5	34.7	31.8	36.9

	Percent change 1972 to 1982	1982	1983	1984	Percent change 1982 to 1983	Percent change 1983 to 1984	State's rank in percent change 1982 to 1983	State's rank in percent change 1983 to 1984	Rank 1982	1983	1984
Total Personal Income (in millions)	235.1	44,652	45,540	48,417	2.0	6.3	48	47	20	21	22
Per Capita Income	189.0	10,211	10,262	10,850	0.4	5.7	48	46	32	36	37
Population (in thousands)	15.9	4,383	4,438	4,462	1.2	0.5	14	31	18	18	18
Population Under Age 5	13.6	392,000	407,000	405,000	3.8	-0.4	14	26	13	13	13

	Score change 1972 to 1982	Average score 1982	1983	1984	Percent change 1982 to 1983	Percent change 1983 to 1984	State's rank in percent change 1982 to 1983	State's rank in percent change 1983 to 1984	1982 score	1983 score	1984 score
SAT Verbal Scores	-14.0	470	469	472	-0.2	0.6	33	8	18	18	18
SAT Math Scores	-21.0	505	502	508	-0.5	1.1	40	8	25	27	25

	Score change 1978 to 1982	Average score 1982	1983	1984	Percent change 1982 to 1983	Percent change 1983 to 1984	State's rank in percent change 1982 to 1983	State's rank in percent change 1983 to 1984	1982 score	1983 score	1984 score
SAT Verbal Scores of Intended Education Majors	39.0	432	423	419	-2.0	-0.9	47	44	12	23	27
SAT Math Scores of Intended Education Majors	30.0	446	449	451	0.6	0.4	19	37	21	21	23

	Change in percent 1972 to 1981	Percent minority enrollment 1972	1976	1981
Percentage of Minority Enrollment	2.4	41.0	41.9	43.4

	Change in percent 1965 to 1980	Percent of all students enrolled in private schools 1965	1970	1980
Percentage of Private School Enrollment	1.9	15.1	15.8	17.0

	Change in percent 1971 to 1983	1971-72	1980-81	1983-84
Graduation Rates	-9.7	66.9	63.7	57.2

	Change in percent 1980 to 1985	Percent unemployed 1980	1984	1985
Unemployment Rates	5.7	6.2	10.4	11.9

	Percent change 1972-73 to 1982-83	1982-83	1983-84	1984-85	Percent change 1982-83 to 1983-84	1983-84 to 1984-85	State's rank in percent change 1982-83 to 1983-84	1983-84 to 1984-85	State's Rank 1982	1983	1984
Public Elementary School Enrollment	-17.2	146,848	144,500	144,136	-1.6	-0.2	40	32	38	38	37
Public Secondary School Enrollment	-7.0	56,138	62,300	63,703	11.0	2.2	1	12	43	43	43
Public Elementary and Secondary Enrollment	-14.3	211,986	207,000	207,839	-2.3	0.4	44	17	38	38	39
Numbers of Public Elementary Teachers	14.8	7,778	7,773	8,187	0.0	5.3	18	8	38	38	37
Numbers of Public Secondary School Teachers	0.6	4,499	4,500	4,323	0.0	-3.9	21	44	40	40	40
Numbers of Public Elementary and Secondary Teachers	9.2	12,277	12,273	12,510	0.0	1.9	20	17	38	38	38
Elementary Teachers' Salaries	76.0	15,755	16,839	17,849	6.8	5.9	25	34	48	47	49
Secondary Teachers' Salaries	76.3	17,073	18,171	19,238	6.4	5.8	24	32	46	45	48
Total Teachers' Salaries	75.7	16,248	17,328	18,329	6.6	5.7	24	35	48	48	49
Per Pupil Expenditures in ADA	214.1	2,624	2,829	3,038	7.8	7.3	26	25	35	33	33
Total Current Expenditures (in thousands)	147.1	560,262	592,554	639,740	5.7	7.9	30	24	39	40	39
Total Revenue Receipts (in thousands)	154.3	549,260	580,554	624,740	5.7	7.6	29	20	41	41	39

	Change in percent 1972-73 to 1982-83	Percent share 1982-83	1983-84	1984-85
Federal Revenue Receipts	0.8	10.1	7.8	7.6
State Revenue Receipts	15.2	49.7	50.9	51.0
Local and Other Revenue Receipts	-16.0	40.2	41.3	41.4

	Percent change 1972 to 1982	1982	1983	1984	Percent change 1982 to 1983	1983 to 1984	State's rank in percent change 1982 to 1983	1983 to 1984	Rank 1982	1983	1984
Total Personal Income (in millions)	166.9	10,261	11,298	12,349	10.1	9.3	5	27	40	40	40
Per Capita Income	143.7	9,031	9,861	10,678	9.1	8.2	4	26	42	39	40
Population (in thousands)	9.5	1,136	1,146	1,156	0.8	0.8	25	22	38	38	38
Population Under Age 5	-3.6	81,000	82,000	82,000	1.2	0.0	35	16	40	40	40

	Score change 1972 to 1982	Average score 1982	1983	1984	Percent change 1982 to 1983	1983 to 1984	State's rank in percent change 1982 to 1983	1983 to 1984	1982 score	1983 score	1984 score
SAT Verbal Scores	-24.0	427	427	429	0.0	0.4	29	19	36	35	35
SAT Math Scores	-17.0	463	464	463	0.2	-0.2	18	42	39	39	42

	Score change 1978 to 1982	Average score 1982	1983	1984	Percent change 1982 to 1983	1983 to 1984	State's rank in percent change 1982 to 1983	1983 to 1984	1982 score	1983 score	1984 score
SAT Verbal Scores of Intended Education Majors	-9.0	389	387	400	-0.5	3.3	36	13	39	42	36
SAT Math Scores of Intended Education Majors	-12.0	417	415	428	-0.4	3.1	28	11	35	39	34

	Change in percent 1972 to 1981	Percent minority enrollment 1972	1976	1981
Percentage of Minority Enrollment	0.2	0.7	0.9	0.9

	Change in percent 1965 to 1980	Percent of all students enrolled in private schools 1965	1970	1980
Percentage of Private School Enrollment	-5.0	12.3	5.9	7.3

	Change in percent 1971 to 1983	1971-72	1980-81	1983-84
Graduation Rates	-4.1	80.8	71.6	76.7

	Change in percent 1980 to 1985	Percent unemployed 1980	1984	1985
Unemployment Rates	-1.1	8.0	7.3	6.9

	Percent change 1972-73 to 1982-83	1982-83	1983-84	1984-85	Percent change 1982-83 to 1983-84	1983-84 to 1984-85	State's rank in percent change 1982-83 to 1983-84	1983-84 to 1984-85	State's Rank 1982	1983	1984
Public Elementary School Enrollment	-32.6	344,147	335,757	328,320	-2.4	-2.2	47	46	25	26	26
Public Secondary School Enrollment	-13.6	355,054	346,398	345,443	-2.4	-0.2	37	28	15	14	15
Public Elementary and Secondary Enrollment	-24.1	699,201	682,155	673,763	-2.4	-1.2	45	43	22	21	22
Numbers of Public Elementary Teachers	16.2	17,344	17,318	17,370	-0.1	0.3	19	32	27	27	27
Numbers of Public Secondary School Teachers	-5.2	20,149	20,119	20,324	-0.1	1.0	25	19	18	17	17
Numbers of Public Elementary and Secondary Teachers	-10.8	37,493	37,437	37,694	-0.1	0.6	21	30	21	21	20
Elementary Teachers' Salaries	99.6	21,780	23,052	24,742	5.8	7.3	32	23	11	11	11
Secondary Teachers' Salaries	102.7	23,142	24,471	26,265	5.7	7.3	31	20	11	10	10
Total Teachers' Salaries	104.2	22,786	24,095	25,861	5.7	7.3	31	23	10	11	9
Per Pupil Expenditures in ADA	193.4	3,488	3,720	4,101	6.6	10.2	33	12	9	11	8
Total Current Expenditures (in thousands)	75.2	2,350,020	2,416,618	2,627,891	2.8	8.7	46	20	17	18	17
Total Revenue Receipts (in thousands)	76.9	2,380,831	2,486,755	2,683,004	4.4	7.8	36	19	17	16	16

	Change in percent 1972-73 to 1982-83	Percent share 1982-83	1983-84	1984-85
Federal Revenue Receipts	-1.0	5.9	5.6	5.7
State Revenue Receipts	-7.6	40.2	39.6	40.4
Local and Other Revenue Receipts	8.6	53.9	54.8	53.9

	Percent change 1972 to 1982	1982	1983	1984	Percent change 1982 to 1983	1983 to 1984	State's rank in percent change 1982 to 1983	1983 to 1984	Rank 1982	1983	1984
Total Personal Income (in millions)	157.3	52,243	56,159	61,374	7.5	9.3	19	27	15	15	15
Per Capita Income	146.2	12,237	13,047	14,111	6.6	8.1	16	29	7	7	8
Population (in thousands)	4.5	4,270	4,304	4,349	0.7	1.0	27	19	20	19	19
Population Under Age 5	-11.9	289,000	298,000	301,000	3.1	1.0	17	10	22	22	21

	Score change 1972 to 1982	Average score 1982	1983	1984	Percent change 1982 to 1983	1983 to 1984	State's rank in percent change 1982 to 1983	1983 to 1984	1982 score	1983 score	1984 score
SAT Verbal Scores	-29.0	425	427	429	0.4	0.4	12	19	39	35	35
SAT Math Scores	-18.0	464	466	468	0.4	0.4	11	27	37	36	37

	Score change 1978 to 1982	Average score 1982	1983	1984	Percent change 1982 to 1983	1983 to 1984	State's rank in percent change 1982 to 1983	1983 to 1984	1982 score	1983 score	1984 score
SAT Verbal Scores of Intended Education Majors	-2.0	394	403	400	2.2	-0.7	11	43	36	31	36
SAT Math Scores of Intended Education Majors	-2.0	415	419	421	0.9	0.4	16	37	36	35	40

	Change in percent 1972 to 1981	Percent minority enrollment 1972	1976	1981
Percentage of Minority Enrollment	8.7	24.8	30.2	33.5

	Change in percent 1965 to 1980	Percent of all students enrolled in private schools 1965	1970	1980
Percentage of Private School Enrollment	-3.0	15.4	13.1	12.4

	Change in percent 1971 to 1983	1971-72	1980-81	1983-84
Graduation Rates	1.0	80.4	75.8	81.4

	Change in percent 1980 to 1985	Percent unemployed 1980	1984	1985
Unemployment Rates	-1.4	6.5	5.8	5.1

	Percent change 1972-73 to 1982-83	1982-83	1983-84	1984-85	Percent change 1982-83 to 1983-84	Percent change 1983-84 to 1984-85	State's rank in percent change 1982-83 to 1983-84	State's rank in percent change 1983-84 to 1984-85	State's Rank 1982	State's Rank 1983	State's Rank 1984
Public Elementary School Enrollment	-9.0	613,974	586,482	578,000	-4.4	-1.4	50	42	12	14	15
Public Secondary School Enrollment	-40.9	311,186	292,619	300,000	-5.9	2.5	50	10	19	19	19
Public Elementary and Secondary Enrollment	-23.0	925,160	879,101	878,000	-4.9	-0.1	50	30	14	14	14
Numbers of Public Elementary Teachers	-24.3	22,000	20,103	21,270	-8.6	5.8	51	7	18	20	18
Numbers of Public Secondary School Teachers	5.4	30,000	28,164	35,063	-6.1	24.4	51	1	10	10	8
Numbers of Public Elementary and Secondary Teachers	-9.6	52,000	48,267	56,333	-7.1	16.8	51	1	13	14	11
Elementary Teachers' Salaries	79.9	21,193	22,240	23,835	4.9	7.1	36	27	15	19	19
Secondary Teachers' Salaries	80.8	21,626	22,700	24,350	4.9	7.2	35	23	18	20	19
Total Teachers' Salaries	80.6	21,440	22,500	24,110	4.9	7.1	34	25	18	20	19
Per Pupil Expenditures in ADA	168.4	2,958	3,176	3,889	7.3	22.4	32	2	24	24	13
Total Current Expenditures (in thousands)	111.4	2,993,931	3,035,535	3,383,865	1.3	11.4	50	4	10	10	10
Total Revenue Receipts (in thousands)	109.2	2,900,000	2,969,533	3,433,235	2.3	15.6	45	2	10	10	10

	Change in percent 1972-73 to 1982-83	Percent share 1982-83	Percent share 1983-84	Percent share 1984-85
Federal Revenue Receipts	-0.4	4.8	4.5	5.5
State Revenue Receipts	15.2	39.4	41.3	42.5
Local and Other Revenue Receipts	-14.9	55.8	54.1	51.9

	Percent change 1972 to 1982	1982	1983	1984	Percent change 1982 to 1983	Percent change 1983 to 1984	State's rank in percent change 1982 to 1983	State's rank in percent change 1983 to 1984	Rank 1982	Rank 1983	Rank 1984
Total Personal Income (in millions)	141.8	69,923	76,463	84,497	9.4	10.5	8	15	10	10	10
Per Capita Income	141.0	12,153	13,260	14,574	9.1	9.9	4	9	10	5	5
Population (in thousands)	0.3	5,750	5,767	5,798	0.2	0.5	39	31	11	11	12
Population Under Age 5	-19.7	351,000	359,000	362,000	2.2	0.8	25	12	17	17	16

	Score change 1972 to 1982	Average score 1982	Average score 1983	Average score 1984	Percent change 1982 to 1983	Percent change 1983 to 1984	State's rank in percent change 1982 to 1983	State's rank in percent change 1983 to 1984	1982 score	1983 score	1984 score
SAT Verbal Scores	-28.0	425	427	429	0.4	0.4	12	19	39	35	35
SAT Math Scores	-17.0	463	463	467	0.0	0.8	25	13	39	41	39

	Score change 1978 to 1982	Average score 1982	Average score 1983	Average score 1984	Percent change 1982 to 1983	Percent change 1983 to 1984	State's rank in percent change 1982 to 1983	State's rank in percent change 1983 to 1984	1982 score	1983 score	1984 score
SAT Verbal Scores of Intended Education Majors	-7.0	388	388	391	0.0	0.7	27	32	41	41	43
SAT Math Scores of Intended Education Majors	-12.0	407	407	414	0.0	1.7	23	21	43	43	43

	Change in percent 1972 to 1981	Percent minority enrollment 1972	Percent minority enrollment 1976	Percent minority enrollment 1981
Percentage of Minority Enrollment	4.2	6.5	7.7	10.7

	Change in percent 1965 to 1980	Percent of all students enrolled in private schools 1965	1970	1980
Percentage of Private School Enrollment	-8.2	20.1	16.8	11.9

	Change in percent 1971 to 1983	1971-72	1980-81	1983-84
Graduation Rates	1.9	75.6	73.1	77.5

	Change in percent 1980 to 1985	Percent unemployed 1980	1984	1985
Unemployment Rates	-0.6	5.3	5.8	4.7

119

	Percent change 1972-73 to 1982-83	1982-83	1983-84	1984-85	Percent change 1982-83 to 1983-84	1983-84 to 1984-85	State's rank in percent change 1982-83 to 1983-84	1983-84 to 1984-85	State's Rank 1982	1983	1984
Public Elementary School Enrollment	-21.5	1,156,597	1,132,701	1,140,000	-2.0	0.6	44	22	5	5	5
Public Secondary School Enrollment	-17.6	604,924	603,180	603,000	-0.2	0.0	17	22	7	7	7
Public Elementary and Secondary Enrollment	-19.7	1,761,521	1,735,881	1,743,000	-1.4	0.4	35	17	7	7	6
Numbers of Public Elementary Teachers	-17.3	39,615	37,766	42,500	-4.7	12.7	49	2	9	9	8
Numbers of Public Secondary School Teachers	-11.1	37,222	35,189	37,400	-5.4	6.3	49	5	6	7	7
Numbers of Public Elementary and Secondary Teachers	-14.4	76,837	72,955	79,900	-5.1	9.6	50	2	8	9	8
Elementary Teachers' Salaries	104.6	26,340	28,650	28,191	8.7	-1.6	8	49	2	2	4
Secondary Teachers' Salaries	98.5	26,800	29,140	28,700	8.7	-1.5	6	49	2	2	3
Total Teachers' Salaries	100.5	26,556	28,877	28,401	8.7	-1.6	9	49	2	2	4
Per Pupil Expenditures in ADA	214.8	3,243	3,498	3,434	7.8	-1.8	26	48	15	15	20
Total Current Expenditures (in thousands)	131.1	5,683,799	5,908,979	6,056,439	3.9	2.4	41	44	5	5	5
Total Revenue Receipts (in thousands)	135.6	6,035,268	6,270,000	6,009,744	3.8	-4.1	38	48	6	6	7

	Change in percent 1972-73 to 1982-83	Percent share 1982-83	1983-84	1984-85
Federal Revenue Receipts	4.3	8.1	4.3	4.2
State Revenue Receipts	-11.5	36.1	35.1	33.9
Local and Other Revenue Receipts	7.2	55.8	60.6	61.9

	Percent change 1972 to 1982	1982	1983	1984	Percent change 1982 to 1983	1983 to 1984	State's rank in percent change 1982 to 1983	1983 to 1984	1982	Rank 1983	1984
Total Personal Income (in millions)	132.6	99,747	104,071	113,600	4.3	9.1	43	30	8	9	9
Per Capita Income	130.4	10,942	11,476	12,518	4.8	9.0	35	19	21	24	23
Population (in thousands)	0.9	9,116	9,069	9,075	-0.5	0.0	51	45	8	8	8
Population Under Age 5	-12.2	686,000	682,000	664,000	-0.5	-2.6	51	46	7	8	8

	Score change 1972 to 1982	Average score 1982	1983	1984	Percent change 1982 to 1983	1983 to 1984	State's rank in percent change 1982 to 1983	1983 to 1984	1982 score	1983 score	1984 score
SAT Verbal Scores	1.0	459	458	461	-0.2	0.6	33	8	26	26	26
SAT Math Scores	21.0	514	511	515	-0.5	0.7	40	15	17	20	18

	Score change 1978 to 1982	Average score 1982	1983	1984	Percent change 1982 to 1983	1983 to 1984	State's rank in percent change 1982 to 1983	1983 to 1984	1982 score	1983 score	1984 score
SAT Verbal Scores of Intended Education Majors	-5.0	423	425	445	0.4	4.7	23	7	19	22	12
SAT Math Scores of Intended Education Majors	-9.0	451	450	474	-0.2	5.3	26	6	16	20	12

	Change in percent 1972 to 1981	Percent minority enrollment 1972	1976	1981
Percentage of Minority Enrollment	5.1	16.2	18.3	21.3

	Change in percent 1965 to 1980	Percent of all students enrolled in private schools 1965	1970	1980
Percentage of Private School Enrollment	-5.0	15.2	12.6	10.2

	Change in percent 1971 to 1983	1971-72	1980-81	1983-84
Graduation Rates	-7.8	81.2	71.3	73.4

	Change in percent 1980 to 1985	Percent unemployed 1980	1984	1985
Unemployment Rates	-0.7	11.1	12.5	10.4

	Percent change 1972-73 to 1982-83	1982-83	1983-84	1984-85	Percent change 1982-83 to 1983-84	1983-84 to 1984-85	State's rank in percent change 1982-83 to 1983-84	1983-84 to 1984-85	State's Rank 1982	1983	1984
Public Elementary School Enrollment	-23.8	353,137	348,193	347,678	-1.4	-0.1	36	31	24	24	24
Public Secondary School Enrollment	-18.1	362,084	329,698	347,714	-8.9	5.4	51	2	13	16	14
Public Elementary and Secondary Enrollment	-21.0	715,221	677,891	695,392	-5.2	2.5	51	6	21	22	21
Numbers of Public Elementary Teachers	-9.6	19,025	18,454	19,000	-3.0	2.9	47	20	23	24	21
Numbers of Public Secondary School Teachers	-11.4	20,711	20,090	20,400	-2.9	1.5	42	16	17	18	16
Numbers of Public Elementary and Secondary Teachers	-10.6	39,736	38,544	39,400	-3.0	2.2	47	15	18	20	19
Elementary Teachers' Salaries	118.5	22,115	23,660	24,970	6.9	5.5	23	36	10	10	10
Secondary Teachers' Salaries	105.8	23,574	25,220	26,790	6.9	6.2	21	29	10	8	9
Total Teachers' Salaries	113.9	22,296	24,480	25,920	9.7	5.8	7	34	12	9	8
Per Pupil Expenditures in ADA	172.2	3,136	3,376	3,408	7.6	0.9	29	44	16	17	23
Total Current Expenditures (in thousands)	92.0	2,335,900	2,452,700	2,471,700	5.0	0.7	36	47	18	17	18
Total Revenue Receipts (in thousands)	93.3	2,406,900	2,581,500	2,593,320	7.2	0.4	19	44	16	14	18

	Change in percent 1972-73 to 1982-83	Percent share 1982-83	1983-84	1984-85
Federal Revenue Receipts	0.0	4.7	4.4	4.1
State Revenue Receipts	-9.1	48.9	54.1	51.9
Local and Other Revenue Receipts	9.1	46.3	41.5	44.0

	Percent change 1972 to 1982	1982	1983	1984	Percent change 1982 to 1983	1983 to 1984	State's rank in percent change 1982 to 1983	1983 to 1984	Rank 1982	1983	1984
Total Personal Income (in millions)	167.1	46,213	49,321	55,014	6.7	11.6	26	6	19	19	19
Per Capita Income	149.9	11,155	11,901	13,219	6.6	11.0	16	4	19	19	13
Population (in thousands)	4.2	4,133	4,144	4,162	0.2	0.4	39	36	21	21	21
Population Under Age 5	4.4	329,000	336,000	330,000	2.1	-1.7	26	39	20	19	19

	Score change 1972 to 1982	Average score 1982	1983	1984	Percent change 1982 to 1983	1983 to 1984	State's rank in percent change 1982 to 1983	1983 to 1984	State's rank in 1982 score	1983 score	1984 score
SAT Verbal Scores	-24.0	485	482	481	-0.6	-0.2	37	44	8	11	13
SAT Math Scores	-4.0	543	538	539	-0.9	0.1	46	36	7	7	10

	Score change 1978 to 1982	Average score 1982	1983	1984	Percent change 1982 to 1983	1983 to 1984	State's rank in percent change 1982 to 1983	1983 to 1984	State's rank in 1982 score	1983 score	1984 score
SAT Verbal Scores of Intended Education Majors	1.0	443	445	440	0.4	-1.1	23	45	7	9	16
SAT Math Scores of Intended Education Majors	-10.0	475	489	475	2.9	-2.8	10	47	5	5	10

	Change in percent 1972 to 1981	Percent minority enrollment 1972	1976	1981
Percentage of Minority Enrollment	3.1	2.8	4.1	5.9

	Change in percent 1965 to 1980	Percent of all students enrolled in private schools 1965	1970	1980
Percentage of Private School Enrollment	-6.3	16.8	13.1	10.5

	Change in percent 1971 to 1983	1971-72	1980-81	1983-84
Graduation Rates	-0.7	91.4	84.5	90.7

	Change in percent 1980 to 1985	Percent unemployed 1980	1984	1985
Unemployment Rates	0.2	6.3	7.6	6.5

	Percent change 1972-73 to 1982-83	1982-83	1983-84	1984-85	Percent change 1982-83 to 1983-84	1983-84 to 1984-85	State's rank in percent change 1982-83 to 1983-84	1983-84 to 1984-85	State's Rank 1982	1983	1984
Public Elementary School Enrollment	-16.1	256,325	255,000	257,101	-0.5	0.8	21	20	31	31	31
Public Secondary School Enrollment	-7.5	206,136	205,000	202,039	-0.5	-1.4	22	40	27	27	27
Public Elementary and Secondary Enrollment	-12.4	462,461	460,000	459,140	-0.5	-0.1	16	30	30	30	30
Numbers of Public Elementary Teachers	3.7	13,634	13,507	13,431	-0.9	-0.5	34	38	32	32	32
Numbers of Public Secondary School Teachers	9.0	11,348	11,357	11,341	0.0	-0.1	21	29	30	30	31
Numbers of Public Elementary and Secondary Teachers	6.0	24,982	24,864	24,772	-0.4	-0.3	24	37	32	31	31
Elementary Teachers' Salaries	107.9	14,083	15,632	15,710	10.9	0.4	2	48	51	51	51
Secondary Teachers' Salaries	105.2	14,604	16,210	16,280	10.9	0.4	3	47	51	51	51
Total Teachers' Salaries	106.8	14,320	15,895	15,971	10.9	0.4	2	47	51	51	51
Per Pupil Expenditures in ADA	198.3	1,895	1,962	2,205	3.5	12.3	48	7	51	51	50
Total Current Expenditures (in thousands)	143.3	895,242	922,098	1,025,112	3.0	11.1	44	6	34	36	34
Total Revenue Receipts (in thousands)	147.6	889,089	915,762	1,021,067	3.0	11.5	41	11	33	34	34

	Change in percent 1972-73 to 1982-83	Percent share 1982-83	1983-84	1984-85
Federal Revenue Receipts	-3.9	23.0	19.4	17.8
State Revenue Receipts	4.3	53.3	55.3	56.7
Local and Other Revenue Receipts	-0.4	23.7	25.2	25.5

	Percent change 1972 to 1982	1982	1983	1984	Percent change 1982 to 1983	1983 to 1984	State's rank in percent change 1982 to 1983	1983 to 1984	Rank 1982	1983	1984
Total Personal Income (in millions)	180.5	19,833	21,098	23,010	6.3	9.0	30	32	32	32	32
Per Capita Income	153.7	7,725	8,155	8,857	5.5	8.6	27	23	51	51	51
Population (in thousands)	10.6	2,569	2,587	2,598	0.7	0.4	27	36	31	31	31
Population Under Age 5	2.8	223,000	226,000	221,000	1.3	-2.2	33	43	29	28	28

	Score change 1972 to 1982	Average score 1982	1983	1984	Percent change 1982 to 1983	1983 to 1984	State's rank in percent change 1982 to 1983	1983 to 1984	State's rank in 1982 score	1983 score	1984 score
SAT Verbal Scores	66.0	479	474	480	-1.0	1.2	45	3	15	16	14
SAT Math Scores	71.0	509	507	512	-0.3	0.9	38	10	23	24	20

	Score change 1978 to 1982	Average score 1982	1983	1984	Percent change 1982 to 1983	1983 to 1984	State's rank in percent change 1982 to 1983	1983 to 1984	State's rank in 1982 score	1983 score	1984 score
SAT Verbal Scores of Intended Education Majors	-67.0	404	432	461	6.9	6.7	5	5	26	15	8
SAT Math Scores of Intended Education Majors	-74.0	406	452	449	11.3	-0.6	1	42	44	16	24

	Change in percent 1972 to 1981	Percent minority enrollment 1972	1976	1981
Percentage of Minority Enrollment	0.5	51.1	49.0	51.6

	Change in percent 1965 to 1980	Percent of all students enrolled in private schools 1965	1970	1980
Percentage of Private School Enrollment	5.9	3.6	7.7	9.5

	Change in percent 1971 to 1983	1971-72	1980-81	1983-84
Graduation Rates	4.3	59.4	59.7	63.7

	Change in percent 1980 to 1985	Percent unemployed 1980	1984	1985
Unemployment Rates	4.3	6.5	11.3	10.8

122

	Percent change 1972-73 to 1982-83	1982-83	1983-84	1984-85	Percent change 1982-83 to 1983-84	Percent change 1983-84 to 1984-85	State's rank in percent change 1982-83 to 1983-84	State's rank 1983-84 to 1984-85	State's Rank 1982	1983	1984
Public Elementary School Enrollment	-24.8	547,057	546,155	545,062	-0.1	-0.2	14	32	16	16	16
Public Secondary School Enrollment	-13.9	255,784	249,298	248,731	-2.5	-0.2	38	28	20	20	21
Public Elementary and Secondary Enrollment	-21.7	802,841	795,453	793,793	-0.9	-0.2	24	34	16	16	17
Numbers of Public Elementary Teachers	-3.8	23,003	23,342	23,726	1.4	1.6	8	25	17	17	17
Numbers of Public Secondary School Teachers	9.9	22,954	23,372	23,514	1.8	0.6	6	21	13	12	13
Numbers of Public Elementary and Secondary Teachers	2.6	45,957	46,714	47,240	1.6	1.1	9	25	16	16	15
Elementary Teachers' Salaries	93.8	17,031	18,800	19,824	10.3	5.4	3	37	41	36	38
Secondary Teachers' Salaries	96.9	18,012	19,799	21,084	9.9	6.4	5	27	39	33	32
Total Teachers' Salaries	95.5	17,521	19,300	20,452	10.1	5.9	5	33	40	35	35
Per Pupil Expenditures in ADA	191.3	2,513	2,714	2,993	7.9	10.2	24	12	38	38	35
Total Current Expenditures (in thousands)	113.6	1,948,607	2,081,002	2,266,361	6.7	8.9	24	17	20	20	19
Total Revenue Receipts (in thousands)	111.1	2,065,000	2,207,379	2,339,454	6.8	5.9	20	34	20	19	20

	Change in percent 1972-73 to 1982-83	Percent share 1982-83	1983-84	1984-85
Federal Revenue Receipts	0.1	8.1	7.2	6.2
State Revenue Receipts	4.5	39.6	39.9	37.2
Local and Other Revenue Receipts	-4.6	52.3	52.9	56.6

	Percent change 1972 to 1982	1982	1983	1984	Percent change 1982 to 1983	Percent change 1983 to 1984	State's rank in percent change 1982 to 1983	State's rank 1983 to 1984	Rank 1982	1983	1984
Total Personal Income (in millions)	149.9	50,423	54,817	60,738	8.7	10.9	11	10	17	16	16
Per Capita Income	139.9	10,188	11,029	12,129	8.2	9.9	9	9	33	29	29
Population (in thousands)	4.2	4,942	4,970	5,008	0.5	0.7	31	26	15	15	15
Population Under Age 5	1.1	372,000	377,000	374,000	1.3	-0.7	33	28	15	15	15

	Score change 1972 to 1982	Average score 1982	1983	1984	Percent change 1982 to 1983	Percent change 1983 to 1984	State's rank in percent change 1982 to 1983	State's rank in percent change 1983 to 1984	1982 score	1983 score	1984 score
SAT Verbal Scores	-18.0	465	466	469	0.2	0.6	18	8	22	20	19
SAT Math Scores	-2.0	510	510	512	0.0	0.3	25	32	21	21	20

	Score change 1978 to 1982	Average score 1982	1983	1984	Percent change 1982 to 1983	Percent change 1983 to 1984	State's rank in percent change 1982 to 1983	State's rank in percent change 1983 to 1984	1982 score	1983 score	1984 score
SAT Verbal Scores of Intended Education Majors	-2.0	426	433	439	1.6	1.3	15	23	17	14	17
SAT Math Scores of Intended Education Majors	8.0	453	457	460	0.8	0.6	17	34	14	12	18

	Change in percent 1972 to 1981	Percent minority enrollment 1972	1976	1981
Percentage of Minority Enrollment	-2.1	16.9	12.8	14.8

	Change in percent 1965 to 1980	Percent of all students enrolled in private schools 1965	1970	1980
Percentage of Private School Enrollment	-2.5	15.5	13.2	13.0

	Change in percent 1971 to 1983	1971-72	1980-81	1983-84
Graduation Rates	-4.2	80.4	73.7	76.2

	Change in percent 1980 to 1985	Percent unemployed 1980	1984	1985
Unemployment Rates	0.6	6.8	8.1	7.4

	Percent change 1972-73 to 1982-83	1982-83	1983-84	1984-85	Percent change 1982-83 to 1983-84	1983-84 to 1984-85	State's rank in percent change 1982-83 to 1983-84	1983-84 to 1984-85	State's Rank 1982	1983	1984
Public Elementary School Enrollment	-8.5	106,900	108,300	108,905	1.3	0.5	3	23	40	40	40
Public Secondary School Enrollment	-18.3	45,500	45,400	45,335	-0.2	-0.1	17	27	45	45	44
Public Elementary and Secondary Enrollment	-11.7	152,400	153,700	154,240	0.8	0.3	2	20	42	42	42
Numbers of Public Elementary Teachers	-3.2	6,430	6,300	6,726	-2.0	6.7	44	3	39	39	39
Numbers of Public Secondary School Teachers	17.0	3,090	3,050	3,030	-1.2	-0.6	32	32	46	46	45
Numbers of Public Elementary and Secondary Teachers	4.8	9,520	9,350	9,756	-1.7	4.3	41	4	41	41	41
Elementary Teachers' Salaries	122.0	18,987	20,126	21,110	5.9	4.8	29	38	28	26	29
Secondary Teachers' Salaries	105.5	20,532	21,764	22,830	6.0	4.8	27	35	26	24	26
Total Teachers' Salaries	118.5	19,488	20,657	21,705	5.9	5.0	28	39	28	26	27
Per Pupil Expenditures in ADA	216.1	3,442	3,631	3,968	5.4	9.2	37	18	10	13	11
Total Current Expenditures (in thousands)	178.2	532,000	565,700	625,900	6.3	10.6	26	8	41	41	40
Total Revenue Receipts (in thousands)	199.2	565,700	603,000	615,690	6.6	2.1	22	42	39	40	40

	Change in percent 1972-73 to 1982-83	Percent share 1982-83	1983-84	1984-85
Federal Revenue Receipts	0.0	8.5	9.1	9.0
State Revenue Receipts	22.2	47.4	45.3	45.0
Local and Other Revenue Receipts	-22.1	44.2	45.6	46.0

	Percent change 1972 to 1982	1982	1983	1984	Percent change 1982 to 1983	1983 to 1984	State's rank in percent change 1982 to 1983	1983 to 1984	Rank 1982	1983	1984
Total Personal Income (in millions)	165.4	7,677	8,121	8,419	5.7	3.6	32	51	45	46	47
Per Capita Income	138.3	9,544	9,945	10,216	4.2	2.7	40	50	38	38	44
Population (in thousands)	11.4	805	817	824	1.4	0.8	12	22	44	44	44
Population Under Age 5	19.0	69,000	71,000	70,000	2.8	-1.4	21	34	41	41	41

	Score change 1972 to 1982	Average score 1982	1983	1984	Percent change 1982 to 1983	1983 to 1984	State's rank in percent change 1982 to 1983	1983 to 1984	State's rank in 1982 score	1983 score	1984 score
SAT Verbal Scores	-25.0	487	480	490	-1.4	2.0	49	1	7	13	7
SAT Math Scores	-3.0	546	535	544	-2.0	1.6	51	5	5	8	7

	Score change 1978 to 1982	Average score 1982	1983	1984	Percent change 1982 to 1983	1983 to 1984	State's rank in percent change 1982 to 1983	1983 to 1984	State's rank in 1982 score	1983 score	1984 score
SAT Verbal Scores of Intended Education Majors	-26.0	431	435	444	0.9	2.0	19	17	13	13	-14
SAT Math Scores of Intended Education Majors	-24.0	476	489	475	2.7	-2.8	12	47	4	5	10

	Change in percent 1972 to 1981	Percent minority enrollment 1972	1976	1981
Percentage of Minority Enrollment	5.2	6.9	9.0	12.1

	Change in percent 1965 to 1980	Percent of all students enrolled in private schools 1965	1970	1980
Percentage of Private School Enrollment	-5.6	10.3	7.6	4.7

	Change in percent 1971 to 1983	1971-72	1980-81	1983-84
Graduation Rates	1.5	81.6	80.7	83.1

	Change in percent 1980 to 1985	Percent unemployed 1980	1984	1985
Unemployment Rates	1.4	6.6	8.8	8.0

	Percent change 1972-73 to 1982-83	1982-83	1983-84	1984-85	Percent change 1982-83 to 1983-84	1983-84 to 1984-85	State's rank in percent change 1982-83 to 1983-84	1983-84 to 1984-85	State's Rank 1982	1983	1984
Public Elementary School Enrollment	-16.8	151,105	149,519	149,497	-1.0	0.0	28	26	36	37	36
Public Secondary School Enrollment	-23.1	117,904	117,479	116,122	-0.3	-1.1	19	39	37	37	37
Public Elementary and Secondary Enrollment	-19.6	269,009	266,998	265,619	-0.7	-0.5	22	38	37	37	36
Numbers of Public Elementary Teachers	-14.7	9,159	8,787	9,327	-4.0	6.1	48	4	36	36	36
Numbers of Public Secondary School Teachers	0.8	8,219	7,998	8,186	-2.6	2.3	41	13	34	34	34
Numbers of Public Elementary and Secondary Teachers	-7.6	17,378	16,785	17,513	-3.4	4.3	48	4	35	35	35
Elementary Teachers' Salaries	103.0	16,650	17,976	19,292	7.9	7.3	12	23	44	41	42
Secondary Teachers' Salaries	95.4	18,173	19598	21,008	7.8	7.1	10	24	37	36	33
Total Teachers' Salaries	99.4	17,412	18,785	20,153	7.8	7.2	12	24	41	37	37
Per Pupil Expenditures in ADA	193.0	2,708	2,927	3,128	8.0	6.8	23	28	33	29	31
Total Current Expenditures (in thousands)	116.8	732,600	767,927	833,000	4.8	8.4	39	22	37	37	37
Total Revenue Receipts (in thousands)	126.6	744,000	790,000	825,000	6.1	4.4	25	39	37	37	37

	Change in percent 1972-73 to 1982-83	Percent share 1982-83	1983-84	1984-85
Federal Revenue Receipts	-1.4	7.1	6.3	5.5
State Revenue Receipts	12.3	27.9	28.5	28.1
Local and Other Revenue Receipts	-10.9	65.0	65.2	66.4

	Percent change 1972 to 1982	1982	1983	1984	Percent change 1982 to 1983	1983 to 1984	State's rank in percent change 1982 to 1983	1983 to 1984	Rank 1982	1983	1984
Total Personal Income (in millions)	145.1	16,942	17,849	19,721	5.3	10.4	35	16	35	35	34
Per Capita Income	134.7	10,641	11,175	12,280	5.0	9.8	31	11	30	28	28
Population (in thousands)	4.5	1,589	1,597	1,606	0.5	0.5	31	31	35	36	36
Population Under Age 5	8.3	130,000	133,000	131,000	2.3	-1.5	23	36	36	36	37

	Score change 1972 to 1982	Average score 1982	1983	1984	Percent change 1982 to 1983	1983 to 1984	State's rank in percent change 1982 to 1983	1983 to 1984	1982 score	1983 score	1984 score
SAT Verbal Scores	39.0	493	494	493	0.2	-0.2	18	44	6	6	6
SAT Math Scores	50.0	552	546	548	-1.0	0.3	48	32	4	4	5

	Score change 1978 to 1982	Average score 1982	1983	1984	Percent change 1982 to 1983	1983 to 1984	State's rank in percent change 1982 to 1983	1983 to 1984	1982 score	1983 score	1984 score
SAT Verbal Scores of Intended Education Majors	10.0	444	447	412	0.6	-7.8	20	51	5	8	29
SAT Math Scores of Intended Education Majors	14.0	489	464	465	-5.1	0.2	50	39	2	10	14

	Change in percent 1972 to 1981	Percent minority enrollment 1972	1976	1981
Percentage of Minority Enrollment	2.4	8.1	7.5	10.5

	Change in percent 1965 to 1980	Percent of all students enrolled in private schools 1965	1970	1980
Percentage of Private School Enrollment	-3.6	15.7	13.8	12.1

	Change in percent 1971 to 1983	1971-72	1980-81	1983-84
Graduation Rates	-1.6	85.7	82.7	84.1

	Change in percent 1980 to 1985	Percent unemployed 1980	1984	1985
Unemployment Rates	1.9	3.9	5.3	5.8

	Percent change 1972-73 to 1982-83	1982-83	1983-84	1984-85	Percent change 1982-83 to 1983-84	1983-84 to 1984-85	State's rank in percent change 1982-83 to 1983-84	1983-84 to 1984-85	State's Rank 1982	1983	1984
Public Elementary School Enrollment	12.2	81,640	81,730	79,400	0.1	-2.8	12	47	44	44	45
Public Secondary School Enrollment	17.9	69,460	69,470	72,200	0.0	3.9	13	5	40	40	40
Public Elementary and Secondary Enrollment	14.7	151,100	151,200	151,600	0.0	0.2	9	25	43	43	43
Numbers of Public Elementary Teachers	34.8	3,838	3,876	4,076	0.9	5.1	9	10	46	46	46
Numbers of Public Secondary School Teachers	40.7	3,384	3,417	3,420	0.9	0.0	13	28	43	43	43
Numbers of Public Elementary and Secondary Teachers	37.5	7,222	7,293	7,496	0.9	2.7	12	10	46	46	45
Elementary Teachers' Salaries	92.0	21,710	22,000	22,110	1.3	0.5	49	46	12	20	24
Secondary Teachers' Salaries	93.2	22,480	23,000	22,960	2.3	-0.1	45	48	13	18	25
Total Teachers' Salaries	92.5	22,070	23,000	22,520	4.2	-2.0	39	50	13	14	25
Per Pupil Expenditures in ADA	141.0	2,758	2,870	2,998	4.0	4.4	45	37	29	32	34
Total Current Expenditures (in tnousands)	181.0	407,465	426,125	465,300	4.5	9.1	40	13	46	46	45
Total Revenue Receipts (in thousands)	166.5	397,244	419,091	460,400	5.5	9.8	30	16	46	46	46

	Change in percent 1972-73 to 1982-83	Percent share 1982-83	1983-84	1984-85
Federal Revenue Receipts	0.9	0.6	5.2	4.0
State Revenue Receipts	22.8	60.6	42.4	39.5
Local and Other Revenue Receipts	-23.7	31.8	52.4	56.5

	Percent change 1972 to 1982	1982	1983	1984	Percent change 1982 to 1983	1983 to 1984	State's rank in percent change 1982 to 1983	1983 to 1984	Rank 1982	1983	1984
Total Personal Income (in millions)	267.6	10,548	11,087	12,038	5.1	8.5	38	36	39	42	42
Per Capita Income	128.2	12,022	12,441	13,216	3.4	6.2	42	45	12	11	14
Population (in thousands)	61.1	876	891	911	1.7	2.2	11	4	43	43	43
Population Under Age 5	43.5	66,000	69,000	70,000	4.5	1.4	13	8	42	42	41

	Score change 1972 to 1982	Average score 1982	1983	1984	Percent change 1982 to 1983	1983 to 1984	State's rank in percent change 1982 to 1983	1983 to 1984	1982 score	1983 score	1984 score
SAT Verbal Scores	49.0	436	441	442	1.1	0.2	5	26	30	29	30
SAT Math Scores	-30.0	481	480	489	-0.2	1.8	34	4	29	29	28

	Score change 1978 to 1982	Average score 1982	1983	1984	Percent change 1982 to 1983	1983 to 1984	State's rank in percent change 1982 to 1983	1983 to 1984	1982 score	1983 score	1984 score
SAT Verbal Scores of Intended Education Majors	-22.0	398	409	428	2.7	4.6	10	8	32	27	23
SAT Math Scores of Intended Education Majors	5.0	420	423	439	0.7	3.7	18	9	31	30	27

	Change in percent 1972 to 1981	Percent minority enrollment 1972	1976	1981
Percentage of Minority Enrollment	4.7	14.2	17.0	18.9

	Change in percent 1965 to 1980	Percent of all students enrolled in private schools 1965	1970	1980
Percentage of Private School Enrollment	-0.1	4.3	3.3	4.2

	Change in percent 1971 to 1983	1971-72	1980-81	1983-84
Graduation Rates	-0.8	75.4	71.5	74.6

	Change in percent 1980 to 1985	Percent unemployed 1980	1984	1985
Unemployment Rates	2.3	5.6	8.5	7.9

126

SUMMARY TABLE 31. New Hampshire

	Percent change 1972-73 to 1982-83	1982-83	1983-84	1984-85	Percent change 1982-83 to 1983-84	Percent change 1983-84 to 1984-85	State's rank in percent change 1982-83 to 1983-84	State's rank in percent change 1983-84 to 1984-85	State's Rank 1982	State's Rank 1983	State's Rank 1984
Public Elementary School Enrollment	-3.4	93,887	92,948	92,632	-1.0	-0.3	28	34	41	41	41
Public Secondary School Enrollment	-4.9	66,312	65,649	65,983	-1.0	0.5	26	18	41	42	41
Public Elementary and Secondary Enrollment	-4.0	160,199	158,597	158,615	-1.0	0.0	28	27	41	41	41
Numbers of Public Elementary Teachers	19.2	5,122	5,101	5,370	-0.4	5.2	26	9	41	42	41
Numbers of Public Secondary School Teachers	24.2	4,636	4,617	4,734	-0.4	2.5	27	12	39	39	39
Numbers of Public Elementary and Secondary Teachers	21.6	9,758	9,718	10,104	-0.4	3.9	24	6	40	40	40
Elementary Teachers' Salaries	69.6	16,438	17,357	18,638	5.5	7.3	33	23	45	45	45
Secondary Teachers' Salaries	65.5	16,678	17,394	18,505	4.2	6.3	39	28	48	49	49
Total Teachers' Salaries	67.7	16,549	17,376	18,577	4.9	6.9	34	27	45	47	48
Per Pupil Expenditures in ADA	165.7	2,687	2,796	2,964	4.0	6.0	45	31	34	35	36
Total Current Expenditures (in thousands)	138.7	417,996	429,585	456,478	2.7	6.2	47	31	45	45	46
Total Revenue Receipts (in thousands)	153.0	427,295	440,277	493,200	3.0	12.0	41	8	45	45	45

	Change in percent 1972-73 to 1982-83	Percent share 1982-83	Percent share 1983-84	Percent share 1984-85
Federal Revenue Receipts	-0.9	3.9	3.7	3.2
State Revenue Receipts	-0.7	6.9	7.1	8.0
Local and Other Revenue Receipts	1.7	89.2	89.2	88.8

	Percent change 1972 to 1982	1982	1983	1984	Percent change 1982 to 1983	Percent change 1983 to 1984	State's rank in percent change 1982 to 1983	State's rank in percent change 1983 to 1984	Rank 1982	Rank 1983	Rank 1984
Total Personal Income (in millions)	206.0	10,179	11,610	12,842	14.0	10.6	1	13	42	39	39
Per Capita Income	151.5	10,721	12,109	13,148	12.9	8.5	2	24	28	16	15
Population (in thousands)	21.6	948	959	977	1.1	1.8	16	6	42	41	41
Population Under Age 5	3.1	66,000	68,000	68,000	3.0	0.0	19	16	42	43	43

	Score change 1972 to 1982	Average score 1982	Average score 1983	Average score 1984	Percent change 1982 to 1983	Percent change 1983 to 1984	State's rank in percent change 1982 to 1983	State's rank in percent change 1983 to 1984	1982 score	1983 score	1984 score
SAT Verbal Scores	-26.0	443	444	448	0.2	0.9	18	4	29	28	28
SAT Math Scores	-21.0	482	481	483	-0.2	0.4	34	27	28	28	29

	Score change 1978 to 1982	Average score 1982	Average score 1983	Average score 1984	Percent change 1982 to 1983	Percent change 1983 to 1984	State's rank in percent change 1982 to 1983	State's rank in percent change 1983 to 1984	1982 score	1983 score	1984 score
SAT Verbal Scores of Intended Education Majors	-2.0	408	400	405	-1.9	1.2	45	25	24	33	31
SAT Math Scores of Intended Education Majors	-10.0	424	420	427	-0.9	1.6	39	24	28	32	36

	Change in percent 1972 to 1981	Percent minority enrollment 1972	1976	1981
Percentage of Minority Enrollment	0.4	0.9	1.1	1.3

	Change in percent 1965 to 1980	Percent of all students enrolled in private schools 1965	1970	1980
Percentage of Private School Enrollment	-10.7	21.7	17.1	11.0

	Change in percent 1971 to 1983	1971-72	1980-81	1983-84
Graduation Rates	-7.3	83.8	77.7	76.5

	Change in percent 1980 to 1985	Percent unemployed 1980	1984	1985
Unemployment Rates	1.2	4.0	4.7	5.2

127

	Percent change 1972-73 to 1982-83	1982-83	1983-84	1984-85	Percent change 1982-83 to 1983-84	Percent change 1983-84 to 1984-85	State's rank in percent change 1982-83 to 1983-84	State's rank in percent change 1983-84 to 1984-85	State's Rank 1982	1983	1984
Public Elementary School Enrollment	-25.0	738,245	725,703	712,027	-1.6	-1.8	40	43	10	10	10
Public Secondary School Enrollment	-18.5	434,275	422,138	405,755	-2.7	-3.8	40	51	10	10	10
Public Elementary and Secondary Enrollment	-22.8	1,172,520	1,147,841	1,117,782	-2.1	-2.6	41	50	9	9	9
Numbers of Public Elementary Teachers	0.2	42,479	41,884	41,893	-1.4	0.0	38	33	8	8	9
Numbers of Public Secondary School Teachers	-11.7	31,824	31,378	30,965	-1.4	-1.3	34	37	9	9	10
Numbers of Public Elementary and Secondary Teachers	-5.5	74,303	73,262	72,858	-1.4	-0.5	35	38	9	8	9
Elementary Teachers' Salaries	83.9	21,142	22,622	24,596	7.0	8.7	19	15	16	13	13
Secondary Teachers' Salaries	85.4	22,061	23,605	25,732	6.9	9.0	21	13	16	14	13
Total Teachers' Salaries	84.5	21,536	23,044	25,125	7.0	9.0	19	12	15	13	12
Per Pupil Expenditures in ADA	224.3	4,428	4,943	5,220	11.6	5.6	4	33	3	2	3
Total Current Expenditures (in thousands)	125.8	4,864,300	5,308,300	5,506,600	9.1	3.7	12	41	8	8	8
Total Revenue Receipts (in thousands)	120.8	4,968,900	5,372,700	5,722,400	8.1	6.5	10	29	8	8	9

	Change in percent 1972-73 to 1982-83	Percent share 1982-83	1983-84	1984-85
Federal Revenue Receipts	-2.3	3.5	3.8	5.7
State Revenue Receipts	13.8	40.0	39.3	40.0
Local and Other Revenue Receipts	-11.7	56.4	57.0	56.6

	Percent change 1972 to 1982	1982	1983	1984	Percent change 1982 to 1983	Percent change 1983 to 1984	State's rank in percent change 1982 to 1983	State's rank in percent change 1983 to 1984	Rank 1982	1983	1984
Total Personal Income (in millions)	145.5	97,599	104,548	114,837	7.1	9.8	22	22	9	8	8
Per Capita Income	142.1	13,169	14,000	15,282	6.3	9.1	19	17	4	4	4
Population (in thousands)	1.4	7,427	7,468	7,515	0.5	0.6	31	29	9	9	9
Population Under Age 5	-14.6	478,000	486,000	485,000	1.6	-0.2	30	25	9	9	9

	Score change 1972 to 1982	Average score 1982	1983	1984	Percent change 1982 to 1983	Percent change 1983 to 1984	State's rank in percent change 1982 to 1983	State's rank in percent change 1983 to 1984	1982 score	1983 score	1984 score
SAT Verbal Scores	-30.0	416	418	418	0.4	0.0	12	34	44	44	44
SAT Math Scores	-17.0	453	455	458	0.4	0.6	11	20	45	45	45

	Score change 1978 to 1982	Average score 1982	1983	1984	Percent change 1982 to 1983	Percent change 1983 to 1984	State's rank in percent change 1982 to 1983	State's rank in percent change 1983 to 1984	1982 score	1983 score	1984 score
SAT Verbal Scores of Intended Education Majors	-3.0	384	384	388	0.0	1.0	27	29	45	45	45
SAT Math Scores of Intended Education Majors	-4.0	405	403	411	-0.4	1.9	28	19	46	47	45

	Change in percent 1972 to 1981	Percent minority enrollment 1972	1976	1981
Percentage of Minority Enrollment	6.8	21.6	24.5	28.4

	Change in percent 1965 to 1980	Percent of all students enrolled in private schools 1965	1970	1980
Percentage of Private School Enrollment	-4.7	20.3	18.3	15.6

	Change in percent 1971 to 1983	1971-72	1980-81	1983-84
Graduation Rates	-1.1	83.8	76.9	82.7

	Change in percent 1980 to 1985	Percent unemployed 1980	1984	1985
Unemployment Rates	-0.4	7.0	7.4	6.6

SUMMARY TABLE 33. New Mexico

	Percent change 1972-73 to 1982-83	1982-83	1983-84	1984-85	Percent change 1982-83 to 1983-84	Percent change 1983-84 to 1984-85	State's rank in percent change 1982-83 to 1983-84	State's rank in percent change 1983-84 to 1984-85	State's Rank 1982	1983	1984
Public Elementary School Enrollment	3.8	149,900	151,332	143,196	0.9	-5.3	5	51	37	36	38
Public Secondary School Enrollment	-12.4	119,211	118,617	117,678	-0.4	-0.7	21	37	36	36	36
Public Elementary and Secondary Enrollment	-4.1	269,111	269,949	260,874	0.3	-3.3	5	51	36	36	37
Numbers of Public Elementary Teachers	8.0	8,160	8,120	7,990	-0.4	-1.6	26	43	37	37	38
Numbers of Public Secondary School Teachers	26.8	6,490	7,410	6,210	14.1	-16.1	2	50	36	35	36
Numbers of Public Elementary and Secondary Teachers	16.9	14,650	15,530	14,200	6.0	-8.5	1	51	37	36	37
Elementary Teachers' Salaries	133.7	19,730	20,360	21,340	3.1	4.8	44	38	23	25	28
Secondary Teachers' Salaries	140.0	21,130	21,810	22,770	3.2	4.4	42	37	21	23	27
Total Teachers' Salaries	136.6	20,470	20,760	22,064	1.4	6.2	46	30	22	25	26
Per Pupil Expenditures in ADA	239.3	2,843	2,921	3,278	2.7	12.2	49	8	27	30	28
Total Current Expenditures (in thousands)	260.4	876,815	1,018,109	1,041,640	16.1	2.3	1	45	35	32	33
Total Revenue Receipts (in thousands)	204.5	838,242	833,048	893,175	-0.6	7.2	51	22	36	36	36

	Change in percent 1972-73 to 1982-83	Percent share 1982-83	1983-84	1984-85
Federal Revenue Receipts	-10.3	10.2	10.8	11.0
State Revenue Receipts	17.8	77.8	77.7	77.4
Local and Other Revenue Receipts	-7.6	12.0	11.5	11.6

	Percent change 1972 to 1982	1982	1983	1984	Percent change 1982 to 1983	Percent change 1983 to 1984	State's rank in percent change 1982 to 1983	State's rank in percent change 1983 to 1984	Rank 1982	1983	1984
Total Personal Income (in millions)	215.8	12,483	13,512	14,707	8.2	8.8	13	35	37	37	37
Per Capita Income	150.4	9,135	9,656	10,330	5.7	6.9	24	41	40	42	43
Population (in thousands)	26.1	1,367	1,399	1,424	2.3	1.7	6	8	37	37	37
Population Under Age 5	24.8	126,000	133,000	133,000	5.5	0.0	9	16	37	36	36

	Score change 1972 to 1982	Average score 1982	1983	1984	Percent change 1982 to 1983	Percent change 1983 to 1984	State's rank in percent change 1982 to 1983	State's rank in percent change 1983 to 1984	1982 score	1983 score	1984 score
SAT Verbal Scores	-12.0	480	484	487	0.8	0.6	6	8	12	9	9
SAT Math Scores	-6.0	517	519	527	0.3	1.5	15	7	14	13	13

	Score change 1978 to 1982	Average score 1982	1983	1984	Percent change 1982 to 1983	Percent change 1983 to 1984	State's rank in percent change 1982 to 1983	State's rank in percent change 1983 to 1984	1982 score	1983 score	1984 score
SAT Verbal Scores of Intended Education Majors	3.0	439	421	462	-4.1	9.7	51	2	10	24	7
SAT Math Scores of Intended Education Majors	-23.0	445	425	464	-4.4	9.1	48	3	22	29	15

	Change in percent 1972 to 1981	Percent minority enrollment 1972	1976	1981
Percentage of Minority Enrollment	9.7	47.3	53.5	57.0

	Change in percent 1965 to 1980	Percent of all students enrolled in private schools 1965	1970	1980
Percentage of Private School Enrollment	-2.2	8.4	6.5	6.2

	Change in percent 1971 to 1983	1971-72	1980-81	1983-84
Graduation Rates	-3.3	74.7	72.9	71.4

	Change in percent 1980 to 1985	Percent unemployed 1980	1984	1985
Unemployment Rates	0.7	7.1	7.9	7.8

129

SUMMARY TABLE 34. New York

	Percent change 1972-73 to 1982-83	1982-83	1983-84	1984-85	Percent change 1982-83 to 1983-84	1983-84 to 1984-85	State's rank in percent change 1982-83 to 1983-84	1983-84 to 1984-85	State's Rank 1982	1983	1984
Public Elementary School Enrollment	-30.3	1,314,575	1,285,800	1,306,300	-2.1	1.5	45	15	3	3	3
Public Secondary School Enrollment	-14.4	1,390,838	1,347,800	1,319,600	-3.0	-2.0	43	42	1	1	2
Public Elementary and Secondary Enrollment	-22.9	2,705,413	2,633,600	2,625,900	-2.6	-0.2	47	34	3	3	3
Numbers of Public Elementary Teachers	-19.0	74,500	74,000	76,200	-0.6	2.9	29	20	3	3	3
Numbers of Public Secondary School Teachers	-6.7	90,700	90,000	88,700	-0.7	-1.4	29	39	1	1	1
Numbers of Public Elementary and Secondary Teachers	-12.8	165,200	164,000	164,900	-0.7	0.5	30	32	3	3	3
Elementary Teachers' Salaries	102.5	24,150	25,850	28,500	7.0	10.2	19	11	5	4	3
Secondary Teachers' Salaries	102.4	25,700	27,500	30,000	7.0	9.0	19	13	3	4	2
Total Teachers' Salaries	102.4	25,000	26,750	29,000	7.0	8.4	19	16	4	4	2
Per Pupil Expenditures in ADA	160.9	4,477	4,845	5,226	8.2	7.8	20	23	2	3	2
Total Current Expenditures (in thousands)	84.4	11,600,000	12,200,000	13,100,000	5.1	7.3	35	26	2	2	2
Total Revenue Receipts (in thousands)	77.3	11,121,000	11,794,235	12,583,325	6.0	6.6	26	27	2	2	2

	Change in percent 1972-73 to 1982-83	Percent share 1982-83	1983-84	1984-85
Federal Revenue Receipts	-1.4	4.0	3.8	4.0
State Revenue Receipts	1.3	41.9	41.3	43.1
Local and Other Revenue Receipts	0.1	54.1	55.0	52.9

	Percent change 1972 to 1982	1982	1983	1984	Percent change 1982 to 1983	1983 to 1984	State's rank in percent change 1982 to 1983	1983 to 1984	Rank 1982	1983	1984
Total Personal Income (in millions)	125.5	217,230	229,922	250,433	5.8	8.9	31	33	2	2	2
Per Capita Income	134.4	12,389	13,014	14,121	5.0	8.5	31	24	6	8	7
Population (in thousands)	-3.8	17,567	17,667	17,735	0.5	0.3	31	40	2	2	2
Population Under Age 5	-16.8	1,171,000	1,182,000	1,183,000	0.9	0.0	38	16	3	3	3

	Score change 1972 to 1982	Average score 1982	1983	1984	Percent change 1982 to 1983	1983 to 1984	State's rank in percent change 1982 to 1983	1983 to 1984	1982 score	1983 score	1984 score
SAT Verbal Scores	-31.0	429	422	424	-1.6	0.4	50	19	35	41	40
SAT Math Scores	-28.0	467	466	470	-0.2	0.8	34	13	34	36	34

	Score change 1978 to 1982	Average score 1982	1983	1984	Percent change 1982 to 1983	1983 to 1984	State's rank in percent change 1982 to 1983	1983 to 1984	1982 score	1983 score	1984 score
SAT Verbal Scores of Intended Education Majors	-3.0	405	400	404	-1.2	1.0	41	29	25	33	32
SAT Math Scores of Intended Education Majors	-7.0	433	430	436	-0.6	1.3	33	28	25	26	28

	Change in percent 1972 to 1981	Percent minority enrollment 1972	1976	1981
Percentage of Minority Enrollment	5.3	26.7	29.7	32.0

	Change in percent 1965 to 1980	Percent of all students enrolled in private schools 1965	1970	1980
Percentage of Private School Enrollment	-5.3	22.1	18.8	16.8

	Change in percent 1971 to 1983	1971-72	1980-81	1983-84
Graduation Rates	-9.2	75.9	67.2	66.7

	Change in percent 1980 to 1985	Percent unemployed 1980	1984	1985
Unemployment Rates	-0.1	7.3	7.7	7.2

	Percent change 1972-73 to 1982-83	1982-83	1983-84	1984-85	Percent change 1982-83 to 1983-84	1983-84 to 1984-85	State's rank in percent change 1982-83 to 1983-84	1983-84 to 1984-85	State's Rank 1982	1983	1984
Public Elementary School Enrollment	-3.6	770,952	761,053	758,402	-1.2	-0.3	33	34	9	9	9
Public Secondary School Enrollment	-7.1	332,528	328,553	336,143	-1.1	2.3	27	11	18	17	16
Public Elementary and Secondary Enrollment	-4.7	1,103,480	1,089,606	1,094,545	-1.2	0.4	30	17	10	10	10
Numbers of Public Elementary Teachers	3.7	33,303	32,970	32,915	-1.0	-0.1	36	37	11	12	12
Numbers of Public Secondary School Teachers	30.6	21,958	21,739	23,169	-0.9	6.5	31	4	16	15	14
Numbers of Public Elementary and Secondary Teachers	12.8	55,261	54,709	56,084	-1.0	2.5	34	13	12	12	13
Elementary Teachers' Salaries	99.9	17,476	18,299	20,620	4.7	12.6	38	6	37	38	33
Secondary Teachers' Salaries	89.4	17,697	18,530	20,788	4.7	12.1	36	5	43	41	35
Total Teachers' Salaries	130.0	17,585	18,014	20,691	2.4	14.8	44	1	38	41	33
Per Pupil Expenditures in ADA	229.2	2,265	2,460	2,588	8.6	5.2	17	34	43	43	45
Total Current Expenditures (in thousands)	192.9	2,439,684	2,609,253	2,727,800	6.9	4.5	22	37	14	15	15
Total Revenue Receipts (in thousands)	146.4	2,503,835	2,654,169	2,787,900	6.0	5.0	26	37	14	13	14

	Change in percent 1972-73 to 1982-83	Percent share 1982-83	1983-84	1984-85
Federal Revenue Receipts	2.6	16.1	11.4	10.3
State Revenue Receipts	-2.6	61.5	61.7	61.5
Local and Other Revenue Receipts	1.9	22.4	26.9	28.2

	Percent change 1972 to 1982	1982	1983	1984	Percent change 1982 to 1983	1983 to 1984	State's rank in percent change 1982 to 1983	1983 to 1984	Rank 1982	1983	1984
Total Personal Income (in millions)	169.2	54,433	59,628	66,322	9.6	11.3	7	7	13	13	13
Per Capita Income	138.4	9,048	9,805	10,758	8.3	9.7	8	13	41	41	38
Population (in thousands)	13.7	6,019	6,082	6,165	1.0	1.3	20	13	10	10	10
Population Under Age 5	-7.6	416,000	421,000	416,000	1.2	-1.1	35	30	12	11	11

	Score change 1972 to 1982	Average score 1982	1983	1984	Percent change 1982 to 1983	1983 to 1984	State's rank in percent change 1982 to 1983	1983 to 1984	State's rank in 1982 score	1983 score	1984 score
SAT Verbal Scores	-15.0	396	394	395	-0.5	0.2	36	26	48	48	48
SAT Math Scores	-7.0	431	431	432	0.0	0.2	25	34	48	48	48

	Score change 1978 to 1982	Average score 1982	1983	1984	Percent change 1982 to 1983	1983 to 1984	State's rank in percent change 1982 to 1983	1983 to 1984	State's rank in 1982 score	1983 score	1984 score
SAT Verbal Scores of Intended Education Majors	10.0	365	360	368	-1.3	2.2	42	15	47	49	49
SAT Math Scores of Intended Education Majors	11.0	393	389	392	-1.0	0.7	41	33	47	49	50

	Change in percent 1972 to 1981	Percent minority enrollment 1972	1976	1981
Percentage of Minority Enrollment	1.1	30.8	31.4	31.9

	Change in percent 1965 to 1980	Percent of all students enrolled in private schools 1965	1970	1980
Percentage of Private School Enrollment	3.0	1.9	4.8	4.9

	Change in percent 1971 to 1983	1971-72	1980-81	1983-84
Graduation Rates	0.8	68.5	67.1	69.3

	Change in percent 1980 to 1985	Percent unemployed 1980	1984	1985
Unemployment Rates	-0.3	5.9	7.3	5.6

131

	Percent change 1972-73 to 1982-83	1982-83	1983-84	1984-85	Percent change 1982-83 to 1983-84	Percent change 1983-84 to 1984-85	State's rank in percent change 1982-83 to 1983-84	State's rank in percent change 1983-84 to 1984-85	State's Rank 1982	1983	1984
Public Elementary School Enrollment	-14.5	80,647	80,903	83,157	0.3	2.8	6	7	45	45	44
Public Secondary School Enrollment	-23.9	35,922	33,862	35,076	-5.8	3.6	49	6	51	51	51
Public Elementary and Secondary Enrollment	-17.6	116,569	114,765	118,233	-1.5	3.0	37	5	45	46	46
Numbers of Public Elementary Teachers	3.5	4,719	4,708	4,608	-0.2	-2.1	21	47	43	43	44
Numbers of Public Secondary School Teachers	6.9	2,780	2,677	2,692	-3.7	0.5	45	22	48	48	47
Numbers of Public Elementary and Secondary Teachers	4.7	7,499	7,385	7,300	-1.5	-1.1	37	44	44	45	46
Elementary Teachers' Salaries	129.2	17,680	19,503	19,610	10.3	0.5	3	46	36	29	39
Secondary Teachers' Salaries	121.1	19,110	21,231	20,340	11.0	-4.1	2	51	32	28	39
Total Teachers' Salaries	127.7	18,390	20,363	19,900	10.7	-2.2	3	51	32	27	40
Per Pupil Expenditures in ADA	259.0	3,055	3,307	3,249	8.2	1.7	20	47	20	20	30
Total Current Expenditures (in thousands)	187.7	383,480	408,165	399,860	6.4	-2.0	25	50	47	47	47
Total Revenue Receipts (in thousands)	149.6	340,500	378,002	352,000	11.0	-6.8	3	50	50	47	50

	Change in percent 1972-73 to 1982-83	Percent share 1982-83	1983-84	1984-85
Federal Revenue Receipts	-3.4	7.3	7.1	7.1
State Revenue Receipts	22.7	51.5	56.4	59.5
Local and Other Revenue Receipts	-19.4	41.1	36.4	33.4

	Percent change 1972 to 1982	1982	1983	1984	Percent change 1982 to 1983	Percent change 1983 to 1984	State's rank in percent change 1982 to 1983	State's rank in percent change 1983 to 1984	Rank 1982	1983	1984
Total Personal Income (in millions)	162.3	7,290	7,937	8,553	8.8	7.7	10	41	47	47	46
Per Capita Income	147.0	10,830	11,664	12,461	7.7	6.8	12	42	24	22	24
Population (in thousands)	6.2	672	680	686	1.1	0.8	16	22	46	46	46
Population Under Age 5	1.8	59,000	61,000	61,000	3.3	0.0	16	16	46	45	45

	Score change 1972 to 1982	Average score 1982	1983	1984	Percent change 1982 to 1983	Percent change 1983 to 1984	State's rank in percent change 1982 to 1983	State's rank in percent change 1983 to 1984	State's rank in 1982 score	1983 score	1984 score
SAT Verbal Scores	-20.0	505	505	500	0.0	-0.9	29	49	3	4	5
SAT Math Scores	-3.0	563	560	554	-0.5	-1.0	40	49	2	2	3

	Score change 1978 to 1982	Average score 1982	1983	1984	Percent change 1982 to 1983	Percent change 1983 to 1984	State's rank in percent change 1982 to 1983	State's rank in percent change 1983 to 1984	State's rank in 1982 score	1983 score	1984 score
SAT Verbal Scores of Intended Education Majors	0.0	0	445	484	-0.1	8.7	33	3	51	9	3
SAT Math Scores of Intended Education Majors	0.0	0	509	502	-0.1	-1.3	25	45	51	3	5

	Change in percent 1972 to 1981	Percent minority enrollment 1972	1976	1981
Percentage of Minority Enrollment	1.1	2.4	6.2	3.5

	Change in percent 1965 to 1980	Percent of all students enrolled in private schools 1965	1970	1980
Percentage of Private School Enrollment	-3.1	11.5	8.7	8.4

	Change in percent 1971 to 1983	1971-72	1980-81	1983-84
Graduation Rates	3.7	91.1	81.9	94.8

	Change in percent 1980 to 1985	Percent unemployed 1980	1984	1985
Unemployment Rates	2.2	5.3	6.6	7.5

	Percent change 1972-73 to 1982-83	1982-83	1983-84	1984-85	Percent change 1982-83 to 1983-84	Percent change 1983-84 to 1984-85	State's rank in percent change 1982-83 to 1983-84	State's rank in percent change 1983-84 to 1984-85	State's Rank 1982	1983	1984
Public Elementary School Enrollment	-24.0	1,148,400	1,130,800	1,108,400	-1.5	-1.9	38	44	6	6	6
Public Secondary School Enrollment	-22.5	708,100	697,300	697,700	-1.5	0.0	28	22	5	6	6
Public Elementary and Secondary Enrollment	-23.4	1,856,500	1,828,100	1,806,100	-1.5	-1.2	37	43	5	5	5
Numbers of Public Elementary Teachers	-4.8	52,940	52,800	50,820	-0.2	-3.8	21	48	5	5	5
Numbers of Public Secondary School Teachers	-14.3	41,190	39,965	43,609	-2.9	9.3	42	3	5	5	5
Numbers of Public Elementary and Secondary Teachers	-9.2	94,130	92,765	94,429	-1.4	1.8	35	18	6	6	6
Elementary Teachers' Salaries	111.7	19,550	20,922	22,183	7.0	6.0	19	33	25	23	23
Secondary Teachers' Salaries	111.9	20,590	22,072	23,383	7.1	5.9	17	31	24	21	24
Total Teachers' Salaries	111.5	20,004	21,421	22,737	7.0	6.1	19	31	24	23	23
Per Pupil Expenditures in ADA	194.2	2,784	3,090	3,315	10.9	7.2	7	26	28	27	25
Total Current Expenditures (in thousands)	117.1	5,080,000	5,570,000	5,865,000	9.6	5.2	8	33	7	7	7
Total Revenue Receipts (in thousands)	115.4	5,310,000	5,790,000	6,100,000	9.0	5.3	9	36	7	7	6

	Change in percent 1972-73 to 1982-83	Percent share 1982-83	1983-84	1984-85
Federal Revenue Receipts	-0.8	5.0	5.2	5.1
State Revenue Receipts	7.4	40.7	43.9	42.6
Local and Other Revenue Receipts	-6.6	54.3	50.9	52.3

	Percent change 1972 to 1982	1982	1983	1984	Percent change 1982 to 1983	Percent change 1983 to 1984	State's rank in percent change 1982 to 1983	State's rank in percent change 1983 to 1984	Rank 1982	1983	1984
Total Personal Income (in millions)	140.3	115,087	120,539	132,404	4.7	9.8	41	22	6	7	7
Per Capita Income	139.4	10,667	11,218	12,314	5.1	9.7	30	13	29	27	26
Population (in thousands)	0.4	10,772	10,746	10,752	-0.2	0.0	48	45	6	6	7
Population Under Age 5	9.6	810,000	808,000	788,000	-0.2	-2.4	49	45	5	5	5

	Score change 1972 to 1982	Average score 1982	1983	1984	Percent change 1982 to 1983	Percent change 1983 to 1984	State's rank in percent change 1982 to 1983	State's rank in percent change 1983 to 1984	1982 score	1983 score	1984 score
SAT Verbal Scores	-5.0	456	458	460	0.4	0.4	12	19	27	26	27
SAT Math Scores	-7.0	502	504	508	0.3	0.7	15	15	26	26	25

	Score change 1978 to 1982	Average score 1982	1983	1984	Percent change 1982 to 1983	Percent change 1983 to 1984	State's rank in percent change 1982 to 1983	State's rank in percent change 1983 to 1984	1982 score	1983 score	1984 score
SAT Verbal Scores of Intended Education Majors	0.0	423	429	426	1.4	-0.6	16	42	19	20	24
SAT Math Scores of Intended Education Majors	3.0	454	452	457	-0.4	1.1	28	30	12	16	20

	Change in percent 1972 to 1981	Percent minority enrollment 1972	1976	1981
Percentage of Minority Enrollment	0.7	14.0	14.0	14.7

	Change in percent 1965 to 1980	Percent of all students enrolled in private schools 1965	1970	1980
Percentage of Private School Enrollment	-2.3	14.4	13.5	12.1

	Change in percent 1971 to 1983	1971-72	1980-81	1983-84
Graduation Rates	1.2	81.0	75.9	82.2

	Change in percent 1980 to 1985	Percent unemployed 1980	1984	1985
Unemployment Rates	3.1	6.6	10.6	9.7

SUMMARY TABLE 38. Oklahoma

	Percent change 1972-73 to 1982-83	1982-83	1983-84	1984-85	Percent change 1982-83 to 1983-84	1983-84 to 1984-85	State's rank in percent change 1982-83 to 1983-84	1983-84 to 1984-85	State's Rank 1982	1983	1984
Public Elementary School Enrollment	-0.1	343,317	344,611	334,000	0.3	-3.0	6	48	26	25	25
Public Secondary School Enrollment	-9.5	250,508	243,427	256,000	-2.8	5.1	41	3	21	21	20
Public Elementary and Secondary Enrollment	-4.3	593,825	588,038	590,000	-0.9	0.3	24	20	25	25	25
Numbers of Public Elementary Teachers	19.8	18,294	18,682	18,300	2.1	-2.0	5	46	25	23	26
Numbers of Public Secondary School Teachers	20.8	16,779	17,011	16,700	1.3	-1.8	10	40	20	20	20
Numbers of Public Elementary and Secondary Teachers	20.2	35,073	35,693	35,000	1.7	-1.9	8	46	22	22	23
Elementary Teachers' Salaries	132.3	17,780	19,503	18,380	9.6	-5.7	6	51	35	29	48
Secondary Teachers' Salaries	132.2	18,790	19,000	19,490	1.1	2.5	49	45	34	39	45
Total Teachers' Salaries	132.1	18,270	18,490	18,930	1.2	2.3	48	44	35	40	47
Per Pupil Expenditures in ADA	263.5	3,039	3,312	3,264	8.9	-1.4	15	46	21	19	29
Total Current Expenditures (in thousands)	246.9	1,865,000	2,026,876	2,017,362	8.6	-0.4	13	49	21	21	22
Total Revenue Receipts (in thousands)	123.0	1,890,000	2,088,860	1,986,000	10.5	-4.9	5	49	21	21	23

	Change in percent 1972-73 to 1982-83	Percent share 1982-83	1983-84	1984-85
Federal Revenue Receipts	0.5	10.3	7.3	7.4
State Revenue Receipts	17.3	60.2	66.7	61.4
Local and Other Revenue Receipts	-17.8	29.5	26.0	31.2

	Percent change 1972 to 1982	1982	1983	1984	Percent change 1982 to 1983	1983 to 1984	State's rank in percent change 1982 to 1983	1983 to 1984	Rank 1982	1983	1984
Total Personal Income (in millions)	241.5	36,121	36,238	38,735	0.3	6.9	49	44	24	25	25
Per Capita Income	185.7	11,247	10,988	11,745	-2.3	6.8	50	42	18	30	32
Population (in thousands)	19.6	3,226	3,298	3,298	2.2	0.0	7	45	25	24	25
Population Under Age 5	24.0	258,000	280,000	281,000	8.5	0.3	2	15	24	24	23

	Score change 1972 to 1982	Average score 1982	1983	1984	Percent change 1982 to 1983	1983 to 1984	State's rank in percent change 1982 to 1983	1983 to 1984	1982 score	1983 score	1984 score
SAT Verbal Scores	-12.0	483	489	484	1.2	-1.0	4	51	10	8	11
SAT Math Scores	-4.0	518	521	525	0.5	0.7	9	15	13	11	14

	Score change 1978 to 1982	Average score 1982	1983	1984	Percent change 1982 to 1983	1983 to 1984	State's rank in percent change 1982 to 1983	1983 to 1984	1982 score	1983 score	1984 score
SAT Verbal Scores of Intended Education Majors	-5.0	442	452	438	2.2	-3.0	11	47	8	7	19
SAT Math Scores of Intended Education Majors	-23.0	448	456	453	1.7	-0.6	15	42	20	13	22

	Change in percent 1972 to 1981	Percent minority enrollment 1972	1976	1981
Percentage of Minority Enrollment	4.4	16.4	22.0	20.8

	Change in percent 1965 to 1980	Percent of all students enrolled in private schools 1965	1970	1980
Percentage of Private School Enrollment	-0.4	3.1	2.9	2.7

	Change in percent 1971 to 1983	1971-72	1980-81	1983-84
Graduation Rates	0.2	79.4	75.4	79.6

	Change in percent 1980 to 1985	Percent unemployed 1980	1984	1985
Unemployment Rates	3.5	4.3	7.3	7.8

134

	Percent change 1972-73 to 1982-83	1982-83	1983-84	1984-85	Percent change 1982-83 to 1983-84	Percent change 1983-84 to 1984-85	State's rank in percent change 1982-83 to 1983-84	State's rank in percent change 1983-84 to 1984-85	State's Rank 1982	1983	1984
Public Elementary School Enrollment	-1.3	276,238	275,330	278,672	-0.3	1.2	16	16	29	29	29
Public Secondary School Enrollment	-13.4	171,946	171,370	168,013	-0.3	-1.9	19	41	30	30	30
Public Elementary and Secondary Enrollment	-6.3	448,184	446,700	446,685	-0.3	0.0	13	27	31	31	31
Numbers of Public Elementary Teachers	23.1	14,817	14,070	14,256	-5.0	1.3	50	26	29	31	30
Numbers of Public Secondary School Teachers	-4.4	10,455	9,920	10,157	-5.1	2.3	48	13	32	32	32
Numbers of Public Elementary and Secondary Teachers	10.7	25,272	23,990	24,413	-5.0	1.7	49	19	31	32	32
Elementary Teachers' Salaries	132.4	21,309	22,374	24,358	4.9	8.8	36	14	14	17	14
Secondary Teachers' Salaries	138.0	22,536	23,663	25,822	5.0	9.1	34	12	12	13	12
Total Teachers' Salaries	132.6	21,746	22,833	24,889	4.9	9.0	34	12	14	17	13
Per Pupil Expenditures in ADA	258.9	3,604	3,771	3,963	4.6	5.0	43	36	7	8	12
Total Current Expenditures (in thousands)	238.7	1,607,012	1,653,664	1,711,191	2.9	3.4	45	42	25	25	27
Total Revenue Receipts (in thousands)	198.4	1,595,946	1,650,080	1,720,000	3.3	4.2	40	40	26	26	26

	Change in percent 1972-73 to 1982-83	Percent share 1982-83	1983-84	1984-85
Federal Revenue Receipts	4.5	8.8	5.6	4.9
State Revenue Receipts	16.5	36.8	28.8	29.0
Local and Other Revenue Receipts	-21.1	54.4	65.6	66.1

	Percent change 1972 to 1982	1982	1983	1984	Percent change 1982 to 1983	Percent change 1983 to 1984	State's rank in percent change 1982 to 1983	State's rank in percent change 1983 to 1984	Rank 1982	1983	1984
Total Personal Income (in millions)	188.5	27,350	28,659	30,973	4.7	8.0	41	39	30	31	31
Per Capita Income	139.1	10,231	10,768	11,582	5.2	7.5	29	36	31	31	34
Population (in thousands)	20.7	2,668	2,662	2,674	-0.2	0.4	48	36	30	30	30
Population Under Age 5	24.6	208,000	209,000	205,000	0.4	-1.9	41	41	30	31	31

	Score change 1972 to 1982	Average score 1982	1983	1984	Percent change 1982 to 1983	Percent change 1983 to 1984	State's rank in percent change 1982 to 1983	State's rank in percent change 1983 to 1984	State's rank in 1982 score	1983 score	1984 score
SAT Verbal Scores	-20.0	435	432	435	-0.6	0.6	37	8	31	34	33
SAT Math Scores	-10.0	473	469	472	-0.8	0.6	45	20	32	33	32

	Score change 1978 to 1982	Average score 1982	1983	1984	Percent change 1982 to 1983	Percent change 1983 to 1984	State's rank in percent change 1982 to 1983	State's rank in percent change 1983 to 1984	State's rank in 1982 score	1983 score	1984 score
SAT Verbal Scores of Intended Education Majors	-11.0	401	406	411	1.2	1.2	17	25	28	29	30
SAT Math Scores of Intended Education Majors	-8.0	420	428	433	1.9	1.1	14	30	31	27	30

	Change in percent 1972 to 1981	Percent minority enrollment 1972	1976	1981
Percentage of Minority Enrollment	3.9	4.6	6.5	8.5

	Change in percent 1965 to 1980	Percent of all students enrolled in private schools 1965	1970	1980
Percentage of Private School Enrollment	-1.6	7.3	8.4	5.7

	Change in percent 1971 to 1983	1971-72	1980-81	1983-84
Graduation Rates	-10.8	83.8	70.6	73.0

	Change in percent 1980 to 1985	Percent unemployed 1980	1984	1985
Unemployment Rates	3.2	7.9	10.1	11.1

135

SUMMARY TABLE 40. Pennsylvania

	Percent change 1972-73 to 1982-83	1982-83	1983-84	1984-85	Percent change 1982-83 to 1983-84	1983-84 to 1984-85	State's rank in percent change 1982-83 to 1983-84	1983-84 to 1984-85	State's Rank 1982	1983	1984
Public Elementary School Enrollment	-28.2	872,629	844,640	832,850	-3.2	-1.3	48	41	7	7	7
Public Secondary School Enrollment	-20.7	911,340	891,860	869,210	-2.1	-2.5	35	47	4	4	4
Public Elementary and Secondary Enrollment	-24.6	1,783,969	1,736,500	1,702,060	-2.6	-1.9	47	47	6	6	7
Numbers of Public Elementary Teachers	-12.5	48,917	48,114	47,744	-1.6	-0.7	39	40	6	6	7
Numbers of Public Secondary School Teachers	-3.9	54,938	54,036	53,406	-1.6	-1.1	36	35	4	4	4
Numbers of Public Elementary and Secondary Teachers	-8.0	103,855	102,150	101,150	-1.6	-0.9	39	42	4	4	4
Elementary Teachers' Salaries	101.5	21,098	22,720	24,289	7.6	6.9	14	29	17	12	15
Secondary Teachers' Salaries	101.1	21,241	22,875	24,561	7.6	7.3	11	20	20	19	18
Total Teachers' Salaries	102.1	21,178	22,800	24,435	7.6	7.1	14	25	19	18	18
Per Pupil Expenditures in ADA	182.4	3,385	3,725	4,002	10.0	7.4	11	24	12	10	10
Total Current Expenditures (in thousands)	99.5	6,160,900	6,553,000	7,014,130	6.3	7.0	26	28	4	4	4
Total Revenue Receipts (in thousands)	108.2	6,204,300	6,523,500	6,946,060	5.1	6.4	31	32	4	4	4

	Change in percent 1972-73 to 1982-83	Percent share 1982-83	1983-84	1984-85
Federal Revenue Receipts	-0.3	7.5	4.3	3.2
State Revenue Receipts	-5.4	45.2	45.4	45.4
Local and Other Revenue Receipts	5.8	47.4	50.3	51.4

	Percent change 1972 to 1982	1982	1983	1984	Percent change 1982 to 1983	1983 to 1984	State's rank in percent change 1982 to 1983	1983 to 1984	Rank 1982	1983	1984
Total Personal Income (in millions)	143.6	129,956	136,409	146,894	5.0	7.7	39	41	5	5	5
Per Capita Income	144.4	10,934	11,468	12,343	4.8	7.6	35	34	22	25	25
Population (in thousands)	-0.3	11,879	11,895	11,901	0.1	0.0	43	45	4	4	4
Population Under Age 5	-12.1	775,000	788,000	778,000	1.6	-1.2	30	32	6	6	6

	Score change 1972 to 1982	Average score 1982	1983	1984	Percent change 1982 to 1983	1983 to 1984	State's rank in percent change 1982 to 1983	1983 to 1984	1982 score	1983 score	1984 score
SAT Verbal Scores	-24.0	424	425	425	0.2	0.0	18	34	42	39	39
SAT Math Scores	-17.0	461	461	462	0.0	0.2	25	34	43	43	43

	Score change 1978 to 1982	Average score 1982	1983	1984	Percent change 1982 to 1983	1983 to 1984	State's rank in percent change 1982 to 1983	1983 to 1984	1982 score	1983 score	1984 score
SAT Verbal Scores of Intended Education Majors	-1.0	398	400	402	0.5	0.5	21	34	32	33	33
SAT Math Scores of Intended Education Majors	-6.0	422	419	424	-0.7	1.1	37	30	30	35	38

	Change in percent 1972 to 1981	Percent minority enrollment 1972	1976	1981
Percentage of Minority Enrollment	1.5	13.3	14.4	14.8

	Change in percent 1965 to 1980	Percent of all students enrolled in private schools 1965	1970	1980
Percentage of Private School Enrollment	-4.1	21.5	19.5	17.4

	Change in percent 1971 to 1983	1971-72	1980-81	1983-84
Graduation Rates	-5.9	85.6	78.7	79.7

	Change in percent 1980 to 1985	Percent unemployed 1980	1984	1985
Unemployment Rates	0.6	7.8	9.6	8.4

136

	Percent change 1972-73 to 1982-83	1982-83	1983-84	1984-85	Percent change 1982-83 to 1983-84	1983-84 to 1984-85	State's rank in percent change 1982-83 to 1983-84	1983-84 to 1984-85	State's Rank 1982	1983	1984
Public Elementary School Enrollment	-40.8	73,591	68,642	68,615	-6.7	0.0	51	26	46	46	46
Public Secondary School Enrollment	-6.1	65,771	67,537	65,419	2.7	-3.1	3	49	42	41	42
Public Elementary and Secondary Enrollment	-27.5	139,362	136,179	134,034	-2.2	-1.5	43	45	44	44	44
Numbers of Public Elementary Teachers	-17.0	3,573	3,581	3,723	0.2	3.9	15	15	47	47	48
Numbers of Public Secondary School Teachers	5.8	3,826	3,860	3,825	0.8	-0.9	15	34	41	41	41
Numbers of Public Elementary and Secondary Teachers	-7.7	7,399	7,441	7,548	0.5	1.4	15	21	45	44	44
Elementary Teachers' Salaries	134.0	24,070	25,593	27,497	6.3	7.4	27	22	6	5	5
Secondary Teachers' Salaries	100.1	22,154	23,555	28,075	6.3	19.1	25	1	15	16	5
Total Teachers' Salaries	130.0	23,175	24,641	27,384	6.3	11.1	26	9	9	7	5
Per Pupil Expenditures in ADA	220.3	3,389	3,720	4,097	9.7	10.1	13	15	11	11	9
Total Current Expenditures (in thousands)	126.9	444,947	469,419	506,670	5.5	7.9	32	24	44	44	43
Total Revenue Receipts (in thousands)	121.1	447,699	469,564	500,293	4.8	6.5	33	29	43	43	44

	Change in percent 1972-73 to 1982-83	Percent share 1982-83	1983-84	1984-85
Federal Revenue Receipts	-3.0	4.7	4.6	4.1
State Revenue Receipts	1.2	37.0	35.8	36.8
Local and Other Revenue Receipts	1.8	58.3	59.5	59.0

	Percent change 1972 to 1982	1982	1983	1984	Percent change 1982 to 1983	1983 to 1984	State's rank in percent change 1982 to 1983	1983 to 1984	Rank 1982	1983	1984
Total Personal Income (in millions)	137.8	10,254	11,173	12,245	8.9	9.5	9	25	41	41	41
Per Capita Income	142.3	10,751	11,694	12,730	8.7	8.8	6	20	26	20	18
Population (in thousands)	-1.8	953	955	962	0.2	0.7	39	26	41	42	42
Population Under Age 5	-17.8	60,000	60,000	60,000	0.0	0.0	43	16	45	46	46

	Score change 1972 to 1982	Average score 1982	1983	1984	Percent change 1982 to 1983	1983 to 1984	State's rank in percent change 1982 to 1983	1983 to 1984	1982 score	1983 score	1984 score
SAT Verbal Scores	-31.0	420	422	424	0.4	0.4	12	19	43	41	40
SAT Math Scores	-19.0	457	459	461	0.4	0.4	11	27	44	44	44

	Score change 1978 to 1982	Average score 1982	1983	1984	Percent change 1982 to 1983	1983 to 1984	State's rank in percent change 1982 to 1983	1983 to 1984	1982 score	1983 score	1984 score
SAT Verbal Scores of Intended Education Majors	-8.0	393	384	398	-2.2	3.6	48	11	38	45	39
SAT Math Scores of Intended Education Majors	-13.0	415	406	416	-2.1	2.4	46	14	36	45	41

	Change in percent 1972 to 1981	Percent minority enrollment 1972	1976	1981
Percentage of Minority Enrollment	3.1	5.1	6.5	8.2

	Change in percent 1965 to 1980	Percent of all students enrolled in private schools 1965	1970	1980
Percentage of Private School Enrollment	-8.0	24.8	20.2	16.8

	Change in percent 1971 to 1983	1971-72	1980-81	1983-84
Graduation Rates	-6.0	81.2	72.6	75.2

	Change in percent 1980 to 1985	Percent unemployed 1980	1984	1985
Unemployment Rates	-1.7	7.5	6.0	5.8

SUMMARY TABLE 42. South Carolina

	Percent change 1972-73 to 1982-83	1982-83	1983-84	1984-85	Percent change 1982-83 to 1983-84	Percent change 1983-84 to 1984-85	State's rank in percent change 1982-83 to 1983-84	State's rank in percent change 1983-84 to 1984-85	State's Rank 1982	1983	1984
Public Elementary School Enrollment	8.9	424,363	420,000	422,420	-1.0	0.5	28	23	20	20	20
Public Secondary School Enrollment	-22.6	184,156	180,800	180,300	-1.8	-0.2	31	28	29	29	29
Public Elementary and Secondary Enrollment	-3.1	608,519	600,800	602,720	-1.2	0.3	30	20	24	24	24
Numbers of Public Elementary Teachers	24.8	20,408	20,430	21,270	0.1	4.1	16	13	20	19	18
Numbers of Public Secondary School Teachers	10.8	11,622	11,640	12,070	0.1	3.6	19	9	29	28	28
Numbers of Public Elementary and Secondary Teachers	19.2	32,030	32,070	33,340	0.1	3.9	19	6	26	25	24
Elementary Teachers' Salaries	101.4	16,027	16,980	19,206	5.9	13.1	29	5	46	46	43
Secondary Teachers' Salaries	108.4	17,183	18,200	20,592	5.9	13.1	30	2	45	44	36
Total Teachers' Salaries	103.2	16,523	17,500	19,800	5.9	13.1	28	2	46	45	41
Per Pupil Expenditures in ADA	152.3	2,247	2,431	2,650	8.1	9.0	22	21	44	44	43
Total Current Expenditures (in thousands)	154.5	1,459,657	1,572,445	1,715,435	7.7	9.0	16	16	29	28	26
Total Revenue Receipts (in thousands)	158.0	1,489,700	1,630,802	1,743,738	9.4	6.9	7	26'	29	27	25

	Change in percent 1972-73 to 1982-83	Percent share 1982-83	1983-84	1984-85
Federal Revenue Receipts	-3.4	13.6	12.0	6.9
State Revenue Receipts	1.4	57.1	59.3	62.8
Local and Other Revenue Receipts	2.0	29.3	28.6	30.3

	Percent change 1972 to 1982	1982	1983	1984	Percent change 1982 to 1983	1983 to 1984	State's rank in percent change 1982 to 1983	State's rank in percent change 1983 to 1984	Rank 1982	1983	1984
Total Personal Income (in millions)	154.2	27,228	29,923	33,248	9.8	11.1	6	9	31	29	29
Per Capita Income	142.6	8,475	9,168	10,075	8.1	9.8	11	11	49	47	46
Population (in thousands)	17.8	3,227	3,264	3,300	1.1	1.1	16	16	24	25	24
Population Under Age 5	3.7	250,000	254,000	252,000	1.6	-0.7	30	28	25	26	27

	Score change 1972 to 1982	Average score 1982	1983	1984	Percent change 1982 to 1983	1983 to 1984	State's rank in percent change 1982 to 1983	State's rank in percent change 1983 to 1984	1982 score	1983 score	1984 score
SAT Verbal Scores	-21.0	378	383	384	1.3	0.2	3	26	51	51	51
SAT Math Scores	-12.0	412	415	419	0.7	0.9	8	10	51	51	50

	Score change 1978 to 1982	Average score 1982	1983	1984	Percent change 1982 to 1983	1983 to 1984	State's rank in percent change 1982 to 1983	State's rank in percent change 1983 to 1984	1982 score	1983 score	1984 score
SAT Verbal Scores of Intended Education Majors	4.0	356	358	356	0.5	-0.5	21	41	49	51	51
SAT Math Scores of Intended Education Majors	6.0	384	382	383	-0.5	0.2	32	39	49	50	51

	Change in percent 1972 to 1981	Percent minority enrollment 1972	1976	1981
Percentage of Minority Enrollment	2.3	41.2	41.8	43.5

	Change in percent 1965 to 1980	Percent of all students enrolled in private schools 1965	1970	1980
Percentage of Private School Enrollment	4.9	2.5	5.8	7.4

	Change in percent 1971 to 1983	1971-72	1980-81	1983-84
Graduation Rates	-3.8	70.0	70.3	66.2

	Change in percent 1980 to 1985	Percent unemployed 1980	1984	1985
Unemployment Rates	1.1	5.7	7.3	6.8

138

SUMMARY TABLE 43. South Dakota

	Percent change 1972-73 to 1982-83	1982-83	1983-84	1984-85	Percent change 1982-83 to 1983-84	Percent change 1983-84 to 1984-85	State's rank in percent change 1982-83 to 1983-84	State's rank in percent change 1983-84 to 1984-85	State's Rank 1982	1983	1984
Public Elementary School Enrollment	-22.3	85,718	85,920	86,228	0.2	0.3	8	25	43	43	43
Public Secondary School Enrollment	-27.1	37,907	36,736	36,590	-3.1	-0.4	46	33	50	50	50
Public Elementary and Secondary Enrollment	-23.8	123,625	122,656	122,818	-0.7	0.1	22	26	45	45	45
Numbers of Public Elementary Teachers	1.3	5,200	5,334	5,387	2.5	0.9	4	30	40	40	40
Numbers of Public Secondary School Teachers	-8.6	2,612	2,655	2,635	1.6	-0.7	8	33	49	49	48
Numbers of Public Elementary and Secondary Teachers	-2.3	7,812	7,989	8,022	2.2	0.4	6	33	43	43	43
Elementary Teachers' Salaries	101.4	15,386	16,200	17,300	5.2	6.7	35	30	49	50	50
Secondary Teachers' Salaries	93.7	15,988	16,700	17,450	4.4	4.4	38	37	49	50	50
Total Teachers' Salaries	97.2	15,595	16,480	17,356	5.6	5.3	32	37	49	50	50
Per Pupil Expenditures in ADA	186.1	2,411	2,657	2,813	10.2	5.8	9	32	41	40	39
Total Current Expenditures (in thousands)	117.0	309,340	335,000	365,500	8.3	9.1	14	13	49	49	50
Total Revenue Receipts (in thousands)	133.0	344,000	371,300	364,500	7.9	-1.8	12	47	48	48	49

	Change in percent 1972-73 to 1982-83	Percent share 1982-83	1983-84	1984-85
Federal Revenue Receipts	-3.2	8.7	8.1	10.6
State Revenue Receipts	14.1	27.6	26.9	26.9
Local and Other Revenue Receipts	-10.9	63.7	65.0	62.6

	Percent change 1972 to 1982	1982	1983	1984	Percent change 1982 to 1983	Percent change 1983 to 1984	State's rank in percent change 1982 to 1983	State's rank in percent change 1983 to 1984	Rank 1982	1983	1984
Total Personal Income (in millions)	154.2	6,676	6,894	7,799	3.2	13.1	45	2	49	49	49
Per Capita Income	144.2	9,582	9,851	11,049	2.8	12.1	44	2	36	40	36
Population (in thousands)	2.1	694	700	706	0.8	0.8	25	22	45	45	45
Population Under Age 5	13.0	61,000	64,000	63,000	4.9	-1.5	11	36	44	44	44

	Score change 1972 to 1982	Average score 1982	1983	1984	Percent change 1982 to 1983	Percent change 1983 to 1984	State's rank in percent change 1982 to 1983	State's rank in percent change 1983 to 1984	1982 score	1983 score	1984 score
SAT Verbal Scores	9.0	522	517	520	-0.9	0.5	43	16	1	2	1
SAT Math Scores	7.0	553	560	566	1.2	1.0	3	9	3	2	2

	Score change 1978 to 1982	Average score 1982	1983	1984	Percent change 1982 to 1983	Percent change 1983 to 1984	State's rank in percent change 1982 to 1983	State's rank in percent change 1983 to 1984	1982 score	1983 score	1984 score
SAT Verbal Scores of Intended Education Majors	1.0	490	495	514	1.0	3.8	18	10	1	1	1
SAT Math Scores of Intended Education Majors	25.0	531	564	539	6.2	-4.4	4	51	1	1	2

	Change in percent 1972 to 1981	Percent minority enrollment 1972	1976	1981
Percentage of Minority Enrollment	5.4	7.8	7.9	2.5

	Change in percent 1965 to 1980	Percent of all students enrolled in private schools 1965	1970	1980
Percentage of Private School Enrollment	-2.3	10.1	6.7	7.8

	Change in percent 1971 to 1983	1971-72	1980-81	1983-84
Graduation Rates	-6.2	91.2	82.0	85.0

	Change in percent 1980 to 1985	Percent unemployed 1980	1984	1985
Unemployment Rates	1.2	4.8	5.0	6.0

SUMMARY TABLE 44. Tennessee

	Percent change 1972-73 to 1982-83	1982-83	1983-84	1984-85	Percent change 1982-83 to 1983-84	Percent change 1983-84 to 1984-85	State's rank in percent change 1982-83 to 1983-84	State's rank in percent change 1983-84 to 1984-85	State's Rank 1982	State's Rank 1983	State's Rank 1984
Public Elementary School Enrollment	8.6	592,002	590,148	583,578	-0.3	-1.1	16	40	14	12	13
Public Secondary School Enrollment	-30.1	238,222	236,322	237,175	-0.7	0.3	24	20	22	22	22
Public Elementary and Secondary Enrollment	-6.3	830,224	826,470	820,753	-0.4	-0.6	14	39	15	15	15
Numbers of Public Elementary Teachers	10.4	24,713	24,264	25,192	-1.8	3.8	42	16	16	16	14
Numbers of Public Secondary School Teachers	-1.5	14,696	14,872	14,816	1.1	-0.3	12	30	24	24	23
Numbers of Public Elementary and Secondary Teachers	5.6	39,409	39,136	40,008	-0.7	2.2	30	15	19	19	18
Elementary Teachers' Salaries	116.6	17,330	17,850	20,020	3.0	12.1	45	8	39	43	37
Secondary Teachers' Salaries	101.1	17,470	17,990	20,180	2.9	12.1	43	5	44	47	42
Total Teachers' Salaries	109.9	17,380	17,900	20,080	2.9	12.1	42	5	43	44	39
Per Pupil Expenditures in ADA	186.6	2,061	2,173	2,349	5.4	8.0	37	22	47	48	46
Total Current Expenditures (in thousands)	160.7	1,763,898	1,830,126	2,004,746	3.7	9.5	42	10	23	23	23
Total Revenue Receipts (in thousands)	165.1	1,695,179	1,736,012	1,958,187	2.4	12.7	44	7	24	24	24

	Change in percent 1972-73 to 1982-83	Percent share 1982-83	Percent share 1983-84	Percent share 1984-85
Federal Revenue Receipts	-0.1	13.0	10.0	9.9
State Revenue Receipts	2.1	47.2	45.9	49.9
Local and Other Revenue Receipts	-2.1	39.8	44.1	40.3

	Percent change 1972 to 1982	1982	1983	1984	Percent change 1982 to 1983	Percent change 1983 to 1984	State's rank in percent change 1982 to 1983	State's rank in percent change 1983 to 1984	Rank 1982	Rank 1983	Rank 1984
Total Personal Income (in millions)	174.7	41,406	44,580	49,055	7.7	10.1	18	18	22	22	21
Per Capita Income	141.5	8,899	9,515	10,400	6.9	9.3	13	16	44	44	41
Population (in thousands)	13.8	4,656	4,685	4,717	0.6	0.6	30	29	17	17	17
Population Under Age 5	0.0	331,000	334,000	329,000	0.9	-1.4	38	34	19	20	20

	Score change 1972 to 1982	Average score 1982	Average score 1983	Average score 1984	Percent change 1982 to 1983	Percent change 1983 to 1984	State's rank in percent change 1982 to 1983	State's rank in percent change 1983 to 1984	1982 score	1983 score	1984 score
SAT Verbal Scores	1.0	480	483	486	0.6	0.6	10	8	12	10	10
SAT Math Scores	11.0	519	519	523	0.0	0.7	25	15	11	13	15

	Score change 1978 to 1982	Average score 1982	Average score 1983	Average score 1984	Percent change 1982 to 1983	Percent change 1983 to 1984	State's rank in percent change 1982 to 1983	State's rank in percent change 1983 to 1984	1982 score	1983 score	1984 score
SAT Verbal Scores of Intended Education Majors	4.0	446	439	458	-1.5	4.3	43	9	4	11	10
SAT Math Scores of Intended Education Majors	-1.0	475	463	481	-2.5	3.8	47	8	5	11	8

	Change in percent 1972 to 1981	Percent minority enrollment 1972	1976	1981
Percentage of Minority Enrollment	3.0	21.6	21.9	24.6

	Change in percent 1965 to 1980	Percent of all students enrolled in private schools 1965	1970	1980
Percentage of Private School Enrollment	3.8	3.9	5.7	7.7

	Change in percent 1971 to 1983	1971-72	1980-81	1983-84
Graduation Rates	-6.9	72.0	71.1	65.1

	Change in percent 1980 to 1985	Percent unemployed 1980	1984	1985
Unemployment Rates	1.7	6.5	8.9	8.2

140

	Percent change 1972-73 to 1982-83	1982-83	1983-84	1984-85	Percent change 1982-83 to 1983-84	Percent change 1983-84 to 1984-85	State's rank in percent change 1982-83 to 1983-84	State's rank in percent change 1983-84 to 1984-85	State's Rank 1982	1983	1984
Public Elementary School Enrollment	23.3	1,663,304	1,668,000	1,687,880	0.2	1.1	8	17	2	2	2
Public Secondary School Enrollment	-16.4	1,322,355	1,327,000	1,371,965	0.3	3.3	8	7	2	2	1
Public Elementary and Secondary Enrollment	5.3	2,985,659	2,995,000	3,059,845	0.3	2.1	5	8	2	2	2
Numbers of Public Elementary Teachers	34.2	92,793	94,607	95,758	1.9	1.2	6	28	2	2	2
Numbers of Public Secondary School Teachers	20.6	74,505	76,489	76,881	2.6	0.5	5	22	2	2	2
Numbers of Public Elementary and Secondary Teachers	27.8	167,298	171,096	172,639	2.2	0.9	6	27	2	1	2
Elementary Teachers' Salaries	121.2	19,0007	19,379	21,965	1.9	13.3	46	4	27	32	25
Secondary Teachers' Salaries	128.8	20,225	20,763	23,390	2.6	12.6	44	3	27	31	23
Total Teachers' Salaries	124.5	19,550	20,100	22,600	2.8	12.4	43	3	27	30	24
Per Pupil Expenditures in ADA	173.7	2,547	2,670	3,287	4.8	23.1	42	1	36	39	27
Total Current Expenditures (in thousands)	207.1	8,184,426	8,700,000	11,125,151	6.2	27.8	28	1	3	3	3
Total Revenue Receipts (in thousands)	231.1	8,311,967	8,800,000	10,362,776	5.8	17.7	28	1	3	3	3

	Change in percent 1972-73 to 1982-83	Percent share 1982-83	1983-84	1984-85
Federal Revenue Receipts	-2.0	10.0	6.8	7.8
State Revenue Receipts	3.7	50.6	47.7	45.6
Local and Other Revenue Receipts	-1.7	39.5	45.5	46.6

	Percent change 1972 to 1982	1982	1983	1984	Percent change 1982 to 1983	Percent change 1983 to 1984	State's rank in percent change 1982 to 1983	State's rank in percent change 1983 to 1984	Rank 1982	1983	1984
Total Personal Income (in millions)	269.6	174,528	183,753	202,031	5.3	9.9	35	21	3	3	3
Per Capita Income	184.4	11,423	11,686	12,636	2.3	8.1	46	29	17	21	20
Population (in thousands)	29.9	15,329	15,724	15,989	2.5	1.6	4	10	3	3	3
Population Under Age 5	27.1	1,329,000	1,415,000	1,440,000	6.4	1.7	4	7	2	2	2

	Score change 1972 to 1982	Average score 1982	1983	1984	Percent change 1982 to 1983	Percent change 1983 to 1984	State's rank in percent change 1982 to 1983	State's rank in percent change 1983 to 1984	State's rank in 1982 score	1983 score	1984 score
SAT Verbal Scores	-30.0	415	412	413	-0.7	0.2	41	26	45	45	45
SAT Math Scores	-23.0	453	453	453	0.0	0.0	25	38	45	47	47

	Score change 1978 to 1982	Average score 1982	1983	1984	Percent change 1982 to 1983	Percent change 1983 to 1984	State's rank in percent change 1982 to 1983	State's rank in percent change 1983 to 1984	State's rank in 1982 score	1983 score	1984 score
SAT Verbal Scores of Intended Education Majors	-10.0	385	385	384	0.0	-0.2	27	39	44	44	46
SAT Math Scores of Intended Education Majors	-8.0	406	406	406	0.0	0.0	23	41	44	45	47

	Change in percent 1972 to 1981	Percent minority enrollment 1972	1976	1981
Percentage of Minority Enrollment	7.9	38.0	40.8	45.9

	Change in percent 1965 to 1980	Percent of all students enrolled in private schools 1965	1970	1980
Percentage of Private School Enrollment	-1.1	6.0	7.2	4.9

	Change in percent 1971 to 1983	1971-72	1980-81	1983-84
Graduation Rates	-0.8	70.2	70.4	69.4

	Change in percent 1980 to 1985	Percent unemployed 1980	1984	1985
Unemployment Rates	1.6	5.6	6.5	7.2

	Percent change 1972-73 to 1982-83	1982-83	1983-84	1984-85	Percent change 1982-83 to 1983-84	1983-84 to 1984-85	State's rank in percent change 1982-83 to 1983-84	1983-84 to 1984-85	State's Rank 1982	1983	1984
Public Elementary School Enrollment	35.3	221,521	225,244	234,437	1.6	4.0	2	3	35	34	33
Public Secondary School Enrollment	4.0	147,817	152,964	155,704	3.5	1.8	2	13	35	34	33
Public Elementary and Secondary Enrollment	20.7	369,338	378,208	390,141	2.4	3.1	1	4	35	34	34
Numbers of Public Elementary Teachers	44.8	9,251	9,416	9,984	1.7	6.0	7	5	35	35	35
Numbers of Public Secondary School Teachers	-4.0	5,826	6,017	6,204	3.2	3.1	4	10	37	37	37
Numbers of Public Elementary and Secondary Teachers	20.8	15,077	15,433	16,188	2.3	4.8	5	3	36	37	36
Elementary Teachers' Salaries	128.0	19,066	19,447	20,700	1.9	6.4	46	32	26	31	32
Secondary Teachers' Salaries	138.8	20,970	21,389	22,388	1.9	4.6	46	36	23	26	29
Total Teachers' Salaries	131.4	19,859	20,256	21,307	1.9	5.1	45	38	26	28	29
Per Pupil Expenditures in ADA	179.6	1,965	1,992	2,182	1.3	9.5	51	16	50	50	51
Total Current Expenditures (in thousands)	228.0	865,510	958,585	1,020,541	10.7	6.4	5	30	36	35	36
Total Revenue Receipts (in thousands)	220.3	886,051	896,882	1,002,619	1.2	11.8	48	9	34	35	35

	Change in percent 1972-73 to 1982-83	Percent share 1982-83	1983-84	1984-85
Federal Revenue Receipts	-3.9	5.2	5.1	5.4
State Revenue Receipts	3.2	56.3	54.7	54.4
Local and Other Revenue Receipts	-0.7	38.5	40.1	40.2

	Percent change 1972 to 1982	1982	1983	1984	Percent change 1982 to 1983	1983 to 1984	State's rank in percent change 1982 to 1983	1983 to 1984	Rank 1982	1983	1984
Total Personal Income (in millions)	220.6	13,790	14,575	16,052	5.6	10.1	33	18	36	36	36
Per Capita Income	134.1	8,820	9,005	9,719	2.0	7.9	47	32	46	49	50
Population (in thousands)	36.9	1,571	1,619	1,652	3.0	2.0	2	5	36	35	35
Population Under Age 5	65.9	204,000	211,000	206,000	3.4	-2.3	15	44	31	30	30

	Score change 1972 to 1982	Average score 1982	1983	1984	Percent change 1982 to 1983	1983 to 1984	State's rank in percent change 1982 to 1983	1983 to 1984	1982 score	1983 score	1984 score
SAT Verbal Scores	-31.0	494	508	503	2.8	-0.9	1	49	5	3	3
SAT Math Scores	-26.0	528	545	542	3.2	-0.5	1	46	10	5	9

	Score change 1978 to 1982	Average score 1982	1983	1984	Percent change 1982 to 1983	1983 to 1984	State's rank in percent change 1982 to 1983	1983 to 1984	1982 score	1983 score	1984 score
SAT Verbal Scores of Intended Education Majors	-68.0	430	468	495	8.8	5.7	3	6	15	4	2
SAT Math Scores of Intended Education Majors	-30.0	463	480	513	3.6	6.8	8	4	9	8	3

	Change in percent 1972 to 1981	Percent minority enrollment 1972	1976	1981
Percentage of Minority Enrollment	1.2	6.1	6.7	7.3

	Change in percent 1965 to 1980	Percent of all students enrolled in private schools 1965	1970	1980
Percentage of Private School Enrollment	-0.5	2.1	1.9	1.6

	Change in percent 1971 to 1983	1971-72	1980-81	1983-84
Graduation Rates	-1.1	85.6	79.4	84.5

	Change in percent 1980 to 1985	Percent unemployed 1980	1984	1985
Unemployment Rates	1.8	5.8	7.2	7.6

142

SUMMARY TABLE 47. Vermont

	Percent change 1972-73 to 1982-83	1982-83	1983-84	1984-85	Percent change 1982-83 to 1983-84	Percent change 1983-84 to 1984-85	State's rank in percent change 1982-83 to 1983-84	State's rank in percent change 1983-84 to 1984-85	State's Rank 1982	State's Rank 1983	State's Rank 1984
Public Elementary School Enrollment	-26.3	48,166	47,415	48,300	-1.5	1.8	38	12	50	50	50
Public Secondary School Enrollment	5.7	43,344	43,623	42,600	0.6	-2.3	5	46	47	46	47
Public Elementary and Secondary Enrollment	-14.0	91,510	91,038	90,900	-0.5	-0.1	16	30	49	49	50
Numbers of Public Elementary Teachers	-6.9	2,941	2,930	2,809	-0.3	-4.1	24	50	49	50	50
Numbers of Public Secondary School Teachers	27.8	3,310	3,305	3,391	-0.1	2.6	25	11	44	44	44
Numbers of Public Elementary and Secondary Teachers	9.3	6,251	6,235	6,200	-0.2	-0.5	22	38	48	49	48
Elementary Teachers' Salaries	73.5	15,794	17,373	18,539	9.9	6.7	5	30	47	44	46
Secondary Teachers' Salaries	71.5	16,747	18,489	19,407	10.4	4.9	4	34	47	42	47
Total Teachers' Salaries	72.6	16,271	17,931	19,014	10.2	6.0	4	32	47	43	45
Per Pupil Expenditures in ADA	128.1	3,102	3,148	3,783	1.4	20.1	50	3	17	25	15
Total Current Expenditures (in thousands)	85.8	278,687	300,651	333,494	7.9	10.9	15	7	51	51	51
Total Revenue Receipts (in thousands)	104.2	287,443	309,084	339,183	7.5	9.7	16	17	51	51	51

	Change in percent 1972-73 to 1982-83	Percent share 1982-83	1983-84	1984-85
Federal Revenue Receipts	0.9	7.0	5.7	6.2
State Revenue Receipts	2.2	35.2	33.8	33.4
Local and Other Revenue Receipts	-3.1	57.8	60.5	60.4

	Percent change 1972 to 1982	1982	1983	1984	Percent change 1982 to 1983	1983 to 1984	State's rank in percent change 1982 to 1983	1983 to 1984	Rank 1982	1983	1984
Total Personal Income (in millions)	166.7	4,909	5,231	5,665	6.5	8.2	27	38	51	51	51
Per Capita Income	139.3	9,478	9,957	10,692	5.0	7.3	31	39	39	37	39
Population (in thousands)	11.4	520	525	530	0.9	0.9	22	20	49	49	49
Population Under Age 5	-2.6	38,000	39,000	39,000	2.6	0.0	22	16	51	51	51

	Score change 1972 to 1982	Average score 1982	1983	1984	Percent change 1982 to 1983	1983 to 1984	State's rank in percent change 1982 to 1983	1983 to 1984	State's rank in 1982 score	1983 score	1984 score
SAT Verbal Scores	-20.0	433	434	437	0.2	0.6	18	8	32	31	31
SAT Math Scores	-11.0	471	472	470	0.2	-0.4	18	45	33	31	34

	Score change 1978 to 1982	Average score 1982	1983	1984	Percent change 1982 to 1983	1983 to 1984	State's rank in percent change 1982 to 1983	1983 to 1984	State's rank in 1982 score	1983 score	1984 score
SAT Verbal Scores of Intended Education Majors	-8.0	399	408	395	2.2	-3.1	11	48	30	28	40
SAT Math Scores of Intended Education Majors	0.0	430	427	409	-0.6	-4.2	33	50	26	28	46

	Change in percent 1972 to 1981	Percent minority enrollment 1972	1976	1981
Percentage of Minority Enrollment	0.5	0.8	1.0	0.5

	Change in percent 1965 to 1980	Percent of all students enrolled in private schools 1965	1970	1980
Percentage of Private School Enrollment	-9.3	16.6	10.1	7.3

	Change in percent 1971 to 1983	1971-72	1980-81	1983-84
Graduation Rates	5.3	79.7	79.4	85.0

	Change in percent 1980 to 1985	Percent unemployed 1980	1984	1985
Unemployment Rates	-0.8	6.4	6.4	5.6

	Percent change 1972-73 to 1982-83	1982-83	1983-84	1984-85	Percent change 1982-83 to 1983-84	1983-84 to 1984-85	State's rank in percent change 1982-83 to 1983-84	1983-84 to 1984-85	State's Rank 1982	1983	1984
Public Elementary School Enrollment	-9.8	600,396	588,476	585,028	-1.9	-0.5	42	37	13	13	12
Public Secondary School Enrollment	-7.1	375,331	377,634	380,194	0.6	0.6	5	17	12	12	12
Public Elementary and Secondary Enrollment	-8.8	975,727	966,110	965,222	-0.9	0.0	24	27	13	13	13
Numbers of Public Elementary Teachers	10.4	33,303	33,141	32,975	-0.4	-0.5	26	38	11	11	11
Numbers of Public Secondary School Teachers	0.4	23,125	23,013	23,888	-0.4	3.8	27	6	12	13	12
Numbers of Public Elementary and Secondary Teachers	6.1	56,428	56,154	56, 863	-0.4	1.2	24	23	11	11	10
Elementary Teachers' Salaries	95.7	17,875	19,170	20,767	7.2	8.3	18	16	34	35	31
Secondary Teachers' Salaries	98.3	19,426	20,830	22,535	7.2	8.1	16	18	30	29	28
Total Teachers' Salaries	96.6	18,535	19,867	21,536	7.1	8.4	18	16	30	31	28
Per Pupil Expenditures in ADA	191.2	2,737	2,967	3,043	8.4	2.5	19	42	30	28	32
Total Current Expenditures (in thousands)	139.9	2,697,940	2,855,848	3,031,039	5.8	6.1	29	32	11	11	11
Total Revenue Receipts (in thousands)	145.2	2,647,167	2,844,950	3,059,978	7.4	7.5	17	21	11	11	11

	Change in percent 1972-73 to 1982-83	Percent share 1982-83	1983-84	1984-85
Federal Revenue Receipts	-3.8	6.6	6.6	6.9
State Revenue Receipts	7.1	41.6	43.0	44.6
Local and Other Revenue Receipts	-3.2	51.8	50.4	48.5

	Percent change 1972 to 1982	1982	1983	1984	Percent change 1982 to 1983	1983 to 1984	State's rank in percent change 1982 to 1983	1983 to 1984	Rank 1982	1983	1984
Total Personal Income (in millions)	186.2	60,576	67,271	73,637	11.1	9.5	3	25	11	11	11
Per Capita Income	151.6	11,056	12,122	13,067	9.6	7.7	3	33	20	14	16
Population (in thousands)	13.7	5,485	5,550	5,636	1.1	1.5	16	11	13	13	13
Population Under Age 5	-3.3	380,000	389,000	391,000	2.3	0.5	23	13	14	14	14

	Score change 1972 to 1982	Average score 1982	1983	1984	Percent change 1982 to 1983	1983 to 1984	State's rank in percent change 1982 to 1983	1983 to 1984	State's rank in score 1982	1983 score	1984 score
SAT Verbal Scores	-18.0	426	427	428	0.2	0.2	18	26	37	35	38
SAT Math Scores	-13.0	462	463	466	0.2	0.6	18	20	42	41	41

	Score change 1978 to 1982	Average score 1982	1983	1984	Percent change 1982 to 1983	1983 to 1984	State's rank in percent change 1982 to 1983	1983 to 1984	State's rank in score 1982	1983 score	1984 score
SAT Verbal Scores of Intended Education Majors	0.0	388	396	401	2.0	1.2	14	25	41	37	34
SAT Math Scores of Intended Education Majors	-8.0	408	418	428	2.4	2.3	13	15	41	37	34

	Change in percent 1972 to 1981	Percent minority enrollment 1972	1976	1981
Percentage of Minority Enrollment	2.7	24.8	25.8	27.5

	Change in percent 1965 to 1980	Percent of all students enrolled in private schools 1965	1970	1980
Percentage of Private School Enrollment	0.9	6.0	7.5	6.9

	Change in percent 1971 to 1983	1971-72	1980-81	1983-84
Graduation Rates	-0.3	76.0	72.0	75.7

	Change in percent 1980 to 1985	Percent unemployed 1980	1984	1985
Unemployment Rates	0.7	4.6	5.4	5.3

	Percent change 1972-73 to 1982-83	1982-83	1983-84	1984-85	Percent change 1982-83 to 1983-84	Percent change 1983-84 to 1984-85	State's rank in percent change 1982-83 to 1983-84	State's rank in percent change 1983-84 to 1984-85	State's Rank 1982	State's Rank 1983	State's Rank 1984
Public Elementary School Enrollment	-7.6	381,411	377,303	383,657	-1.0	1.6	28	14	23	23	23
Public Secondary School Enrollment	-5.4	357,207	357,061	357,229	0.0	0.0	13	22	14	13	13
Public Elementary and Secondary Enrollment	-6.6	738,618	734,364	740,886	-0.5	0.8	16	13	19	19	19
Numbers of Public Elementary Teachers	-1.3	18,165	18,028	18,904	-0.7	4.8	30	12	26	26	23
Numbers of Public Secondary School Teachers	14.3	15,956	15,951	16,251	0.0	1.8	21	15	23	22	22
Numbers of Public Elementary and Secondary Teachers	5.4	34,121	33,979	35,155	-0.4	3.5	24	9	23	23	22
Elementary Teachers' Salaries	124.6	23,120	24,392	25,221	5.5	3.3	33	43	9	8	9
Secondary Teachers' Salaries	118.5	23,906	25,221	26,056	5.5	3.3	32	42	9	7	11
Total Teachers' Salaries	121.1	23,488	24,780	25,610	5.5	3.3	33	42	8	6	11
Per Pupil Expenditures in ADA	191.2	2,878	3,106	3,437	7.9	10.6	24	11	26	26	19
Total Current Expenditures (in thousands)	180.0	2,435,243	2,559,104	2,798,353	5.0	9.3	36	12	16	16	14
Total Revenue Receipts (in thousands)	134.2	2,248,039	2,423,561	2,625,828	7.8	8.3	13	18	18	18	17

	Change in percent 1972-73 to 1982-83	Percent share 1982-83	Percent share 1983-84	Percent share 1984-85
Federal Revenue Receipts	-3.3	5.4	4.4	3.9
State Revenue Receipts	28.0	75.2	75.1	74.9
Local and Other Revenue Receipts	-24.6	19.4	19.2	19.4

	Percent change 1972 to 1982	1982	1983	1984	Percent change 1982 to 1983	Percent change 1983 to 1984	State's rank in percent change 1982 to 1983	State's rank in percent change 1983 to 1984	Rank 1982	Rank 1983	Rank 1984
Total Personal Income (in millions)	216.6	49,111	52,301	55,356	6.5	5.8	27	48	18	18	18
Per Capita Income	157.1	11,466	12,162	12,728	6.0	4.6	21	49	16	13	19
Population (in thousands)	36.9	4,276	4,300	4,349	0.5	1.1	31	16	19	20	19
Population Under Age 5	21.5	333,000	343,000	345,000	3.0	0.5	19	13	18	18	18

	Score change 1972 to 1982	Average score 1982	Average score 1983	Average score 1984	Percent change 1982 to 1983	Percent change 1983 to 1984	State's rank in percent change 1982 to 1983	State's rank in percent change 1983 to 1984	1982 score	1983 score	1984 score
SAT Verbal Scores	-22.0	468	463	463	-1.0	0.0	45	34	20	24	24
SAT Math Scores	-7.0	514	510	505	-0.7	-0.9	44	48	17	21	27

	Score change 1978 to 1982	Average score 1982	Average score 1983	Average score 1984	Percent change 1982 to 1983	Percent change 1983 to 1984	State's rank in percent change 1982 to 1983	State's rank in percent change 1983 to 1984	1982 score	1983 score	1984 score
SAT Verbal Scores of Intended Education Majors	-11.0	431	431	433	0.0	0.4	27	36	13	17	21
SAT Math Scores of Intended Education Majors	-13.0	454	451	454	-0.6	0.6	33	34	12	19	21

	Change in percent 1972 to 1981	Percent minority enrollment 1972	Percent minority enrollment 1976	Percent minority enrollment 1981
Percentage of Minority Enrollment	7.1	7.0	10.1	14.1

	Change in percent 1965 to 1980	Percent of all students enrolled in private schools 1965	Percent of all students enrolled in private schools 1970	Percent of all students enrolled in private schools 1980
Percentage of Private School Enrollment	-0.7	7.6	6.3	6.9

	Change in percent 1971 to 1983	1971-72	1980-81	1983-84
Graduation Rates	-9.1	84.6	74.2	75.5

	Change in percent 1980 to 1985	Percent unemployed 1980	1984	1985
Unemployment Rates	2.0	7.4	10.0	9.4

145

SUMMARY TABLE 50. West Virginia

	Percent change 1972-73 to 1982-83	1982-83	1983-84	1984-85	Percent change 1982-83 to 1983-84	Percent change 1983-84 to 1984-85	State's rank in percent change 1982-83 to 1983-84	State's rank in percent change 1983-84 to 1984-85	State's Rank 1982	1983	1984
Public Elementary School Enrollment	-2.0	225,253	220,825	214,029	-1.9	-3.0	42	48	34	35	35
Public Secondary School Enrollment	-16.7	149,862	150,426	148,912	0.3	-1.0	8	38	34	35	35
Public Elementary and Secondary Enrollment	-8.5	375,115	371,251	362,941	-1.0	-2.2	28	49	34	35	35
Numbers of Public Elementary Teachers	32.3	12,229	12,652	12,427	3.4	-1.7	3	44	33	33	33
Numbers of Public Secondary School Teachers	13.2	9,930	9,765	10,130	-1.6	3.7	36	8	33	33	33
Numbers of Public Elementary and Secondary Teachers	23.5	22,159	22,417	22,557	1.1	0.6	11	30	34	34	34
Elementary Teachers' Salaries	119.8	16,923	16,726	19,530	-1.1	16.7	51	2	42	48	40
Secondary Teachers' Salaries	108.8	17,813	18,461	19,603	3.6	6.1	41	30	42	43	44
Total Teachers' Salaries	113.9	17,322	17,482	19,563	0.9	11.9	49	6	44	46	44
Per Pupil Expenditures in ADA	205.8	2,465	2,587	2,866	4.9	10.7	41	10	40	41	37
Total Current Expenditures (in thousands)	177.0	943,036	989,465	1,057,037	4.9	6.8	38	29	32	34	32
Total Revenue Receipts (in thousands)	190.1	949,546	1,023,120	1,137,249	7.7	11.1	15	13	32	32	32

	Change in percent 1972-73 to 1982-83	Percent share 1982-83	1983-84	1984-85
Federal Revenue Receipts	-3.9	9.0	9.2	9.1
State Revenue Receipts	5.6	62.4	61.2	63.6
Local and Other Revenue Receipts	-1.8	28.5	29.6	27.3

	Percent change 1972 to 1982	1982	1983	1984	Percent change 1982 to 1983	Percent change 1983 to 1984	State's rank in percent change 1982 to 1983	State's rank in percent change 1983 to 1984	Rank 1982	1983	1984
Total Personal Income (in millions)	168.3	17,142	17,999	19,223	4.9	6.8	40	46	34	34	35
Per Capita Income	147.6	8,758	9,160	9,846	4.5	7.4	38	37	47	48	48
Population (in thousands)	8.4	1,961	1,965	1,952	0.2	-0.6	39	51	34	34	34
Population Under Age 5	1.4	143,000	143,000	136,000	0.0	-4.8	43	51	35	35	35

	Score change 1972 to 1982	Average score 1982	1983	1984	Percent change 1982 to 1983	Percent change 1983 to 1984	State's rank in percent change 1982 to 1983	State's rank in percent change 1983 to 1984	1982 score	1983 score	1984 score
SAT Verbal Scores	-7.0	462	466	466	0.8	0.0	6	34	24	20	23
SAT Math Scores	7.0	506	512	510	1.1	-0.3	5	44	24	19	23

	Score change 1978 to 1982	Average score 1982	1983	1984	Percent change 1982 to 1983	Percent change 1983 to 1984	State's rank in percent change 1982 to 1983	State's rank in percent change 1983 to 1984	1982 score	1983 score	1984 score
SAT Verbal Scores of Intended Education Majors	-17.0	397	412	425	3.7	3.1	7	14	34	26	25
SAT Math Scores of Intended Education Majors	-26.0	411	440	435	7.0	-1.1	3	44	39	24	29

	Change in percent 1972 to 1981	Percent minority enrollment 1972	1976	1981
Percentage of Minority Enrollment	-0.6	4.9	4.5	4.3

	Change in percent 1965 to 1980	Percent of all students enrolled in private schools 1965	1970	1980
Percentage of Private School Enrollment	-0.1	3.3	4.6	3.2

	Change in percent 1971 to 1983	1971-72	1980-81	1983-84
Graduation Rates	4.3	73.1	72.6	77.4

	Change in percent 1980 to 1985	Percent unemployed 1980	1984	1985
Unemployment Rates	4.2	9.2	16.5	13.4

146

	Percent change 1972-73 to 1982-83	1982-83	1983-84	1984-85	Percent change 1982-83 to 1983-84	1983-84 to 1984-85	State's rank in percent change 1982-83 to 1983-84	1983-84 to 1984-85	State's Rank 1982	1983	1984
Public Elementary School Enrollment	-22.6	449,982	446,807	451,474	-0.7	1.0	25	18	18	18	18
Public Secondary School Enrollment	-19.2	334,848	327,839	316,068	-2.0	-3.5	34	50	17	18	18
Public Elementary and Secondary Enrollment	-21.1	784,830	774,646	767,542	-1.2	-0.9	30	40	17	17	18
Numbers of Public Elementary Teachers	5.8	26,674	26,100	25,100	-2.1	-3.8	45	48	13	14	15
Numbers of Public Secondary School Teachers	-2.2	22,364	21,500	20,250	-3.8	-5.8	46	46	15	16	18
Numbers of Public Elementary and Secondary Teachers	2.1	49,038	47,600	45,350	-2.9	-4.7	46	49	15	15	16
Elementary Teachers' Salaries	102.2	21,062	22,540	24,190	7.0	7.3	19	23	19	14	17
Secondary Teachers' Salaries	100.0	22,024	23,570	25,190	7.0	6.8	19	25	17	15	14
Total Teachers' Salaries	100.9	21,496	23,000	24,780	6.9	7.7	22	21	16	14	14
Per Pupil Expenditures in ADA	201.7	3,380	3,553	3,880	5.1	9.2	40	18	13	14	14
Total Current Expenditures (in thousands)	134.5	2,571,853	2,714,810	2,933,731	5.5	8.0	32	23	12	12	12
Total Revenue Receipts (in thousands)	122.7	2,609,889	2,724,554	2,761,444	4.3	1.3	37	43	12	12	15

	Change in percent 1972-73 to 1982-83	Percent share 1982-83	1983-84	1984-85
Federal Revenue Receipts	1.5	5.4	4.4	3.9
State Revenue Receipts	6.8	37.4	37.9	39.5
Local and Other Revenue Receipts	-8.3	57.2	57.7	56.7

	Percent change 1972 to 1982	1982	1983	1984	Percent change 1982 to 1983	1983 to 1984	State's rank in percent change 1982 to 1983	1983 to 1984	Rank 1982	1983	1984
Total Personal Income (in millions)	157.8	51,033	53,699	58,668	5.2	9.3	37	27	16	17	17
Per Capita Income	143.3	10,725	11,311	12,309	5.4	8.8	28	20	27	26	27
Population (in thousands)	5.9	4,745	4,747	4,766	0.0	0.4	45	36	16	16	16
Population Under Age 5	0.8	363,000	364,000	358,000	0.2	-1.6	42	38	16	16	17

	Score change 1972 to 1982	Average score 1982	1983	1984	Percent change 1982 to 1983	1983 to 1984	State's rank in percent change 1982 to 1983	1983 to 1984	State's rank in 1982 score	1983 score	1984 score
SAT Verbal Scores	-26.0	476	473	475	-0.6	0.4	37	19	16	17	17
SAT Math Scores	-8.0	535	533	532	-0.3	-0.1	38	40	8	9	11

	Score change 1978 to 1982	Average score 1982	1983	1984	Percent change 1982 to 1983	1983 to 1984	State's rank in percent change 1982 to 1983	1983 to 1984	State's rank in 1982 score	1983 score	1984 score
SAT Verbal Scores of Intended Education Majors	-9.0	430	454	439	5.5	-3.3	6	49	15	5	17
SAT Math Scores of Intended Education Majors	-14.0	471	486	476	3.1	-2.0	9	46	7	7	9

	Change in percent 1972 to 1981	Percent minority enrollment 1972	1976	1981
Percentage of Minority Enrollment	2.6	6.7	8.0	9.3

	Change in percent 1965 to 1980	Percent of all students enrolled in private schools 1965	1970	1980
Percentage of Private School Enrollment	-7.7	24.1	19.9	16.4

	Change in percent 1971 to 1983	1971-72	1980-81	1983-84
Graduation Rates	-5.5	89.5	81.1	84.0

	Change in percent 1980 to 1985	Percent unemployed 1980	1984	1985
Unemployment Rates	0.8	7.0	8.7	7.8

147

	Percent change 1972-73 to 1982-83	1982-83	1983-84	1984-85	Percent change 1982-83 to 1983-84	1983-84 to 1984-85	State's rank in percent change 1982-83 to 1983-84	1983-84 to 1984-85	State's Rank 1982	1983	1984
Public Elementary School Enrollment	30.6	58,254	57,505	59,887	-1.2	4.1	33	2	47	47	47
Public Secondary School Enrollment	5.6	43,411	43,460	43,300	0.1	-0.3	11	31	46	47	46
Public Elementary and Secondary Enrollment	18.9	101,665	100,965	103,187	-0.6	2.2	20	7	47	47	47
Numbers of Public Elementary Teachers	78.1	4,575	4,566	4,720	-0.1	3.3	19	19	44	44	43
Numbers of Public Secondary School Teachers	47.1	2,172	2,493	2,270	14.7	-8.9	1	48	51	50	50
Numbers of Public Elementary and Secondary Teachers	62.4	6,747	7,059	6,990	4.6	-0.9	4	42	47	47	47
Elementary Teachers' Salaries	148.4	23,210	24,000	26,172	3.4	9.0	41	12	8	9	6
Secondary Teachers' Salaries	157.6	24,710	25,100	27,817	1.5	10.8	47	9	6	9	8
Total Teachers' Salaries	158.2	23,690	24,500	26,709	3.4	9.0	41	12	7	8	6
Per Pupil Expenditures in ADA	222.5	4,022	4,488	4,809	11.5	7.1	5	27	4	4	4
Total Current Expenditures (in thousands)	369.5	499,800	559,275	610,666	11.9	9.1	4	13	42	42	41
Total Revenue Receipts (in thousands)	286.8	464,000	537,060	592,000	15.7	10.2	1	15	42	42	41

	Change in percent 1972-73 to 1982-83	Percent share 1982-83	1983-84	1984-85
Federal Revenue Receipts	-5.3	4.0	2.6	3.7
State Revenue Receipts	0.9	34.7	29.6	28.7
Local and Other Revenue Receipts	4.4	61.3	67.8	67.6

	Percent change 1972 to 1982	1982	1983	1984	Percent change 1982 to 1983	1983 to 1984	State's rank in percent change 1982 to 1983	1983 to 1984	Rank 1982	1983	1984
Total Personal Income (in millions)	294.0	6,205	6,130	6,437	-1.2	5.0	51	49	50	50	50
Per Capita Income	172.4	12,211	11,920	12,586	-2.3	5.5	50	47	8	18	21
Population (in thousands)	44.7	509	514	511	0.9	-0.5	22	50	50	50	50
Population Under Age 5	66.7	50,000	53,000	52,000	6.0	-1.8	7	40	47	47	48

	Score change 1972 to 1982	Average score 1982	1983	1984	Percent change 1982 to 1983	1983 to 1984	State's rank in percent change 1982 to 1983	1983 to 1984	1982 score	1983 score	1984 score
SAT Verbal Scores	-27.0	484	492	489	1.6	-0.6	2	48	9	7	8
SAT Math Scores	-17.0	533	530	545	-0.5	2.8	40	3	9	10	6

	Score change 1978 to 1982	Average score 1982	1983	1984	Percent change 1982 to 1983	1983 to 1984	State's rank in percent change 1982 to 1983	1983 to 1984	1982 score	1983 score	1984 score
SAT Verbal Scores of Intended Education Majors	-17.0	402	401	482	-0.2	20.1	34	1	27	32	4
SAT Math Scores of Intended Education Majors	-20.0	453	420	485	-7.2	15.4	51	1	14	32	6

	Change in percent 1972 to 1981	Percent minority enrollment 1972	1976	1981
Percentage of Minority Enrollment	-1.8	9.3	8.7	7.5

	Change in percent 1965 to 1980	Percent of all students enrolled in private schools 1965	1970	1980
Percentage of Private School Enrollment	-1.5	4.5	3.9	3.0

	Change in percent 1971 to 1983	1971-72	1980-81	1983-84
Graduation Rates	-2.4	84.1	79.2	81.7

	Change in percent 1980 to 1985	Percent unemployed 1980	1984	1985
Unemployment Rates	0.0	4.0	8.0	0.0

NOTES

1. Feistritzer Associates, The American Teacher, (Washington: Feistritzer Publications, 1983), p. 1.

2. The Metropolitan Life Survey of the American Teacher, (New York: Metropolitan Insurance Companies, 1984), p. 11.

3. Ibid.

4. Ibid.

5. National Education Association, Nationwide Teacher Opinion Poll, 1983 (Washington: 1983), p. 5.

6. National Education Association, Estimates of School Statistics 1984-85, (Washington: 1984), p. 35.

7. Metropolitan Life Survey of the American Teacher, 1984, 11.

8. C. Emily Feistritzer, The Condition of Teaching: A State-by-State Analysis, (Princeton, N.J.: The Carnegie Foundation for the Advancement of Teaching, 1983), p. 27.

9. Market Data Retrieval, 1985-86 Educational Mailing Lists, (Westport, Conn.: 1985), pp. 2-8.

10. The Condition of Teaching, 1983, p. 28.

11. Metropolitan Life Survey of the American Teacher, 1984, p. 19.

12. National Education Association, Nationwide Teacher Opinion Poll 1983, p. 9.

13. National Education Association, Status of the American Public School Teacher 1980-81, (Washington: 1982), p. 75.

14. Nationwide Teacher Opinion Poll 1983, 1983, p. 9.

15. Ibid.

16. Status of the American Public School Teacher 1980-81, 1982, p. 76.

17. C. Emily Feistritzer, Cheating Our Children: Why We Need School Reform, (Washington: National Center for Education Information, 1985), pp. 23-24.

18. Ibid., pp. 8-9.

19. C. Emily Feistritzer, The Making of a Teacher: A Report on Teacher Education and Certification, (Washington: The National Center for Education Information, 1984), p. 1.

20. U. S. Department of Education, National Center for Education Statistics, Condition of Education 1983, pp. 214 and 216.

21. Press Release: "A Gallup Survey Conducted for the National Education Association," July 1, 1985, p. 10.

22. Ibid., p. 11.

23.   The Making of a Teacher, 1984, pp. 1-5.

24.   The Condition of Education, 1983, p. 186.

25.   Ibid. p. 188.

26.   The Making of a Teacher, 1984, pp. 9-11.

27.   Ibid. 1984, p. 26.

28.   Ibid., p. 28.

29.   Ibid., p. 36.

30.   National Association of State Directors of Teacher Education and Certification, Manual on Certification and Preparation of Educational Personnel in the United States, (Sacramento, Calif.: 1984), p. 4.